IDENTITIES

IDENTITIES

An Anthology of
West of Scotland Poetry, Prose and Drama

Edited by
GEDDES THOMSON
Principal Teacher of English
Allan Glen's Secondary School, Glasgow

Introduction by
EDWIN MORGAN

HEINEMANN EDUCATIONAL BOOKS
LONDON AND EDINBURGH

Heinemann Educational Books Ltd
22 Bedford Square, London WC1B 3HH

LONDON   EDINBURGH   MELBOURNE   AUCKLAND
HONG KONG   SINGAPORE   KUALA LUMPUR   NEW DELHI
IBADAN   NAIROBI   JOHANNESBURG
EXETER (NH)   KINGSTON   PORT OF SPAIN

All photographs by Ken MacGregor
except cover photograph of
child, reproduced by courtesy
of George Outram & Co. Ltd.

*The publishers acknowledge the financial assistance of the
Scottish Arts Council in the publication of this volume*

British Library CIP Data
Identities.
1. English literature—Scottish authors
2. English literature—20th century
820'.8'09411   PR8644
ISBN 0435 14901 6

Printed and bound in Great Britain
by Morrison & Gibb, Edinburgh

CONTENTS

PREFACE

Thematic anthologies have proliferated in recent years, so it is fair that an editor should explain what makes his particular offering different. This anthology consists of poetry, prose and drama selected from the writing produced by west of Scotland authors over the last two decades—the first such collection published. Its basic aim is well-expressed in the opening sentence of *Scottish Literature in the Secondary School* (HMSO 1976): 'One of the ways in which any society attempts to lead its young to an understanding of what they are as individual and social beings is by introducing them to the literature of their own country'.

The anthology is arranged in universal themes, and the quality and insight of the literature make it suitable both for the general reader and for use in schools for pupils aged fourteen and upwards.

Part One of the anthology is retrospective, examining childhood experience, while Part Two explores the concerns of adolescence and young adulthood. Both the themes and individual extracts are lengthier than in many anthologies. In general, the material within each theme becomes progressively more sophisticated so that pupils of all abilities can explore the themes through the literature and their own experience.

Notes on the poems and extracts indicate other relevant material, especially by Scottish writers, while the glossary at the back of the book may prove helpful.

Finally, although the anthology is as representative as possible, considerations of space and thematic balance have led to the exclusion of writers whom the editor would have liked to include. Some of these writers are mentioned in the Select Bibliography.

Geddes Thomson

INTRODUCTION

A writer inhabits many worlds. Emily Brontë wrote about her native place, Joseph Conrad wrote about everywhere except his native place, yet *Wuthering Heights* and *Lord Jim* are both fine imaginative achievements: real and convincing on one level, mysterious and unfathomable on another. Good writing can come from any sort of experience and any sort of place, but it has somehow to produce that shock of surprise that jumps us beyond our comfortable expectancies, in addition to presenting us with a well realized world which we can relate to the world we know. For example, when the boy in Alan Spence's short story 'Tinsel' looks through the window at the end and sees the reflection of his own kitchen stretching outside into the dark, this is a perfectly ordinary thing to see, but in the boy's imagination, and in the imagination of the author which he is passing on through the boy to us his readers, that simple optical illusion is transformed into something magic, into something symbolic. You can see a similar process at work in the idea of 'walking through seaweed' in Ian Hamilton Finlay's play of that title, in the vividly recalled yet almost ghostly grate and gas-mantle of W. S. Graham's poem 'The Dark Dialogues II', or in the hilarious memorability—why *was* it memorable?—of Uncle Hughie's fight with the egg in William McIlvanney's novel *Remedy is None*.

If I emphasize this quality of imagination, it is perhaps because writers from Glasgow and the west of Scotland are sometimes thought of as being very down-to-earth characters, realistic, knowing, quick and sharp, Caledonian New Yorkers, hard-men whose chibs happen to be non-detachable typewriter-keys. No one would deny that there is an element of truth in this—Glasgow is after all a splendidly abrasive place, and it would be surprising if no abrasiveness got into the writing—but it is far from being the whole picture. What is true is that the writing from this area, as it has emerged in the last two decades or so, has a strong basic human interest, and the editor of this anthology does not have any forced or artificial search for his categories of family life, growing up, school, work, rituals, violence, and love. The dangers of such writing are obvious enough, and we have not always escaped them: nostalgia, the golden glow, reminiscence for its own sake. But a recurrent hard-edged quality has kept that to a minimum (Williams, Trocchi, Rae, Leonard), as has also, in a quite different way, an unsentimental sensitiveness (Spence, Kelman, Lochhead, Conn). Two sections of the anthology are, it seems to me, of particular interest. 'A

Sense of Place' and 'Language' are both concerned with establishing, preserving, criticizing and recreating identity, whether identity of environment or identity of speech. A sense of place, and it may be the place he was born or grew up in, or the place he works in, or the place he leaves and comes back to, is of great importance to a writer; and this is true whether it is a town like Kilmarnock or Greenock, not widely known beyond Scotland, or a city like Glasgow almost strangled with its own fame and notoriety. In every instance the writer has to wrestle with the truth and meaning of his own place, to define it or redefine it, in relation to his own life and the changes of the time. Change!—that is the writer's apple that he sinks his teeth into with a kind of energetic anguished delight. And the traumatic changes which have affected the west of Scotland during the last generation are certainly one of the reasons why so many writers from this area have been impelled to express themselves. Here, the environment may press so hard that, as Archie Hind's hero Mat says in *The Dear Green Place*, 'all this moved him in a way that art could only be secondary to'—yet, even as we find ourselves assenting to this, by a sort of double-take we realize that it is through art that Hind is telling us. Almost the opposite method is used in W. S. Graham's moving poem 'Greenock at Night I Find You': we are made aware right from the opening lines that words are being put together in an unusual and special way, a way that is art and not life, and then as we read on into the poem we find more and more that life comes forward and speaks to us—about a place, about memory, about a son and his father: shining simplicities caught in good words.

It is when writers become aware of the changing society round about them, or of the wider sense in which 'the times they are a-changin', that certain themes, and indeed literature itself, may snap into life. One of these awarenesses in recent years has been the awareness of language. Although the prose and verse extracts in the 'Language' section of the anthology refer to different kinds of Scottish speech, rural and urban, the point they are making is the same: that there is something dangerous, or desperately wrong, about a system which forces children to unlearn or to give up the language they naturally talk. Gordon Williams shows that the end-result may be chaotic, a weird mixture of Scottish and English words and pro-nunciations (even if the chaos has its causes and its social nuances); William McIlvanney brings out in a more directly attacking way (notice how the 'English' equivalent which the boy writes for *breeks* is itself Scottish, *troosers*) the sense of loss when everyday words are replaced by alien forms; and Tom Leonard takes the argument a step further by using the condemned 'language of the gutter' throughout, with wonderful ironic effect. There is no easy means of resolving Scotland's language problems. It is a fact, however, that at the moment there are a number of people with sharp ears, listening hard and writing well. It is not reportage that is wanted, but perhaps something like what the American poet Charles Bukowski has done with American speech, using a racy and outspoken colloquial basis but deploying it with the tact and subtle movement of high art.

The society shown in the anthology is predominantly working-class, and this is a fair reflection of the writing that has recently appeared. It is no doubt also a fair reflection of Glasgow and the west of Scotland, except that there are omissions which must continue to tantalize the inquirer. Middle-class Glasgow, rich and strange as it is, calls out for a great deal more literary embodiment than it gets. Social satire is remarkably thin on the ground. Where are the Jane Austens of Bearsden, the Evelyn Waughs of Newton Mearns? Where is a Kingsley Amis to turn a beady eye on the aspiring Hampsteaders of East Kilbride? Maybe even asking the questions will sow a seed or two, who knows.

At any rate, I hope the present collection will show something of the variety and vitality of what is being written in these parts. The editor has brought together with real success, I think, that mixture of the local and the general which can recommend itself to a range of readers: authenticity yes, but set alight by imagination.

Edwin Morgan

ACKNOWLEDGEMENTS

The editor gratefully acknowledges the help and advice of Stewart Conn, Kenneth Goodwin, Edwin Morgan, Hugh C. Rae, Allan Shearer and Bette Stevenson in the preparation of this anthology; also the patience and indispensable help of his wife, Lucy, who typed the manuscript.

The editor and publishers wish to thank the following for permission to reproduce copyright material:

John Calder for extracts from *Mr Alfred MA* by George Friel and *The Aquarium* by Stewart Conn; Ian Hamilton Finlay for the extract from *Walking through Seaweed*; Maurice Lindsay for his poems 'Accident Report' and 'Attending a Football Match' from *This Business of Living* (Akros Publications); Alan Spence for the extracts from 'Boom Baby' from *Jock Tamson's Bairns—Essays on a Scots Childhood*, ed. Trevor Royle (Hamish Hamilton); Collins for 'Tinsel' and 'Sheaves' from *Its Colours they are Fine* and 'Sailmaker' from *Scottish Short Stories*, all by Alan Spence; Stephen Mulrine for 'The Coming of the Wee Malkies' from *Poems* (Akros Publications); Tom Leonard for 'The Good Thief' and 'The Miracle of the Burd and the Fishes' from *Poems* (The O'Brien Press, Dublin), 'The Dropout' from *Bunnit Husslin* (The Third Eye Centre, Glasgow), and 'Unrelated Incident (i) and (iii) from *Three Glasgow Writers* (Molendinar Press); Carl MacDougall for 'The Blind Reading' from *Scottish Short Stories* (Collins) and 'The Six Travellers' from *A Scent of Water* (Molendinar Press); Molendinar Press for extract from *The Sash* by Hector Macmillan and for 'Fifty Pence' by James Kelman in *Three Glasgow Writers*; Liz Lochhead for 'Poem on a Daytrip', 'The Choosing', 'For my Grandmother Knitting' and 'Poem for my Sister' from *Memo for Spring* (Reprographia), 'The Lady of Shalott', and extracts from 'A Protestant Girlhood' from *Jock Tamson's Bairns—Essays on a Scots Childhood*, ed. Trevor Royle (Hamish Hamilton); Edwin Morgan for 'Glasgow 5 March 1971' from *Instamatic Poems*; Carcanet Press for 'Glasgow Sonnet i' from *From Glasgow to Saturn* by Edwin Morgan; Edinburgh University Press for 'Trio', 'King Billy' and 'In the Snack-bar' from *The Second Life* by Edwin Morgan; Catherine Lucy Czerkawska for 'Keystone Cop' from *White Boats* (Garret Arts, Edinburgh) and extracts from 'A Sheltered Wilderness' from *Jock Tamson's Bairns—Essays on a Scots Childhood*, ed. Trevor Royle (Hamish Hamilton); Canongate Publishing for the extract from *The Bevellers* by Roddy McMillan; John Farquharson for 'Children Playing', 'Grandmother' and 'Incident' from *The Longships in Harbour* (Eyre & Spottiswoode), extracts from *Remedy is None* (Eyre & Spottiswoode) and Docherty (Allen & Unwin), all by William McIlvanney; Faber & Faber for the extract from 'Growing Up in the West' by William McIlvanney from *Memoirs of a Modern Scotland*, ed. Karl Miller, 'Ships' from *Terry Street*, and 'The Competition' and 'Renfrewshire Traveller' from *Love or Nothing*, by Douglas Dunn; Secker & Warburg for extracts from *From Scenes Like These* by Gordon Williams; W. S. Graham for 'The Dark

Dialogues II' from *Malcolm Mooney's Land* and 'Greenock at Night I Find You' from *Implements in their Places* (Faber & Faber); Pan Books for the extract from *Billy Connolly—the Authorized Version* by Billy Connolly; Curtis Brown for extracts from *Dancing in the Streets* by Clifford Hanley (Hutchinson); A. M. Heath for the extract from *Jean in the Morning* by Janet Sandison (Macmillan); Anthony Blond for extracts from *The Saturday Epic* and *Night Pillow* by Hugh C. Rae; Anthony Shiel for 'Remote Country' from *The Swans of Berwick* by Sidney Tremayne (Chatto & Windus); William Heinemann for the extract from *The Galloway Shepherd* by Ian Niall; George MacBeth for 'The Miner's Helmet' from *The Broken Places* (Macmillan); Hutchinson for 'Harelaw', 'Todd', 'Ayrshire Farm' and 'Lion Tamer' from *Stoats in the Sunlight*, 'Family Visit' from *An Ear to the Ground*, and 'Afternoon Visit' from *Under the Ice*, all by Stewart Conn, and for extracts from *Shoes were for Sunday* and *Best Foot Forward* by Molly Weir, *In a Marmalade Saloon* by Patrick O'Connor, *The Dear Green Place* by Archie Hind, and *The Taste of Too Much* by Clifford Hanley.

PART ONE

I

TO BE A CHILD

Jesus Loves Me

When I was five years old I went to school and the very first thing I learned was 'Jesus loves me'. At first I was very much afraid of school because it was new and everything new was frightening. I went there on the first day with a big girl called Maisie Anderson who lived upstairs from us and she led me in through the iron gates in the wall with the iron railings on top, across the concrete playground and into the grey stone building to a big room which had dark brown paint half-way up the walls, a lot of long wooden forms with desks in front of them and there was a queer dry stale smell. Maisie led me to a high desk that stood all alone in the middle of the floor and here there was a lady, sitting on a high chair with a pen in her hand and a big book in front of her. She had a thin face, spectacles that pinched her nose and she looked down at me sternly and said:

'Name?'

'Tell your name,' Maisie whispered and gave me a prod in the back.

'Jean Robertson,' I said and the pen scratched in the book.

'Address?' the lady said now. I did not know what she meant.

'Where do you live?' she asked impatiently.

'Railway Terrace, miss,' said Maisie.

'Number?' the teacher asked Maisie now.

'Same close as me but down the stair,' said Maisie.

'Down the stair *what*?' said the teacher very sternly.

'Miss,' said Maisie.

'Which side?'

Maisie looked up at the ceiling and I knew that she was imagining herself standing at the mouth of our close. She held out her right hand.

'Number three,' said the teacher, scratching with the pen again and then to me: 'Go and sit over there and no talking. Next. Name?'

That was how I found out what an address was and what my own address was so perhaps that was the first thing I learned at school and not 'Jesus loves me' but 'Jesus loves me' must have been the second thing.

After all the names and addresses had been scratched into the book the teacher said that if there was any more fidgeting or talking she would strap every one of us and that we were to pay attention because we were going to learn 'Jesus loves me'. After that, every morning, school began with 'Jesus loves me' and the people who could not say it by themselves on Friday morning got the strap. I did not get the strap because I could say it. I had been able to say it on Tuesday, the very first day but, of course, I did not know what it meant. I had never heard of Jesus; I had never heard of love and I had never heard of the Bible and this lesson that came first every morning was called 'Bible'. To the best of my knowledge, I belonged to my mother and father and not to Jesus and although I was said to be little for my age, I was not weak but quite healthy, probably as strong for my age as Jesus.

From *Jean in the Morning* by Janet Sandison

My Primary School

That was what it was like, to be a child. The place, the people. Soon you went to school. You don't want to go back there, you've been padding it out with bits about your parents and so on. Why go back there anyway? You know how you hate it when you find yourself back there with no choice, in Dreams. And you're always running along the corridors, you're late and this is always the primary school and the corridors are spiked with pegs and coats with a damp dog-like smell and you keep swinging through doors into classroom after classroom looking for your class, your empty place. And can't find it. Or there's the dream where it's always the high school and the history class and suddenly there you are out in the middle of the floor wearing nothing but your vest. A too-short vest. You pull it down in front of you, then the back of you, don't know which way to turn. Everyone is laughing. And you don't know which part to expose.

So why try to tell it? Not for nostalgia. Not to say ah when we were wee. Not for all that merely. Easy, too easy to write a kind of proletarian Molesworth compleat with French-teachers-who-couldn't-keep-order. Yes, there were a lot of real-life cliche characters, you could without one word of a lie dredge up the Recognisable Particular. Something to have people smile to remember. Except that would not be honest enough, to thereby imply that it was any of it absolutely harmless. So go back, dig deep, but know that you'll not get at any of the things you accepted most easily, that hurt you the most. You will be the last person to know what they are.

Newarthill Primary School. A big black stone-built place with railings around it. Old, it had the date 1897 cut into the stone between the Boys Entrance and the entrance marked Girls. I was five. My mother took me to enrol and on the way back she said she hoped I'd stay on at school, go to University if I had it in me, she and my father would make every sacrifice. It was a great shame my father had never had the chance.

We were taught by Look and Say. Apple says ah. Miss Brown was not particularly pleased that I knew how to recite Ay Bee See Dee and recognise the characters, said the Parents didn't know the damage they did. But I learned to read very quickly. Most of the class did. We learned by rote. Off by heart. Tables: nine sixes are fifty-four ten sixes are six-ty; Similes: as black as coal, as green as grass; Singulars and Plurals: hoof, hooves, sheep, sheep, fish, fish or fishes, spoonful, spoonsful. We chanted aloud like a prayer.

The school did seem to be staffed by a collection of remarkably similar mainly maiden ladies. The odd widow. Does my memory lie to me in showing me so many Miss Jean Brodies twenty years beyond their prime? Each time before you moved up a class you were afraid, had heard the shouting spill into the corridor, had heard the rumours of beltings for Nothing, knew that this was going to be the most terrifying class in the school. But it always turned out to be much the same. The teachers had their moods. The sums got harder.

Each day started off with the Lord's Prayer, half an hour or so of Bible. The Story of Joseph read verse each around the class, a chapter a day, missing out Chapter thirty-nine, being the spicy one where Potiphar's wife stages her seduction scene. But I was suspicious enough, had the sense to read it anyway. Or we had to repeat what we'd learned at home a verse a night, Isaiah 53, or the gibberish of a Scottish Paraphrase.

5

Oh god of Be-ethel by hoosand
thy pe-ople Still are fed
Who through the Weary
Wild-er-ness has stole our father's leg.

After the Bible then Reading, your homework piece, without a stammer. Aloud. Then Spelling. Every night you had to learn one group from the little red and white Schonell's Essential Spelling Book. Every day we wrote them down.

see	six	by
tree	fix	cry
been	box	try
sky	sweet	fox

More than two wrong got the belt. Hugh Gilmour and Jeannie Nielson got the belt every day. For the Spelling and for other things. Remember his pink flush, his orange hair, his gallus grin, how cock of the walk he was when he swaggered back to his seat. He kept count of his beltings, his boast was that he could take it. Farm Jeannie Nielson was big and cow-dumb. Smelt of the byre, carried it in on her shoes. Her eyelashes were matted together with a sticky affliction called Sleep. She cried easy. Sat alone at the front to see the board. When one of us nice girls or clever boys was Bad we were moved down to sit beside her as punishment. She cried easy. Still she was belted for her Spelling Errors.

Can that be true? Can they have been so cruel, those dedicated ladies with their flowery smocks to keep the chalk-dust from their good-wool dresses, with their churchy peppermint mothball breaths. They all played a club-footed piano, taught songs. Flow gently Sweet Afton. On their autumn window-sills bulbs split their sides in purple crocks, in spring milky frogspawn quickened into wriggling punctuation marks. The weather chart was filled in up to date. They taught us to tell a tree by its leaves. Once, thanks to my teachers, I knew the difference between the Mute and the Bewick's Swan. Nature Study was the gentle ladies' favourite subject. Once for weeks we had a snuffling hedgehog in a cardboard box. They loved animals.

Everything was a competition.

Every Friday there was a reshuffle, you were moved in descending order from the back row to the front, according to your marks, according to your stars.

Every summer there was a week of Tests. From this was decided the list of prizewinners. *Black Beauty*—for General Excellence Elsie Lochhead has been awarded Third Prize (Equal) in Class Primary V says this florid label, laurel leaves, a garland. My mother thought this poor and to be honest I had not thought to sink so low. One place lower next year and it would be a mere Certificate of Merit. No book.

6

And there was the Gala Day to consider too. Newarthill Miners Welfare Association organised it. There was a marquee, the sweet smell of cut grass under canvas, a tombola, a ride around the village on the back of a crepe-paper-decorated lorry, milk and a bag of buns. And every year from the Top Class of the Primary School there was the Gala Queen, the cleverest girl in all the school, not the prettiest, the most popular, not the voted-for. The miners respected education above all. Like everything else this was a glittering prize for cleverness, the true worth. No one questioned it. The Girl Dux, the Queen, and the Boy Dux her Champion. Led around on a white horse. Made to wear brown velvet doublet and hose, usually wrinkled. And the Queen in a white dress in a car like a wedding car.

Even the colour of your sewing was a prize. Twice a week at the end of the afternoon for an hour we were Split Up. The boys from the girls. The boys got handwork, raffia mats, the girls sewing. We made lap bags of linen to keep our knitting in. Learned in theory to turn a heel. The linen was in three colours. Miss Ferguson gave the cleverest—according to last weeks Test Marks—first choice. Pink, blue or helio. No one liked helio. Miss Ferguson said the stupid did not deserve a choice in anything. Had to take what they got.

History and Geography. The Tulipfields of Holland. Bruce and the Spider. Or Composition. A Day In the Life of a Penny. A Walk In the Rain. Never use the word got or a preposition to end a sentence with. Mine were usually best, sometimes they even got Read Out and I'd be extra proud, go home with something good to tell. To maybe make up for the six out of ten sums. I loved Composition. I knew what they wanted you to write. I knew to be one of the Winners, the Clever Ones, you had to be clean and neat and quiet and eager and just anxious enough under the tense time-counting pressure of Mental Arithmetic or Dictation. I loved school.

Except for that Worst Day. Remember it. Go back. Before your bath on Friday nights your mother combed your hair in her lap with a fine-tooth comb, carefully checking. There was once she found Something, said who had you been playing with, never never to try on anyone else's pixie. Next day she bought a bottle from the Chemists called Suleo Emulsion. Smelt horrible. A sticky pomade. You had to keep it on for at least forty-eight hours, so on Monday you had to go to school slicked with it, your hair in ratstails. You prayed the nit-nurse would not come that day. She did not come often, five times, six times in the seven years of Primary School. But that day she came. You could not believe it, you wanted to die, you wished you'd wake up and it wasn't true. Your class went to the hall. You queued up. Girls first. She lifted all your skirts quickly, tested your eyes, made you read a row of letters, looked in your ears, looked at your hair. You felt sick and dumb. She said Hmm, and stay behind please. The rest of the class went back to the classroom, looking back. Your best friend

7

waved. You were left these with Jeannie Nielson and Hugh Gilmour. The Nurse said did you realise you had a Dirty Head. You explained about your mother checking, the stuff she'd put on, on Saturday. She said Ah yes but this should have been noticed Before. But there was probably no need to notify the parents as it was being dealt with. She gave Jeannie Nielson and Hugh Gilmour a Letter to Take Home. You went back to the classroom, burning, heard whispers, kept your head down over your sums, tried to concentrate. You were in the Very Back Seat, were Top that week, all the morning heads kept turning round, the people who had been your friends hissing Did You Get A Note. You did not answer. Later you said you had really been kept back because you might need glasses.

My mother was angry when I told her at lunchtime. Said what had the nurse meant should have been noticed before, she checked every week in life. My grandmother was there on a visit, said it was a disgrace and if my mother did not go and see the headmaster then she would. I said please granny don't come, just leave it. It was a whisper.

All afternoon you dread it. Kept looking at the glass above the door waiting for her smart felt hat to show, for the rap of her knuckles. Eventually the headmaster came, asked to see you, took you to his office. Asked for the whole story. Your grandmother was on her high horse, saying it was a well-known fact they'd rather leave a Dirty Head for a clean one. The Nurse was there, flustered. The headmaster was saying the whole thing was Very Regrettable. You felt terrible.

From *A Protestant Girlhood* by Liz Lochhead

The Competition

When I was ten, going to Hamilton
On the Leyland bus named for Eddlewood,
A boy with an aeroplane just like mine
Zoomed at his war games in the seat in front.
I'd never seen such a school uniform—
As brown as the manure in Cousar's coup
Where someone's city cousin had jumped in
Having been told it was 'just sand'—
One of Glasgow's best fee-paying places,
Brown as barrowloads from the blue-bottled byre.
I couldn't help it; I had to talk to him
And tell him I, too, had a Hurricane.
His mother pulled him to her, he sat sullen,
As if I'd spoiled his game. I spoke again,
And he called me a poor boy, who should shut up.

I'd never thought of it like that.
The summer tenements were so dry I cried.
My grandfather wouldn't give *him* sixpence;·
He'd never have a grudge as lovely as mine.

Years later, running in a race, barefooted
As I'd trained my spikes to ruin, convinced
My best competitor was him, I ran into
The worst weathers of pain, determined to win,
But on the last lap, inches from the tape, was beaten
By someone from Shotts Miners' Welfare Harriers Club.

Douglas Dunn

Sheaves

The patch of wasteground had always been called the Hunty. Nobody
knew why. Nobody even knew what the name meant. It was roughly
rectangular, the same length as the tenement block that backed on to
it. There had once been a line of walls, railings and middens
separating the Hunty from the actual back courts, but progressive
decay, wind and rain, and several generations of children had eroded
this barrier almost completely.

Aleck and Joe had crossed into the Hunty and were crouching
down playing at farms. Aleck had a toy tractor and a few plastic
animals, and Joe had a Land-Rover and trailer, and some soldiers to
use as farmworkers.

Using bits of slate, they scraped up a patch of dirt and divided it
into fields which they furrowed with lollipop sticks. Joe crammed
some scrubby grass into his trailer and Aleck made a primitive
farmhouse out of a cornflakes packet.

They were both wearing T-shirts and khaki shorts, and for the first
time since the start of the endless summer, Aleck suddenly shivered.
The wind was cold. His clothes were too thin. That morning his
mother had said it was the first day of autumn.

'Gawn tae Sunday school this efternin?' asked Joe.

'Ach aye,' said Aleck. 'Mightaswell. Anywey, it's harvest the day.'

There had been a harvest service on the wireless that morning.
Aleck had been half listening to it during breakfast. That was
probably what had made him think about farms and bring out the
toys they were playing with.

'We aw slept in fur Chapel,' said Joe. 'Huv tae go the night.'

Apart from the rough grass, all that grew on the wasteground were
nettles and dandelions. Aleck plucked a dandelion clock. Fluffy ball

that had once been a bright yellow flower. Peethebed. He began blowing on it, sending the seeds drifting through the air, counting to tell the time.

One . . . Two

Each seed would hang, parachute down, land somewhere else and grow again.

Three . . . Four

Joe had grown tired of farming and he was using his soldiers as soldiers. They took over the cornflakes packet and killed some of the animals for food.

Five . . . Six

Joe made aeroplane noises and dive-bombed the farm with stones and clods of earth. The soldiers and animals were scattered, the fields churned up, laid waste.

Seven . . . Eight

Aleck wondered why dandelions were called peethebeds. Maybe you wet the bed if you ate them.

Nine.

Aleck's mother opened the window and shouted him up. That meant it must be time to get ready for Sunday school. About half past one.

He gathered up his things.

'Mibbe see ye efter,' said Joe.

'Prob'ly,' said Aleck.

As he crossed the back court towards his close, he decided that the time told by a dandelion clock was magic. That was why it was different from ordinary time. If you caught one of the seeds you could make a secret wish. That proved they were magic. Only special people knew how it worked. Like Jesus and witches and medicine men. Magic time.

He could see his mother working at the sink, the window slightly open. He stopped and cradled his toys against him with one arm, almost dropping them as he waved up at her.

The theme music for the end of *Family Favourites* was crackling out above the rush of the tap. Behind the sports page, his father absently was singing along, adding the words here and there.

'With a song in my heart
Da da dee, da da dee, da da dee . . .'

His mother, at the sink, was washing and cutting vegetables for soup, a pot with a bone for stock simmering away on one gas ring. On the other, a kettle of water for Aleck to wash himself was just coming to the boil.

'Ah'll let ye in here tae get washed in a minnit son.'

'Och ah'm quite clean mammy. Ah'll jist gie ma hands'n face a wee wipe.'

'A cat's lick an a promise ye mean! Naw son, ye've goat tae wash yerself right. Ah mean yer manky. Ye canny go tae Sunday school lik that.'

'Da da dee da doo
I will live life through
With a song in my heart
FOOOOR YEW!'

On the last line of the song his father stood up, arms outstretched, still holding the newspaper, hanging on to the long nasal concluding note, crescendo drowning out the radio, hearing himself as a miraculous combination of Al Jolson and Richard Tauber and Bing Crosby.

'Whit a singer!' he said, patting his chest.

'Whit a heid ye mean!' said his mother.

'Ah'm tellin ye, ah shoulda been on the stage.'

'Aye, scrubbin it!' they replied, in unison, and they all laughed.

She shifted the vegetables on to the running board, emptied the basin and unclogged the sink of peelings. Then she cleaned out the basin and poured in hot water from the kettle.

'Right!' she said, handing him a towel.

Stirring the water with his hands, he made ripples and waves, whirlpools and storms. He squeezed the soap so that it slipped up and out of his grasp and blooped into the basin. He slapped the water with his palm, ruffled it up till its surface was a froth of bubbles. Then he washed his hands and arms, face and neck.

'Aboot time tae!' said his mother. 'Yirra mucky pup, so yar.'

She laid a sheet of newspaper on the floor in front of the fire and lifted the basin on to it.

'Feet an legs!' she said. He looked down at his grubby knees and didn't bother to complain.

Sometimes he didn't mind being clean. It could give you a warm feeling inside, like being good. It was just so much of an effort.

His mother laid out his shirt and his suit, his heavy shoes and a pair of clean white ankle socks.

This was the horrible part, the part that was really disgusting. The clothes made him feel so stiff and uncomfortable.

Slowly, sadly, he put them on.

The shoes were solid polished black leather and he consciously clumped round the kitchen. He found it impossible to feel at ease. Clumpetty shoes and cissy white socks. He glowered down at his stupid feet, his shirt collar chafing his neck. He put away his blue socks and white sandshoes. They were what he liked to wear. When he wore them he could run fast, climb dykes, pad and stalk like an Indian. Playing football he could jink and dribble without making one wrong move. Blue and white flashing. A rightness. A sureness of touch. The feel of things.

Clump!

'Whit's the matter?'

'Eh?'

'Yer face is trippin ye.'

'Nothin.'

'Yer no gonnae start aboot thae shoes'n socks again ur ye?'

'Naw. Ah'm awright mammy, honest.'

He knew he couldn't explain and he knew if he tried she would just go on about how lucky he was to have a decent set of clothes to wear. Then his father would chip in about when he was at school—bare feet or parish boots.

His father had laid down the paper, so he picked it up and looked for the jokes and cartoons. Oor Wullie. The Broons. Merry Mac's Fun Parade.

Oor Wullie, Your Wullie, A'body's Wullie. That always made him snigger because of the double meaning.

Wullie and Fat Boab were being chased by P.C. Murdoch because they'd knocked off his helmet. As usual, everything ended happily. As usual, Murdoch had a kindly knowing twinkle in his eye. As usual, Wullie was on his bucket in the last frame, slapping his thighs and laughing.

Real policemen didn't wear helmets any more. They wore caps with black and white checks. They swore at you and moved you on for loitering and booked you for playing football in the street. Joe had been booked about three weeks before and he was waiting for a summons to go to court. There had been about eight of them playing, but only Joe had been caught. He'd been using his jacket as a goalpost and when he'd stopped to pick it up he'd fallen behind. The others had charged through closes and escaped across the Hunty. Aleck had torn his knee on some barbed wire and he'd worn an ostentatious bandage for a week. When anyone had asked what was wrong he'd tried to look sinister like a gangster and spat out his reply.

'Ah goat it runnin fae the polis.'

And he'd hoped it conjured up a picture of himself, gun-toting masked desperado in a running shoot-out across Govan. Wanted. Hunted.

Clump!

'An mind an keep thae shoes clean an don't go gettin them scuffed playin football.'

'Ah kin jist see me playin football in Sunday school!'

'Less a your cheek boy! Yer mother's right. We canny be forever buyin ye new shoes wi you kickin the toes outy them.'

In one frame, Wullie was skulking, head hung, shoulders hunched, and above his head was the word GUILTY.

That was the name of one of Aleck's comics. It had JUSTICE TRAPS THE in small letters across the top, with GUILTY in big red print above blue-uniformed American policemen machine-gunning their way into a roomful of gangsters. Into a plastic bag his mother put a little of each of the vegetables she was using for the soup. Carrot, turnip, potato, celery, onion, leek. This was to be his offering for the service. She added an apple and laid the bag on the table, together with his bible and a penny for the collection.

'There. That's you.'

He was over at the stove, looking in the pot. The broth was coloured red-gold and the fatty stock made the surface shine, globules bubbling, catching the light.

'Smells good.'

'Well, ye kin get intae that when ye get back. Noo c'mon or ye'll be late.'

On his way out of the close he was about to take a running kick at a tin can but he remembered about his shoes and he stopped, restrained. At the next corner were three or four boys he knew, boys his mother was always telling him to stay away from, because every time he got into trouble, it just happened to be with them. They saw him crossing the road and they whistled and shouted at him.

'Waell!'

'Gawn yersel!'

'Heh Aleck, yer luvly!'

'Ah'll get ye!'

One of them began singing and clapping his hands in time.

'Will ye come to the mission
Will ye come will ye come
Will ye come to the mission
Will ye come.'

Aleck laughed back at them but he was blushing and he felt hot and confused. He wanted to go to Sunday school, but at the same time he envied them their freedom and their dirt. His walk was suddenly clumsy and awkward and he was happy to take a short-cut through a close, away from their taunting.

The mission hall was a converted shop, stuck between a close and a Handy Store. The flaking paint on its front was an indeterminate colour—a dirty green or brown. Above the door was the name GLASGOW CITY MISSION and on one of the boarded-up windows was a list of the week's activities. Sunday School. Bible Class. Christian Endeavour. Band of Hope.

Mr Neil was at the door to welcome everybody in, grinning, nodding, pushing up his glasses which kept slipping down his nose. He was not much taller than most of the older children.

'Hello Aleck. Hello. Comeaway in.'

Inside, the place was cool and dark, the only sunlight getting in through the open door. Aleck could smell the different fruits and flowers and vegetables that most of the children had brought, above the usual smell of damp and polished wood and musty old books. The seats were arranged in groups of five or six, the children grouped according to age. At the far end was a small raised platform, with a piano, a lectern and a table draped with a white cloth. On the table stood a wooden cross and a vase of mixed flowers—yellow and red.

At the piano was Mrs Neil, a big woman with greying hair. She wore a white hat and glasses with frames that turned up at the side, like wings. She was talking to Jim, the teacher for Aleck's group, who waved to him as he came in.

Aleck went and sat at his place, making too much noise with his chair. There were four other boys in the group—David, Robert, Martin and John. They all looked up and said hello.

'Learned yer text Aleck?' asked David. David was the only one of the group that Aleck really thought of as a friend. The others had returned their attention to their bibles and were soundlessly mouthing the text over and over.

'Jist aboot,' said Aleck. He opened his bible at the place, which he'd marked by inserting his attendance card and his membership card for the Life Boys.

He went over the words into himself.

'Mark 4: 28 and 29—For the earth bringeth forth fruit of herself; first the blade, then the ear, after that the full corn in the ear. But when the fruit is brought forth, immediately he putteth in the sickle, because the harvest is come.'

'Quite a long wan this week, intit,' said David.

'Aye, so it is,' said Aleck. 'An ah canny get ma tongue roon that "putteth in the sickle".'

'Aye it's hard right enough. Whit is a sickle anywey?'

'It's wan a they things fur cuttin grass. Lik a big knife wi a blade lik that . . .' and Aleck drew an arc in the air with his forefinger.

He went on, 'D'ye remember they kerds ye goat wi Flags bubble-gum?'

'Aye.'

'Well, d'ye remember the Russian wan ah hid, the wan ah widnae swap?'

'Aye, aye it was a red flag.'

'Well, thoan wee things in the coarner wis a hammer an sickle, croassed lik that.' He crossed his forefingers in front of him.

'Aw aye, ah remember. Huv ye ever seen a real wan?'

'A red flag?'

'Naw, a sickle.'

'Naw. Huv you?'

'Naw. Bet it wid be some chib, eh?'

They hadn't heard Jim coming up behind them. He tapped David on the head with his bible.

14

'What would be some "chib"?' he asked, sitting down at the head of the group.

'A sickle,' said David, slicing the air to demonstrate. 'Schuk!'

'Bloodthirsty shower!' said Jim.

Aleck asked him if he'd seen a real sickle.

'Och yes,' he replied. 'We've got one at home. In the toolshed.'

Aleck had forgotten that Jim lived in a house with a garden. He only came to Govan to teach at the mission. He was about twenty-five and he always had a redfaced, clean and scrubbed look. He smelled of soap and haircream, and he always wore a sports jacket with a Christian Endeavour badge in the lapel.

'Ah'm glad you all managed to bring something for the service,' he said. 'Have you all learned the text?'

He got five different replies, from Yes through Silence to No.

'Ach well, we'll see anyway. Would you like to pass me your cards?'

While he was taking in the attendance cards, David turned again to Aleck.

'Didye go tae the pictures last night Aleck?'

'Naw. Ah jist steyed in. Did you?'

'Aye. Ma big brurra took us tae the Lyceum. It was a war picture. Aboot Korea. Terrific! Ah'll tell ye aboot it efter.'

Jim took each of them in turn, and with varying degrees of assurance and hesitancy they intoned the text for the day in the same monotone of incantation that characterized the way they would recite the alphabet or the multiplication tables or any other memorized litany. Then he marked their cards, once for attendance, once for reciting the text. He also marked Aleck's Life Boy card.

The Junior Division of the Boys' Brigade. Sure and Steadfast.

'That's fine,' said Jim. 'Now if you'd all like to open your bibles at the place, we'll have a wee look at it. Mr Neil's going to talk about it after, so I won't spend too much time on it. Right, well what's the text about then?'

'Harvest,' said Robert.

'Right, and what's that?'

'Time a year when aw the crops ur ready,' said David. 'Corn an wheat an stuff.'

'Fine,' said Jim. 'In fact all the crops we need to make food. To live. And that's why we celebrate harvest specially. To give thanks for our food. Now. Do you remember what a parable is?'

'A story,' said Aleck.

'That's right, but it's a special kind of story that Jesus told. If you look at the top of the page it says The Parable of the Sower. Now Jesus told stories like this when he wanted to explain something in a way people could understand. This one starts at verse 3.

'... Behold there went out a sower to sow ...' And Jim read them the whole story, about some seed falling by the wayside and some on stony ground and some among thorns and some on good soil, and when nobody understood, Jim explained about the sower being Jesus.

'If you could look at verse 14,' he went on, 'it says "the sower soweth the word". So Jesus is trying to make something grow from his words. Now, what do you think it is?'

Everybody shrugged or looked at the floor.

'Look at verses 30 to 32.'

Five heads scanning the books.

Silence, except for rustling pages and shuffling feet and creaking chairs.

'No? Oh well. It is quite difficult I suppose. It's talking about the Kingdom of God, growing up like a tree.

'So if Jesus is the sower, trying to make it grow by spreading his words, what d'you think it means about the different kinds of soil?'

Another silence. Then Aleck said, 'Different kindsa people?'

'Yes!' said Jim. 'Good. Good. We're getting there!'

When he finished explaining he said, 'I suppose these things'll be easier when you're older,' and he smiled and added, 'like me'.

The singing of hymns left Aleck feeling strange, though he didn't know why. Sometimes he felt like crying. Sometimes he felt his face flush. Everything seemed very real but far away, as if he was watching it on a film.

Above the platform hung a single light bulb with a pink plastic shade. Aleck was looking at it as if he'd never seen it before. There was a dark crack on the shade, running from the rim about half way up. Aleck hated pink. The colour was like the sound of the word, like the taste of the pink pudding they sometimes had in the school dinner-hall.

Mr Neil with his wife at the piano had led them in singing the hymns. Heavenly sunshine. This little light of mine. This is my story. Give me oil in my lamp.

Cracked pink plastic shade. Sickly insipid pink.

Now Mr Neil was talking, about harvest and parables, about the day's text. The miracle of the growing corn. Man's labour in tending and growing. He putteth in the sickle, because the harvest is come.

'And I know,' he was saying, 'that it's difficult for us in a place like Glasgow, and especially in a place like Govan, to appreciate what harvest really means. I mean it's only in the country that people can really be aware of the changing seasons and what they mean, because there it matters, and so much of your life is bound up with these changes and the actual growing of the food we eat depends on them. Now as you know, the food you eat is just bought by your mothers from the shops. More than likely it comes in packets and tins. The whole process of getting the food from where it's produced to your table is so...so vast and complicated that it's easy to lose sight of the fact that it all still depends on those same basic changes. On the sun and the rain. On the goodness of the soil. On human effort, and patience, and skill. And you know, I've been thinking about all this and about these parables that Jesus told. Like the one you've been talking about today—the parable of the Sower. And I've been thinking especially about the way Jesus used parables—with one meaning on the surface that is obvious and easy to see, but with another far deeper, far greater meaning which is there for us to find.

'And in this parable of the Sower—at one level it's just a wee story about a man planting his seeds, and what happens to them. But when we see that the Sower is Christ, then we see that other meaning, and we think of the harvest that He will reap. And there are so many passages from the bible, so many hymns that tell us the same story, that "All the world is God's own field". And you are that harvest, boys and girls. You are his children. And if you grow in his light, you will

> "stand at the last accepted,
> Christ's golden sheaves for evermore
> to garners bright elected."

And you will be gathered to Him, to dwell with Him in Heaven.

'And no matter what happens to you, even if the dirt of the world seems to have settled on you and made you forget what you really are, deep inside you are still his golden sheaves. And no matter how drab and grey and horrible our lives and this place may sometimes seem, remember that this is only the surface. And even the muck of hundreds of years cannot hide that other meaning which is behind all things. The meaning that we are here to celebrate. That God is Love and Christ is Life.

'And now boys and girls, if you will pray with me in the name of our Lord Jesus Christ, The Light of the World, The Sower of the Word, who taught us when we pray to say . . .

"Our Father . . ."

And everyone stood and joined in—

> "whichartinheaven
> hallowedbethyname
> thykingdomcome
> thywillbedone
> inearth
> asitisinheaven
> giveusthisday
> ourdailybread
> andforgiveusourdebts
> asweforgiveourdebtors
> leadusnot
> intotemptation

butdeliverus
fromevil
forthineisthekingdom
andthepower
andtheglory
forever
amen.

'Now then,' said Mr Neil, 'whose turn is it to take the collection?'

A small girl from one of the younger groups raised her hand.

'Ah yes, Cathy. Here you are then.' And he handed her the collection bag.

Another two girls from the same group were appointed to gather in the harvest offerings. These they collected in a large laundry basket made of bright yellow plastic, which Mr Neil brought out from behind the table. And as the girls performed the little ceremony with as much slow solemnity as they could, Mrs Neil played Bringing in the Sheaves.

With Mr Neil's help, they raised the basket on to the table, between the flowers and the cross. Then he gave thanks once more and everyone stood as he led them in the closing hymn—We plough the fields and scatter.

This was one of Aleck's favourite hymns. It had the same kind of thumping triumphant feel as the tunes they sang at the match or played in the Orange Walk.

> 'We plough the fields and scatter
> The good seed on the land
> But it is fed and watered
> By God's almighty hand;
> He sends the snow in winter
> The warmth to swell the grain
> The breezes and the sunshine
> And soft refreshing rain.'

And Mr Neil conducted some vast imagined angelic choir, clenching his fists and jabbing the air, raising high his cupped hands, stretching wide his arms. And the voices rose with each wobbling note on the piano, up and out across the back courts and the tenements, the puddles and the rubbish, and the broken walls and railings and the sad sparse tufts of grass and nettle that encroached regardless.

> 'All good gifts around us
> Are sent from heaven above;
> Then thank the Lord, O thank the Lord,
> For all His love.'

As David and Aleck crossed the back court, David was describing and acting out scenes from the Korean war film he'd seen at the Lyceum.

'Anywey ther's this Yankee pilot gets shot doon bi the communists, an ye see um fightin is wey oot the cockpit wi aw these flames roon aboot um. 'Nen e manages tae bale oot. An ye jist see is face lookin up, really shitin is sel. Then ye jist see um gawn lik that...Nyaaa!' And with his finger he indicated the spiralling fall.

'But did you say they wur fightin communists?'

'Aye.'

'An the yanks ur the goodies?'

'Aye.'

'But your da's a communist.'

'Aye. Ah know. Ah couldnae understaun that either. But ah didnae bother. It was a great picture.'

Aleck left David at his own close and carried on down the road. At the corner were the same boys he'd passed earlier. They were kicking a ball about. He wondered if they would be gathered to Heaven too. They didn't go to Sunday school. He didn't know.

In his mind the whole day was a confusion; of dandelions and playing and hymns, of soldiers and communists and golden sheaves, harvest and parables and magic time.

The ball bounced across towards him, and instinctively he trapped it and chipped it back. One or two of them gave a sarcastic cheer. The ball went to Shuggie, who was in Aleck's class at school. He shouted across to him.

'Come doon efter if ye want a gemm. We'll be playin roon the Hunty.'

'Thanks,' said Aleck. 'Ah might dae that.' And he started off towards home. Suddenly he laughed and began to run. His dinner would be ready. He would change into his old clothes, and after he'd eaten he would go to the Hunty and play till it was dark.

In his path was a piece of stone chipped from a brick and without slowing down he booted it hard across the road and went charging on towards his close.

From *Its Colours they are Fine* by Alan Spence

NOTES

'Jesus Loves Me' is taken from Chapter 1 of *Jean in the Morning* (Macmillan) by Janet Sandison, a realistic unsentimental description of Jean Robertson's childhood in a Scottish Lowland village during World War I. Several later episodes, particularly the village children's revolt against a tyrannical head-master, are of interest.

The opening chapter of Joyce's *A Portrait of the Artist as a Young Man* (Penguin), Chapter 2 of Dickens' *David Copperfield* and the first four chapters of Dylan Thomas's *Portrait of the Artist as a Young Dog* (Dent) are useful comparisons with this extract. See also Alan Spence's short story, 'Tinsel', elsewhere in this anthology.

'My Primary School', apart from the interest of the subject-matter, is distinguished by the writer's creative use of such devices as capital letters, hyphens, minor sentences and questions. This essay, 'A Protestant Girlhood', appears in *Jock Tamson's Bairns—Essays on a Scots Childhood* (Hamish Hamilton), a collection of essays by younger Scottish writers, which is a key source for the post-war Scottish childhood experience. Particularly recommended are Alan Spence's 'Boom Baby' and Bill Bryden's 'Member At?'.

Cider with Rosie by Laurie Lee (Penguin) and *Village School* by Miss Read (Penguin) contain interesting descriptions of first days at school. A good Scottish version of the theme is Janetta Bowie's *Penny Buff* (Constable).

'The Competition': Stephen Spender's poem, 'Children who were Rough', is a suitable companion piece.

'Sheaves': Alan Spence's collection of short stories. *Its Colours they are Fine* (Collins), is an almost definitive imaginative re-creation of a Glasgow working-class childhood, local yet universal.

2

FAMILY MATTERS

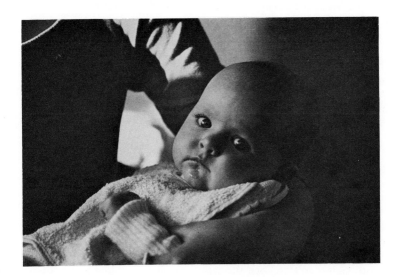

A Baby in the House

'Aw, it's yerself, Charlie,' he said. 'Welcome tae the mad-house.'

'That's a sair oxter ye've got, John,' Charlie said, chucking wee John on the cheek.

'Aye. An' sometimes Ah canny get sleepin' for it at nights. Hang yer coat up there.'

The pegs, like everything else in the hall, were new. The house was a re-let and John was systematically obliterating the signs of former tenancy. He had finished decorating the hall and the living-room and was starting on the kitchen.

As they went into the living-room, Margaret shouted 'Hullo' from the kitchen. The room had that occupied air that the presence of a baby brings. Fender, chairs, and table were no more than improvised billets for the paraphernalia attendant on babyhood. Vests and a nightgown lay in neat array on the table. A pile of laundered nappies was on one chair and on another, one nappy was laid out ready for use. Talcum and cream stood ready by the fire. A rubber mat lay on the hearth rug.

'Just wait till Ah fit Bronco wi' a silencer,' John said, crossing to turn down the volume of the television. The horses galloped on in silence.

'An' how's the Scarlet Pimpernel the night? Ye've been doin' yer invisible man lately, right enough.'

'Aye, Ah haven't been about much,' Charlie conceded.

'About much? Ah thought we were goin' tae have tae send out the police message. Whitehall 1212 stuff.'

John was preoccupied with completing the stripping of the baby that Charlie had interrupted. He laid him on the carpet and unpinned his nappy, averting his head from the contents.

'Oh, son. Ye'll need tae come fae a' that. That's inhuman. Ye'll no' make many friends that way. Ah've heard o' B.O., but that's goin' too far.'

The baby lay unconcernedly while he was wiped. Then John started to hold him above his head, raising and lowering him while he gurgled regularly like a mechanical toy.

'There he is. Look at 'im,' John said. 'Five months an' he hasn't struck a blow yet. They say they've got nothing for 'im at the Broo. He's still to say a word, too. Definitely backward. Spell "constipation". Ye can't, can ye? Well, if ye can't spell it, what about getting it? Eh? Before the hoose gets condemned.' A thread of saliva trailed from the baby's mouth. 'Ye can see the intelligence looking out 'im though, can't ye? See the witty way he's drooling at me there? Ye've got a great career ahead of ye, lad. Remember that. The sky's the limit for you. You could be slaverer to royalty if ye put yer mind to it. Hup, 2, 3, 4. Hup, 2, 3, 4.'

Margaret came in carrying a large basin steaming faintly with hot water.

'Stop it, John,' she said. 'You'll make 'im sick. An' how's Charlie? John. Ah've told ye already.'

She bustled out and back in again, bringing with her a yellow square of foam-rubber that she submerged in the basin. Charlie realized how much she had changed since the baby was born. She had become much more defined as a person, had gained a new authority. The way she went about bathing John junior typified it.

'Ye're just in time for the big performance, Charlie,' she said. 'First house.'

She spread a towel on her knees, took the baby and eased him into the water, cooing him into a sense of security. Conversation between John and Charlie was only incidental to the performance that was taking place in front of them. It had the natural rightness about it that makes people look at a flying bird or accord a few minutes' silent homage to the running of a river. Margaret was no more than an elemental extension of the baby, her hands providing the protection he couldn't yet give himself. He turned placidly this way and that in her grip, prismatically reflecting pleasure in whatever he was facing, the flames of the fire, his father, the edge of the basin, while the water was laved about him. Dry-docked on his mother's lap, he lay like an apprentice Michelin man, radiating with wrinkles, while John supplied Margaret with the required articles in turn, muttering tersely as he did so.

'Cream. Talcum. Nappy,' he said dramatically. 'Do you think the patient will live, Doctor? Look at it. Isn't it fantastic the amount of care that's lavished on the human bum? It's no' that it's a braw thing, either. But that's all weans are, when ye think of it. A pickle o' flesh round two openings. Entrance and exit. It's no'a human bein' we've got at a', Margaret. It's a one-way street for chuck.'

Margaret was unimpressed by John's philosophical insight.

'Never mind, son,' she said. 'It's just yer daft daddy talking.'

Now that he was nappied and nightgowned, hunger came on him like a conditioned reflex. It started as a preliminary wail and was maturing into a howl by the time Margaret had taken the bottle from the fireside, tested the heat of the milk on her wrist, and plugged his mouth with it. The yell transmuted to a gurgle and the gradual lowering of his eyelids registered his progress to satiety. In the silence that ensued, muffled voices could be heard from the television.

From *Remedy is None* by William McIlvanney

A Family Scene

Nearly fifty years of life and nearly twenty-five years of marriage, and nothing to show for it except a houseful of people who had come from God knows where. Samuel Haddow often said the country was overrun with people.

It was a remark that had started as a fresh joke and flattened into a habit. There was a pair of socks in his chair, even.

'They're your own socks,' his wife told him, before he could complain. 'Peter hasn't got any black socks.'

'What do you mean, Peter hasn't got any black socks? Does he think he's taking these? He can go out and dirty a pair of white socks. My God, nothing's private.'

His son Peter stood in bare feet and underpants, with his back to the living-room fire and when Samuel glared at him, the boy shrugged his bony shoulders as if he was pleading innocence. Samuel didn't know whether this was more irritating than words. The boy seemed to have a genius for driving him over the edge of exasperation even by doing nothing at all.

'Oh, take the damn socks,' he muttered. What was so important about a pair of socks, that he should go mad over them? He had promised himself he would let it all flow over him and keep his temper. Fathers were supposed to be fond of their children, but a great deep well of irritation always opened up inside him as soon as he came home and found them there; especially Peter. The boy can't be as bad as that. I would give the damned socks away to a beggar and never miss them. But a beggar wouldn't take them for granted, that's the truth.

'You don't want him to look wrong when he's going to the school dance,' Mrs Haddow said apprehensively, trying to sound casual and businesslike. Her manner merely underlined her anxiety to avoid an outbreak of Samuel's temper, and this somehow irritated him even more.

'I said he could have the socks, I don't care about the socks, you're ironing that crease squinty.'

'Now you're not going to tell me how to press trousers after all these years,' Mrs Haddow said testily. 'Men don't know everything.'

'Here,' said Peter. 'I'll press the pants, and you can go and make the tea, Mum.'

'*You'll* press the pants!' Samuel's well of irritation bubbled again. 'You'll look sweet dancing wi' a hole the shape of an iron on your backside.'

'I'll be careful, Dad.' Peter said, quite reasonably.

'Aye, sure, you'll be careful.' Samuel forced himself to look at his evening paper. The boy *would* be careful, he wasn't in the habit of doing things badly. There was just something about the way he did them.

'I've got some nice spiced beef ham for your tea, Samuel,' his wife said brightly. Appeasing the monster. It was so transparent that a grin twitched at Samuel's mouth. What a bloody life. I'm a monster. Emily surrendered the iron to Peter reluctantly, convinced that he would ruin his good trousers. Men didn't have the touch for jobs like that.

But in the jumble of thoughts that lived in her head, she never lost sight of the need to take care of Samuel, even if Peter *did* arrive at the dance with his backside showing. Men were like babies, especially fathers, and it was important to let them see that they weren't being neglected in favour of their children. She had read it somewhere and its beautiful simplicity had startled her like a revelation of the Light.

The trousers were laid on a folded bedsheet on the living-room table, and Peter was pressing the iron on a damp cloth in a one-two, one-two-three rhythm and humming to himself. His feet began to twitch in sympathy. Samuel caught sight of them, past the edge of his newspaper, and grinned again. The boy was a bloody clown.

'You'd be better goin' in your bare feet,' he remarked. The derision in his voice was mere ingrained custom. 'Socks'll just hide that fancy toe stuff.'

'Yes, I do have rather pretty feet,' Peter said in a thoughtful, yah-yah voice, and Samuel looked to heaven and muttered, 'Oh God, he's got modesty like a wasting disease.' Julie, ten years old, came into the living-room, skinny and self-contained, and stared at Peter with a sneer.

'You look stupid,' she said. Peter answered with a wolfish smile and laid his right foot flat against his left thigh.

It was always the same, there was always something going on, kids spilling over the whole house. Who were they? Christine, twenty, came home from work to find Peter dressed except for his shoes; wriggling the waistband of his trousers to try to make them hang lower. She swooped on him as if she had just created him and started tweaking his tie.

'Dere's a handsome wee brother,' she cooed. 'All nice and clean for his first dance.'

'Dere's a nice wee sister asking for a belt right in the chops,' Peter said. Samuel looked up sharply and then shrugged his shoulders.

'Who's taking you home tonight, Petesy-wetesy?' Christine asked. 'Whose heart is going to be broken?'

'Whose teeth are going to be broken in a minute?' Peter asked her, and she chuckled merrily.

'There, doesn't he look handsome, Mum?' Christine insisted. 'I think our wee Peter's too good for any of these schoolgirls.'

'Don't be silly, Christine,' Mrs Haddow said sharply. 'Peter's too young to be thinking about girls.'

'That's right, Mum—' Peter was saying patiently, when his father answered, 'He'll be dancin' wi' whippets.'

'—Corporation buses.' Peter finished, and his father grinned at him triumphantly. 'You're no' the only comic in the world,' he said. And Peter cried, 'Everybody gets inta de act!' Mrs Haddow looked vexed and uncomprehending, and Samuel and Peter exchanged a rare smile of collusion.

From *The Taste of Too Much* by Clifford Hanley

Poem for my Sister

My little sister likes to try my shoes,
to strut in them,
admire her spindle-thin twelve-year-old legs
in this season's styles.
She says they fit her perfectly,
but wobbles
on their high heels, they're
hard to balance.

I like to watch my little sister
playing hopscotch,
admire the neat hops-and-skips of her,
their quick peck,
never-missing their mark, not
over-stepping the line.
She is competent at peever.

I try to warn my little sister
about unsuitable shoes,
point out my own distorted feet, the callouses,
odd patches of hard skin.
I should not like to see her
in *my* shoes.
I wish she could stay
sure footed,
                    sensibly shod.

Liz Lochhead

The Night that Uncle Hughie
Fought the Egg

'What wis this about an egg?' his uncle Hughie asked. He had an insatiable passion for all tricks, riddles, and feats of general curiosity.

'Ye must've seen it done,' Charlie's father said. 'It's just a matter o' tryin' tae break an egg longways.'

'An egg?' Uncle Hughie said incredulously.

'A comming or garding egg,' Charlie's father said, warming to the fact that it was new to Uncle Hughie. 'Ye just haud it at the two tips between yer hands. And ye canny break it. That's a fact.'

Charlie's father demonstrated the prescribed method of holding the egg.

26

'Ach, get away wi' ye!' Uncle Hughie's lip curled sceptically.

'That's as sure as Ah'm sitting here, Hughie. Ah've tried it maself.'

Uncle Hughie appealed to an invisible synod. As he looked back at Charlie's father his scorn was tempered with sympathy.

'Ye mean tae tell me, John, that you're goin' tae sit there, a grown man, an' tell me that ye couldny break an egg?'

'Ah'm tellin' ye mair than that. *You* couldny break an egg, if ye haud it the way Ah'm talkin' aboot.'

The slur on his manhood was too much for Uncle Hughie, six feet in his woollen socks, half as many broad, with arms like pit-props, reputed to be one of the strongest men in the shire in his prime, who had made a habit of lifting derailed hutches loaded with coal back on to the lines single-handed, who had once carried a huge concrete ball thirty yards from one gatepost to another, whose party piece was so to fill his jacket-sleeve with a flexed forearm that you couldn't move the cloth a millimetre (though some of the family were cynical about the last achievement, believing it to depend on the connivance of Uncle Hughie's tailor). Uncle Hughie's past prowess rose crowing in him like a cock.

'Ah'll lay a' the tea in China that Ah can break every egg frae here tae John o'Groats. An' the hens that laid them.' The last thrown in as a magnanimous afterthought.

'Ye can have London tae an orange,' Charlie's father said adamantly, not to be outdone in generosity.

The rather intractable geographical dimensions of the wager were scaled down to the more finite terms of an even dollar, and four bright half-crowns were tiered ceremoniously on the mantelpiece.

'Elizabeth,' Charlie's father said. 'Would ye go through an' bring us an egg, please, hen?'

'Oh that's no' fair, Father,' Elizabeth's lips pursed righteously. 'You ken fine it canny be done.'

'Are you anither yin, Lizzie?' Uncle Hughie looked like Samson among the Philistines. 'You go through an' fetch me an egg, an' we'll see if it canny be done. This man's got you as bad as himself.'

'Anyway,' Elizabeth said, 'we don't hae eggs to throw away like that.'

'Ah'll buy ye a dozen eggs wi' ma winnings, hen,' Uncle Hughie promised.

'Yer egg'll go back the way it came, Elizabeth,' Charlie's father said. 'Don't fash yourself aboot that. I'll have it for ma breakfast first thing the morra morning.'

'I'll get ye an egg,' Charlie said.

'All right. All right.' Elizabeth could hold out no longer against a united front. 'I'll fetch it for them.'

'Ye'd better strip to the waist, Hughie,' Charlie's father said seriously. 'It'll make an awfu' mess when that egg bursts.'

27

Uncle Hughie took him at his word. He peeled off shirt and vest as one, and stood naked to the waist, revealing a huge craggy torso with fine dark coal-scars running over the left shoulder, and tattooed forearms. On his left forearm what looked like some sort of dancing girl stood with her arms tirelessly upraised, a faded relic of the romantic past who had aged with Uncle Hughie. On his right forearm two pale pink hearts had grown anaemic with the years.

Elizabeth entered like a handmaiden, carrying the egg. A space was cleared in the middle of the floor, and Elizabeth sat down beside Charlie on the settee like a ringside seat. Everything was done with formal propriety, as if it was all according to the eggbreakers' handbook. Uncle Hughie was set in the middle of the cleared space and Charlie's father stood with his hand on his shoulder, giving him a brief run-through of the rules. Uncle Hughie was nodding quietly, not missing a trick. Charlie almost expected to see him shake hands with the egg, and started to give a tense sibilant commentary in Elizabeth's ear.

'I want a good clean fight,' he was saying. 'And break when I say "break". You both know the rules. I won't hesitate to disqualify either you or the egg. So come out fighting and may the best egg win.'

Uncle Hughie was ready. He laced the fingers of both hands carefully together and held them cupped upwards while Charlie's father painstakingly placed the egg between his palms. Uncle Hughie's hand closed impatiently on the egg, but Charlie's father halted him and ran his fingers lightly round the edges of the egg to make sure that it was being held only by the tips.

'Right, Hughie,' he said. 'Away ye go.'

Uncle Hughie started to press.

'Feeling is running high at the Garden tonight,' Charlie resumed in Elizabeth's ear. 'This is something of a needle match, Hughie versus The Egg. Human dignity hangs in the balance.'

Uncle Hughie was now visibly putting on the pressure. The dancing girl writhed sensuously. His right forearm had angina pectoris in duplicate. Huge veins rose and fell on his neck like organ-stops. His forehead, ploughed with effort, slowly took on a faint dew of sweat. His body, like an over-heated boiler, became suffused with an unnatural red glow, as if combustion was imminent. And at the middle of this gigantic exertion, in the still centre of the hurricane, lay the egg, a tribute to the grit of Danish hens.

Uncle Hughie relaxed and took a breather. His palms glittered decoratively, sequined with sweat, and he wiped them on the seat of his trousers.

'Ah wouldny have believed that,' he said.

'There y'are,' Charlies father said, vindicated. 'Ye'll maybe no' be so cocky the next time.'

He resumed his grip on the egg, with Charlie's father sitting confidently watching. Charlie became aware that Elizabeth was struggling to hold in her laughter. She snittered once briefly, like a horse neighing, and cut it short. Glancing at her, Charlie saw her lips twisting nervously in an attempt to suppress the laughter which showed beneath her composure like a kitten under a coverlet. Then he felt laughter lit like a slow fuse in himself, rising steadily, coming nearer to ignition, until it flashed and exploded from his mouth, simultaneous with Elizabeth's. Just at that moment the egg slipped in Uncle Hughie's perspiring hands and burst. Egg-yolk exploded dramatically like shrapnel, and catherine-wheeled in all directions. It spattered sideboard and mirror. It clung like a canker to an artificial flower. A fragment of it fried merrily on the fire. It spotted Uncle Hughie like an exotic acne. The laughter of the other three overtook the last particle of it before it found a resting-place. They hosed Uncle Hughie mercilessly with laughter, while he stood in the centre of the floor, dripping egg. They laughed and coughed and grasped for breath and laughed again. Charlie fell off the settee on to the floor and lay there helplessly, epileptic with laughter.

'For my next trick . . .' Uncle Hughie said.

And they became a quartet of laughers in unison, modulating, improvising, giving new interpretations to the situation through their laughter, until Uncle Hughie went through to get washed and returned spruce and eggless. While he was putting his shirt on again, Charlie's father tried to give him back his money but he insisted it had been fairly lost. In the end it was decided that the money should be given to charity, namely Charlie and Elizabeth. The incident had generated laughter that lasted throughout that night and beyond.

He remembered how they had all felt after it. They were all conscious of having made something among them. A night had been baptized. That was The Night That Uncle Hughie Fought The Egg. It was salvaged from the anonymity of other nights. It would be remembered, along with The Night The Dog Took A Fit, when John, playing vets, muzzled Queenie with an elastic band, and its head inflated ominously and it frothed like a drawing pint, charging chairs, butting sideboards, running a canine reign of terror until his father came in and unloosened the elastic; The Massacre Of The Chickens, when his father put a hundred day-old chickens in a ramshackle hut with a floor like a sieve and during the night the cats pulled them down through the floor like manna and his father came out next morning to a cenotaph of feathers; The Siege Of The Lavatory, when Elizabeth locked herself in the toilet and couldn't get back out and the rest of the family spent most of an hour huddled round the door broadcasting instructions to her and sending messages of hope, and in the end his father had to climb the rone and break a window to get her out, tear-stained and penitent; The Quest For The Canary, when the pet canary, which had the run of the house, flew out of a window inadvertently left open and the scheme turned out to watch his father, holding aloft a cage and rattling a packet of birdseed, wander the streets calling 'Joey, Joey, Joey', to the roof-tops until Joey alighted on his head and he nudged him back into his cage and returned home in an aureole of Franciscan awe.

To their canon of occasions another night had been added. That was how they had felt.

From *Remedy is None* by William McIlvanney

Grandmother

By the time I knew my grandmother she was dead.
Before that she was where I thought she stood,
Spectacles, slippers, venerable head,
A standard-issue twinkle in her eyes—
Familiar stage-props of grandmotherhood.
It took her death to teach me they were lies.

My sixteen-year-old knowingness was shocked
To hear her family narrate her past
In quiet nostalgic chorus. As they talked
Her body stiffened on the muted fast
Though well washed linen coverlet of her bed.
The kitchen where we sat, a room I knew,
Took on a strangeness with each word they said.
How she was born where wealth was pennies, grew
Into a woman before she was a girl,
From dirt and pain constructed happiness,
Shed youth's dreams in the fierce sweat of a mill,
Married and mothered in her sixteenth year,
Fed children from her own mouth's emptiness
In an attic rats owned half of, liked her beer.
Careless, they scattered pictures: mother, wife,
Strikes lived through, hard concessions bought and sold
In a level-headed bargaining with life,
Told anecdotes in which her strength rang gold,
Her eyes were clear, her wants as plain as salt.
The past became a mint from which they struck
Small change till that room glittered like a vault.
The corpse in the other room became to me
Awesome as Pharaoh now, as if one look
Would show me all that I had failed to see.

The kitchen became museum in my sight,
Sacred as church. These were the very chairs
In which her gnarled dignity grew frail.
Her hard-won pride had kept these brasses bright.
Her tireless errands were etched upon the stairs.
A vase shone in the sun, holy as grail.
I wanted to bring others to this room,
Say it's nothing else than this that people mean,
A place to which humility can come,
A wrested niche where no one else has been
Won from the wastes of broken worlds and worse.
Here we can stay. Stupid and false, of course.
Themselves to the living is all we have to give.

Let this be
To her, for wreath, gift, true apology.

William McIlvanney

Father and Son

War's Remedy. Let the soldier be abroad if he will, he can do nothing in
this age. There is another personage—a personage less imposing in the eyes
of some—perhaps insignificant. The schoolmaster is abroad, and I trust to
him, armed with his primer, against the soldier in full military array.

Lord Brougham, Speech, 1828

Conn's voice had baulked on the name, his hesitation advancing and
receding like someone contemplating a jump. Finally he had settled
for Bruffam, pronounced almost inaudibly. In compensation he
declaimed the date with impressive sonorousness.

His father said, 'Read that again.'

While Conn did, slanting the book towards the window to snare the
last of the light, Tam's lips moved silently in pursuit of the words.

'That's true, son,' he said. 'That is true.'

Conn recognised in his father's tone the implication that it was
especially true for Conn. Before Conn had said anything, his father
was already arguing with his silence, because he knew the stubborn
attitudes that lay behind it. Conn found himself wishing that his
grandfather hadn't gone to bed so early or that Angus would come in
or that his mother hadn't found it necessary to go down to Kathleen's
house. Why did Kathleen need to be having a baby anyway? Feeling
himself in the familiar position of being betrayed by a conspiracy of
adult whims, Conn surrendered himself to the inevitability of having
to confront his father's mood alone, to undergo a 'serious talk'.

Tam was lighting one of the many clay pipes he had started

31

recently to use. As the shred of newspaper flared in his fingers, face and throat inhabited for a second the poetry of the flame, achieved in the half-dark a vivid isolation of line and texture held focused in the concentration of a trivial act, like a luminous painting instantly destroyed. Tam fluttered the charred paper, serrated like a feather, into the fire.

'Is that no' whit Ah've been tryin' tae tell ye a' along?' Conn waited. 'It's education, son. That's whit ye've got tae hiv. You're clever enough tae go oan et the schil. Ah ken ye are. Yer mither's got a note there fae a teacher. A lassie. Whit's her name?'

'Miss Anderson.'

'Miss Anderson. That's who it wis. Miss Anderson. She says ye're capable. An' so ye are. But why are ye no' interested?'

Conn shuffled in the chair.

'Ah jist want tae work in the pits.'

'Christ, son. The pits! Ponies work in the pits, son. That's as mony brains as ye need tae work in the pits. They go blin'. Did ye ken that? They're doon in the dark that long that they canny see. An' they're no' the only wans. Ah've been blin' fae Ah wis ony age masel'. That's whit it does tae ye. When Ah wis your age, Ah had ideas, son. Things Ah could see that Ah wid like tae dae. But the pits took care o' that. Ah'm jist a miner noo. Ma days don't belong tae me. Ah'm doon there. An' Ah canny see beyond the seam that Ah'm tryin' tae howk.'

Tam spread his arms and shook his head, as if offering the image of himself to Conn as irrefutable proof of the failure he couldn't find words to convey. Paradoxically, what Conn saw were the forearms bulging from the rolled up sleeves, the hands that looked as tough as stone. The whole person emitted an aura of impunity as cautionary as an electric fence. Sitting there, self-deprecating man and hero-worshipping boy, they made an irony of each other, Tam imparting to his son a conviction he had no words to counteract, Conn interpreting his father's silence against itself.

'Ye see that pair auld man through there? He's leeved a slave an' he's deein' a slave. They can gi'e it ony ither name they like. But that's whit he is. An' ye ken why?' Tam jabbed a forefinger against his own temple. 'Because they took ower in there. That's the only wey ye'll ever bate them, son. By findin' oot the truth fur yerself an' keepin' it in there. Yer gran'feyther's nearly seeventy. An' he's waitin' tae leeve his furst day as his ain man.'

Tam sat looking into the fire, his head cocked delicately as if he was listening. He nodded to his own thoughts and, watching him, Conn experienced a moment that had the eeriness of a seance. He became conscious of the shadows emerging from the fire's meeting with the approaching darkness, and they were assembling themselves around him in the room, like ghosts with whom his father was communing. A minute jet of gas burst from a break in the coal with a sound like a centuries old moan, before it ignited to a separate incandescence within the fire's burning.

'Yer Uncle James. Ah've never telt ye aboot him yet. Hiv Ah, Conn?' Conn shook his head, his boredom animating for the first time into interest at the prospect of a story, at the thought of hearing about a man instead of all this incomprehensible talk about 'them' and 'education'. 'He wis fae Cronberry, then. Yer Granny's nephew. Ma cousin, Ah suppose. Worked in the pits as weel. But a clever, clever boay. Ye ken what he did? Every day he did his shift in the pits. But at nichts. He studied and he re-studied. Tired tae the marrow o' his bones he wis. Aye. But every nicht, right reason or nane—the studyin'! It wis a'...' Tam's rhetoric lost course for a moment in an absence of facts—'the rocks an' that. You ken. Stanes an' the earth. Whit is it?'

'Geology.' Conn felt casually and impressively knowledgeable, a state of mind he was careful not to spoil by dwelling on the fact that he had only learned the word from the teacher the day before.

'That's the wan.' Tam paused as if about to repeat it but didn't bother. 'Oot in a' wathers. Wi' his trooser-legs rowed up. Wadin' the burns. Lookin' fur jist the special stane that he wid be efter at the time. Chappin' them up wi' a wee mell. Makin' his notes. The names he had fur them! He could come oot wi' a name that wid choke a horse. An a' it wid be wis a wee thing like a causey. Ye've nae conception, son. Well. He persevered. An' he wisny stuffy, either. In fact, he knew that he wis deein'. An' him jist in his twinties. But he went oan. He wis efter some kind o' qualification thing. Like letters ahint his name or that. He took his examinations. An' ye ken. The week he dee'd, the word came through the post. The boy had passed. A certificate kinda thing. His mither his it in the hoose yet. Twinty-seeven when he dee'd. An' she his a drawer there in her big dresser that she keeps the way he left it. The first time we're up, Ah'll get her tae show ye it. It's a thing tae see. Jist fu' o' stanes every colour o' the rainbow. Every wan found by James himsel'. An' every wan wi' its wee caird, an' oan the caird the special thing they ca' it. Names ye never thocht were poassible. By, that's some drawer. It's no' a drawer, son. It's a monument.'

There was a silence of some seconds for the legendary James. Tam was remembering holding that certificate in his hands. The name on it was James's but the official wording was relevant to all of them, an amnesty from the inevitability of the narrowness of their lives. Conn was imagining the drawer. He saw the stones like jewels, heaped fragments of blinding iridescence, having no point in his mind beyond their own beauty, a dead man's treasure trove.

'The man's richt.' Tam nodded at the book, *A Treasury of Prose and Poetry,* resting on Conn's knee with his finger keeping the place. 'Hoo can war help *us*? We'll be in the same mogre when it's a' by. Poor Mick. He's daein' whit he has tae dae. But it's no' gonny make ony

33

difference. That's the thing, Conn. Yer brither's life's at stake. An whoever wins, it canny be us. We loast before it stertit.' Caught in the renewed intensity of an old realisation, Tam looked for hope. 'Conn. Why will ye no' see the sense o' goin' oan at the schil, son. Why no'?'

'Ah jist don't want tae, feyther.'

'But whit is it? Why no'?'

'Ah don't like it.'

'Is it the teachers? His somebody goat it in fur ye?'

'Naw. It's no' that.'

'Ah don't understand ye, son. Ah mean, that's where ye could make somethin' o' yerself. See Mr Pirrie. He's aff the same kinna folk as oorselves, Ah hear. An' ye see whit he's made o' himself. Noo is that no' an example fur ye?'

Clumsily, Tam had activated Conn's antagonism towards school, which had so far remained in the lethargy of long-established attitudes. Now, mobilising against that name, past convictions mustered confusedly in his head, the more determined for being inarticulate. So irrational as to be anonymous forces, those convictions nevertheless represented areas of real experience for Conn. They related to truths he had earned for himself, no matter how incapable he was of proving his right to them with words, to the fact that nothing he was taught at school took the slightest cognizance of who he was, that the fundamental premise underlying everything he was offered there was the inferiority of what he had, that the vivid spontaneity of his natural speech was something he was supposed to be ashamed of, that so many of the people who mouthed platitudes about the liberating effects of education were looking through bars at the time, that most teachers breathed hypocrisy, like tortured Christians trying to convert happy pagans, that the classroom wasn't a filter for but a refuge from reality. His indignation came in a welter of incoherent images, a mob of reasons that drowned reason, and the only expression of it all he could achieve was a dogged, sullen silence.

'Mr Pirrie. Noo is that no' somebody ye could look up tae an' try tae dae the same?'

Seeing his father so mistaken in his estimation of himself, Conn couldn't let it pass. It was all right being silent on the question of staying on at school. He had made up his mind on that one. Nothing short of being taken there in handcuffs every day would have induced him to stay on after he was fourteen. But it depressed him to see the way his father was so misled about the school. Mr Pirrie. Why did his father reduce himself to an admiring boy in front of someone who wasn't a match for him? Conn struggled to say something he knew. What came out, like a hiccup after long meditation, was:

'Och, feyther. Ye could easy win him.'

Conn didn't just mean it physically. There was in him a hazy desire to express the result of some ultimate and ideal confrontation of the two men. The words were an attempt to convey a deep faith in his father, something which had survived in spite of what they had taught him in the school, an unshakeable commitment, not unlike 'I love you'.

His father's response was to burst out laughing, shake his head in a patronising way, and then to seem saddened by his son's remark. Conn held in his hurt.

'Whit are ye talkin' aboot, son? Whit's that got tae dae wi' onything? Life's a bit mair complicated than a fist-fight. Ah've maybe goat muscles. But maist o' them are in ma heid. Naw, son. Ye need education.'

They sat hopelessly together in the darkening room, their shapes unfinished sculptures in the firelight, affirming the worth of each other and injuring each other in the affirmation. Conn turned the book over in his hand. He had always loved the feel of it, bound in soft leather and on the front two circles, one within the other, embossed in gold, like a medallion, inside which was the figure of a lady in a wide, sweeping dress. But at the moment he resented it. Running his fingers over the braille of that design, it was as if the gesture taught him he was blind, as if the book could only be a tactile object for him, and he and his father were locked out from the rest of it, rejected by the complex patterns of words which it contained. The sensation which his fingers casually imparted to him now was never entirely to leave him, like a burn that mutes all subsequent touches to a partial memory of itself, one of those perceptions that remain precisely because their truths outreach our rational comprehension, have no need of it, though our comprehension will repeatedly come back to illumine them, intensifying the mystery.

So, in later years, holding again this book, Conn as a man was to understand this evening better, and so many others like it. He would realise how much it had meant to his father, to have this, the only book in the house, given to him at the corner by somebody whose possession of it remained unexplained. He would understand the balm his father felt in listening to the words Conn read from it, those extracts which were often incomprehensible to both of them but which had another meaning for his father, the statement that there were men who understood what was happening to them, that somewhere out there there was meaning. He would even appreciate his father's respect for that leather parcel of words, so that, passing it to his son, he handled it as if it was TNT. But all these laggard insights would only deepen the mystery of what the book had been for both of them, conceal in more impenetrable shadows what it was they had really been trying to say in those evenings of stumbling talk among the carefully cultivated words of strangers.

For Conn later understood what was so obvious, that his father couldn't have afforded to keep him on at school anyway. It had never been a serious possibility. It did, in fact, take all of Tam's tenacity not to accept exemption for Conn, by which he would have been able, due to financial circumstances, to start work at twelve. So why had his father taken so much trouble so often to try to convince him of the wisdom of staying on? Was he perversely hoping that Conn would convince him that it was better to leave, and so assuage his guilt? Or did he console himself with attempting to establish in Conn at least the principle of continued education if he couldn't present to him the fact of it? Was he teaching Conn to condemn his own inability to keep him on at school by way of an apology?

It was to seem to Conn that those evenings, so apparently incidental at the time, their content totally unmemorable, contained the baffling essence of his relationship with his father, that their shy attempts at thought and hobbled gestures held a communication which no eloquence could have paraphrased, and the irrelevant book, which had fallen accidentally between them, was a bridge across which they had trafficked with themselves. The constraint and hurt that traffic had sometimes involved wasn't to be regretted, because it was real.

'Read us somethin' else, son.'

Conn crouched forward in his seat, holding the book almost vertically towards the fire. He flicked the roughly cut pages, looking for a bit that wasn't too big. The heading 'Nature's Records' attracted him. He read aloud:

> Nature will be reported. All things are engaged in writing their history. The planet, the pebble, goes attended by its shadow. The rolling rock leaves its scratches on the mountain: the river its channel in the soil; the animal its bones in the stratum; the fern and the leaf their modest epitaph in the coal. The falling drop makes its sculpture in the sand or the stone. Not a foot steps into the snow or along the ground, but prints in characters more or less lasting a map of its march. Every act of the man inscribes itself in the memories of his fellows and in his own manners and face. The air is full of sounds; the sky, of tokens; the ground is all memoranda and signatures, and every object is covered over with hints which speak to the intelligence.
>
> R. W. Emerson, *Representative Men*

The room had now abandoned the definition of its contours to the darkness. Only the fire salvaged them a space. But Tam made no move to light the mantle. His face was tightened on itself in concentration, as if the words were a knot he couldn't unravel.

'Read that again, Conn.'

While someone released a flare of laughter in the street outside, Conn read again, wishing his mother and Angus would come back, the strangeness of some of the phrases occurring like discomfort in his mouth, and his father listened in utter stillness, as if they were the pagan scriptures.

From *Docherty* by William McIlvanney

Family Visit

Laying linoleum, my father spends hours
With his tape measure,
Littering the floor
As he checks his figures, gets
The angle right; then cuts
Carefully, to the music
Of a slow logic. In despair
I conjure up a room where
A boy sits and plays with coloured bricks.

My mind tugging at its traces,
I see him in more dapper days
Outside the Kibble Palace
With my grandfather, having
His snapshot taken; men firing
That year's leaves.
The Gardens are only a stone's throw
From where I live . . . But now
A younger self comes clutching at my sleeve.

Or off to Innellan, singing, we would go,
Boarding the steamer at the Broomielaw
In broad summer, these boomps-a-daisy
Days, the ship's band playing in a lazy
Swell, my father steering well clear
Of the bar, mother making neat
Packets of waste-paper to carry
To the nearest basket or (more likely)
All the way back to Cranworth Street.

Leaving my father at it
(He'd rather be alone) I take
My mother through the changed Botanics.
The bandstand is gone, and the great
Rain-barrels that used to rot
And overflow. Everything is neat
And plastic. And it is I who must walk
Slowly for her, past the sludge
And pocked marble of Queen Margaret Bridge.

Stewart Conn

From *The Dark Dialogues II*

Almost I, yes, I hear
Huge in the small hours
A man's step on the stair
Climbing the pipeclayed flights
And then stop still
Under the stairhead gas
At the lonely tenement top.
The broken mantle roars
Or dims to a green murmur.
One door faces another.
Here, this is the door
With the loud grain and the name
Unreadable in brass.
Knock, but a small knock,
The children are asleep.
I sit here at the fire
And the children are there
And in this poem I am,
Their mother through his mother.
I sit with the gas turned
Down and time knocking
Somewhere through the wall.
Wheesht, children, and sleep
As I break the raker up,
It is only the stranger
Hissing in the grate.
Only to speak and say
Something, little enough,
Not out of want,
Nor out of love, to say
Something and to hear
That someone has heard me.
This is the house I married
Into, a room and kitchen
In a grey tenement,
The top flat of the land,
And I hear them breathe and turn
Over in their sleep
As I sit here becoming
Hardly who I know.

I have seen them hide
And seek and cry come out
Come out whoever you are
You're not het I called
And called across the wide
Wapenshaw of water.
But the place moved away
Beyond the reach of any
Word. Only the dark
Dialogues drew their breath.
Ah how bright the mantel
Brass shines over me.
Black-lead at my elbow,
Pipe-clay at my feet.
Wheesht and go to sleep
And grow up but not
To say mother mother
Where are the great games
I grew up quick to play.

W. S. Graham

NOTES

'A Baby in the House': possible companion pieces are Hemingway's 'Indian Camp' and Frank O'Connor's 'My Oedipus Complex', both widely anthologised. A splendid Scottish short story, which involves a baby, is Neil Paterson's 'Scotch Settlement' (*The Penguin Book of Scottish Short Stories* edited by J. F. Hendry).

Chapters 25 to 28 of Bill Naughton's *A Roof over your Head* (Blackie) contain a moving account of a child's birth and death from the father's point of view, while Sylvia Plath's poem 'Morning Song' is a good description of mother and baby.

'Poem for my Sister' is a good starting-point for the exploration of relationships among children of different ages within the family.

'Grandmother': this moving tribute can be compared with Liz Lochhead's 'For my Grandmother Knitting'.

The child's first experience of a close relative's death is a significant sub-theme in Scottish literature. Two relevant poems are James Rankin's 'Grandpa' (*Scottish Poetry 2*, Edinburgh University Press) and Duncan Glen's 'My Faither', which appears in various anthologies. Fred Urquhart's short story 'Alicky's Watch' (*Further Modern Scottish Stories* edited by Millar and Low, Heinemann Educational) deals with the same theme.

'Father and Son': William McIlvanney is the prose-poet of Scottish working-class family life, its relevance, values, dignity and mythology. No apologies are offered for his dominance of this section of the anthology, because examples of the negative vision of Scottish family life are not hard to find, from *Weir of Hermiston* and *The House with the Green Shutters* onwards. Conn's father, the miner Tam Docherty, is one of the great figures in Scottish fiction. This chapter from *Docherty* (Allen & Unwin) has its difficulties, but is well worthwhile.

'Family Visit': Seamus Heaney's 'Follower' and John Daniel's '2 Clocks' (both in *Exercises in Practical Criticism*, John O'Neill, Gibson) are similar poetic treatments of the effect of time on family relationships. See also Stewart Conn's 'To my Father' (*An Ear to the Ground*, Hutchinson).

'The Dark Dialogues II': the haunting and mysterious music of this poem recalls some of the traditional Scots lullabies.

3

STREET GAMES

Street Songs

Even in our asphalt jungle, summer was very noticeable. Windows would be thrown up and left that way all day, instead of being closed tightly against damp and cold. Fires were kept just high enough to do the cooking, and the long days seemed always to be warm and golden. This was the time for our running games and our singing games. These songs were surely handed down from generation to generation, and we acted and chanted them, following a ritual which came from we didn't know where. But every movement and gesture was as exact as though it had been choreographed. It seemed as though we had always known words, tune and movement, and I only remember consciously learning one song during my entire childhood. This was 'Ah loast ma hurl on the barra'. It was after Sunday School when I learned it. The big boy and girl who lived in the next close took me home with them to get a taste of their mother's baking of pancakes. As we waited for the hot pancakes to be lifted off the girdle and spread with margarine, the boy started singing 'Oh the bonnie wee barra's mine', and my ears pricked with interest. For ages I'd sung, 'The barra broke at ten o'clock an' ah loast ma hurl on the barra', and I thought that was the entire song. Now it seemed there was more. 'Sing it again, Henry,' I begged him with great excitement. 'Oh sing it again, I want to know the rest of it.' And by the time we'd finished our pancakes we were all three lustily singing:

> The barra broke at ten o'clock
> An' ah loast ma hurl on the barra.
> Aw the bonnie wee barra's mine,
> It disnae belang tae O'Hara,
> The fly wee bloke, stuck tae ma rock,
> But ah'm gonny stick tae his barra.

I remember teaching a wee English boy, who was on a summer visit to his grannie, to sing:

> Missus MacLean had a wee wean
> She didnae know how to *nurse* it,
> She gi'ed it tae me, an' ah gi'ed it some tea,
> An' its wee belly *burstit*.

I was enchanted to hear this old Glasgow song rendered with a prissy English accent, and kept making him sing it for me. I was astounded one day when he refused. 'But why?' I asked him, 'I thought you liked that wee song.' 'My grannie says I'm not to sing it any more,' he said primly. 'She says it's vulgar.' Vulgar! I'd never heard the word before, and didn't know what it meant. When I asked my grannie, she laughed and said, 'Och well, you ken whit the English are like. Butter widnae melt in their mooths, to hear them. The word "belly" will likely be too coorse for them.' Belly too coarse! But it was in the Bible, and we called our navels our belly buttons without shame or thought. I wondered what else I said that was vulgar. I'd have to be careful. Maybe I was constantly being vulgar without knowing it. Grannie dismissed my fears, and said there was nothing wrong with the wee harmless songs we sang, and I was to go out and play and not to be so daft.

So we saw nothing to cause a raised eyebrow when we chanted as we ran through the closes:

A hundred and ninety-nine,
Ma faither fell in the bine,
Ma mother came oot wi' the washin' cloot,
An' skelped his bare behind!

One which caused us great hilarity because of the cheeky wee soldier's behaviour in church was:

Ma wee laud's a sojer,
He comes fae Maryhull,
He gets his pey on Friday night,
An' buys a hauf-a-juH.
He goes tae church on Sundays,
A hauf an 'oor late.
He pulls the buttons aff his shirt,
An' pits them in the plate!

And there was one we used to act, just showing our heads out of the staircase window, as though we weren't properly dressed and daren't lean out farther:

Ah'm no' comin' oot the noo, the noo,
Ah'm no' comin' oot the noo.
Ah'm very sorry Lizzie MacKay, for disappointin' you.
Ma mother's away wi' ma claes tae the pawn
To raise a bob or two.
An' ah've juist a fur aroon' ma neck,
So ah'm no' comin' oot the noo.

In our songs it was the wives who left the husbands, for there was something funny in a man being left to look after the house.
There was a lilting one which went:

Ma wife ran awa' an' left me,
Left me a' ma lane.
Ah'm a simple chap.
Ah widnae care a rap,
If she hadnae run awa' an' left the wean.

And a slower chant, which we sang in a slurred tone as if we'd had a wee bit too much to drink:

Wha's comin' wi' me?
Ah'm oot on the spree.
Ma wife's awa' on the train,
Ah hope ah niver see her again.
Ah'm havin' the time of my life,
Plenty of L.S.D.,
I'm off the teetotal,
I've ta'en tae the bottle.
So wha's comin' wi' me?

And a nice one for singing with a sob in the throat was:

Ah've got the dishes tae wash,
An' the flairs tae scrub.
Nicht an' day ah'm niver away
Fae the washin' tub.
She does whitever she likes,
An' ah dae the best ah can.
Jimmy McPhee can easily see
Ah'm a mere, mere, man.

These were the Glasgow back-court songs which we added to our repertoire of the games played all over the country at their appropriate season. 'Queen Mary, Queen Mary my age is sixteen', 'Broken bridges falling down'. 'The bonnie bunch o' roses', 'Down in yonder valley where the green grass grows', and 'Water water wallflower, growing up so high'. We moved delicately through the movements, oblivious of mothers and grannies who occasionally glanced our way from their tenement windows, self-absorbed and transported into a graceful mannered world.

We were merciless on those who couldn't or wouldn't learn the movements fast enough, and who spoilt the rhythm, and we'd pounce on the hapless novice and put her through it again and again until she got fed up.

From *Shoes were for Sunday* by Molly Weir

The Big Sui and the Lucky Middens

When I was still quite young, I had my own gang—THE CONNOLLYS—and we used to fight with The Sinclairs, who came from round the corner. We made tomahawks with tin cans and sticks: you bashed the can over a stick with a brick and made a sort of hatchet affair. And we would fill a tin can full of ashes, shove it in a nylon stocking, whirl it round our heads and hurl it into the enemy camp, leaving this big smokey trail behind it. I can't recall anyone being hurt, though there was a fair bit of walloping going on; but no slashing or anything like that.

There used to be these air-raid shelters all over the place and we would leap around on top of them. There was the 'Shelter-to-Shelter' jump, which was legendary. They were like mountaineering passes and routes: the White Patch, the Wee Sui and the Big Sui, which was short for suicide.

The Day I Jumped the Big Sui...oh, the feeling. It was like suddenly maturing, like the Indian brave's initiation rites, passing into

44

manhood. And being able to jump the Big Sui was no mean feat. Maybe it was because I was a wee boy, but it seemed like one *hell* of a distance to jump. It was from the top of the air-raid shelter, across a void with railings in the middle of it that divided one back court from another, and then you had to land on top of this midden with a sloped roof. You had to stop dead there or you were right off over the other side.

Geordie Sinclair's attempt at it—what picturesque memories I have of my childhood—I remember well. Geordie was wearing these boots that a lot of the boys wore at the time. Parish boots they were called; all studded and tackety and funny. And he was running like a madman, like a dervish, across the shelter, then leapt into the air and Did the Big Sui. But when he hit the midden, he went into an incredibly fast slide and ended up in mid-air in a sitting position, with a trail of sparks coming from his studs. Landed right on his arse in the back green.

Gerald McGee, who lived in the same close, had a famous attempt at it, too. His toes hit the edge of the midden and he went PLOOOONK; the toes were hanging on and then he lost his grip and his chin hit the edge. He was in a semi-conscious state when we got down to him, eating tea leaves in the midden. He didn't know what time of day it was at all.

When, years later, I moved into Hyndland Road in the West End of Glasgow, I told my wife we had a Lucky Midden. It was just a rented house that we'd moved to from Maryhill Road, but it was a really nice area and I was actually living in a house whose midden I had raided when I was a wee boy.

The Lucky Middens were where all the posh people lived and they would throw out really nice things sometimes. I got a great primus stove once, a real beauty, made of chrome, which I used for many years when I was cycling around. And I found a beautiful stainless steel Spitfire—which my father threw out.

I almost got a guy the jail once, too. I think he was a docker whose house had been raided or else he was hiding stuff... anyway, he had these big two-pound tins of jam in his midden. My aunt threw them out into our midden, wouldn't let me keep them and wouldn't open them, and some other kids found them and their parents took them to the police. Red plum jam, I'll never forget it. And it was stamped on the top; it had come from Canada and must have been military supplies or something. The police came round to our house and asked me where I got them and I told them the midden. And it would have been really easy to go up the stair and ask everybody 'What dae ye dae for a livin'?' And the docker would be away with the prize.

There were all sorts of things you could find in middens. And I would always get thrashed when I got home, my shoes would be all grey with ash and it would be:

'Ye've been in the midden!'

'No—I havenae!'

'Liar!'

THUMP!

I used to wonder how my parents had this amazing psychic ability to tell where I had been playing. And of course all the time I must have smelt exactly like a bloody midden!

Another one was Setting Fire to the Middens. You would put a light to about twelve of them in one back court and then look at it. It was magic. And you could go off and watch it from a distance, all glowing . . . Aye, we made our own entertainment then.

Tying two doors together was another great favourite. You would get two doors opposite each other on a tenement landing, tie the both of them with a piece of rope, ring the bells, stand back and watch. You would do it not quite terribly tight, so that they could open it just a little and be pulling against each other. I loved that. And I remember watching two guys pulling against each other, the two doors slamming, then a knife coming out round the door trying to cut the rope. The guy's shouting and swearing and there's this wee knife working away. Hysterical it was.

The girls didn't take much part in it all. They would do girlie things, like singing a lot. They would play ball against the wall and sing these lovely songs while they were doing it:

A shepherdess was walking
Ding dong, ding dong,
Come along,
Ding dong.

All those wee daft songs. And in the summer evenings they would all join hands and sing and chant 'Be-Baw Babbity'. But the boys were very much boys and the girls were—well, they just got on with it. Occasionally we would play with them; some of the guys were very good at skipping and no one ever called you a pansy for doing it; they'd call you a pansy if you were *bad* at it.

From *Billy Connolly—the Authorized Version*

Children Playing

They gravitate to the edge of each event,
Tease tedium till it snaps. They woo the worst.
Inventing the gamuts they will have to run,
They make a tightrope of mundanity, and give
Catastrophe the odour of their sweat.

Only so do they earn themselves and learn to keep
Their pact of contest with the act of breath.
Returning from imagined distances,
They bring their eyes like trophies freshly won.
Their cuts are badges and their bruises maps.

William McIlvanney

Geordie

When he was a boy there had been an unroofed lavatory in his school
with walls made of red glazed brick which were topped with half-
round glazed brick tops put there to prevent boys from walking along
the top of the wall. After school hours several boys would often take
the urge to climb up round the lavatory and jump from one wall to
another. Mat hated when they did this because the more daring ones
would shout 'Feartie', and taunt anyone unwilling to climb up on the
walls along with them and share their risk. He was so terrified also of
the sickeningly hard concrete floor of the lavatory, that however much
they taunted him he would never attempt to climb up. In a way he
wasn't even ashamed of being afraid. Trees were different, being full
of branches and leaves and rough bark and knobs which you could
cling to, and if you slipped all you got was your knees and elbows
skinned. Across the road from the school in an empty yard there was
an old brick mill with an iron fire escape that went away up higher
than even the roof of the school. Mat wasn't afraid to climb that and it
was much higher than the lavatory walls. Of those implacable tiled
walls he was afraid. Once when he had been playing at a game which
the boys called 'hudgies', that is stealing rides on the backs of motor
lorries, he had fallen off a lorry that had accelerated suddenly and
cracked his head on the ground. He remembered how odd he had felt
and how he had wandered about for some time saying funny things
and not quite knowing what he was doing. Now when he looked at
those dizzy, slippery walls and that hard wet lavatory floor he would
think of what it would be like to fall into that awful square chasm and
he would feel as if his head had gone empty and his skull had been
rung like a bell.

Once Mat had come out of school with his pal Geordie and they
had stood in the playground arguing about what they would do. Some
of the bigger boys had already gathered about the lavatory walls and
Geordie wanted to stay and climb them. Mat tried to coax him off
elsewhere.

'C'mon and watch the waterworks,' he had said.

Geordie was disgusted. 'The waterworks! You're always wanting to go and watch the waterworks. There's nothing there. Nae fun.'

They had gone across to the yard beside the factory and walked up and down, arguing and scrunching their feet in the piles of broken glass which seemed to collect there. Mat couldn't understand why Geordie liked climbing the walls. Nothing, not the attraction of the bigger boys' company, not even the fact that sooner or later someone would eventually summon up the nerve to climb over into the adjoining chocolate works and come back with some cartons of stolen chocolate, could get Mat over his aversion for these walls.

'You stay if you like,' he said. 'I'm going to the waterworks.'

'The waterworks!' Geordie was scornful and as he ran away from Mat towards the school he kept turning back and shouting, 'Feartie, feartie.' Mat stood and watched him go, but he didn't care.

Near the school there were quite a few high tenements and buildings which were either warehouses or factories and all the streets around were bustling with life; the dust never seemed to settle anywhere with the continual stir. On a piece of waste ground there was a game of football going on and Mat could hear the uncomfortable gritty sound of the ball as it bounced and scraped on the stony hard packed earth. And the ragged scraping sound which the boys made as they scuffled and dunted with one another set his teeth on edge. He moved away from all this torrid congestion, looking back from time to time until a bend in the road cut out the sight of the wall. The last Mat saw of Geordie was his tiny figure straining up, his arm outstretched as someone sitting astride the wall leaned down and tried to pull him up.

*　　*　　*

It was later, after tea-time, when he was coming home from a message which his mother had sent him, that Mat met Geordie's sister. She was quite excited by the news she had to tell him, full of importance and unaware of the seriousness of what she was saying.

'Geordie fell off the lavvy wall and landed on the back of his head and he's got a mark just here'—she pointed to the back of her skull— 'and it'll never go away. I've got to go a message. Cheerio!'

When he got back to the house his mother had asked him about Geordie's accident. Her questions showed her anxiety that Mat should not be implicated in the affair.

'Were you there?'

'Naw.'

'And did you see him climb?'

'Naw.'

'Did you fall out with him?'

'Naw. I don't even know what has happened.'

'He broke his skull,' Ma said. Mat felt his head go all empty and he

48

could imagine the cracking of bone on the lavatory floor. His mother continued, 'The ambulance took him to hospital.'

After this Mat sat in a corner brooding. He had to try not to think of the sheer walls from which Geordie had fallen. Instead he tried to think of the waterworks. Just about half-an-hour before bedtime a knock came at the door and his mother went to answer it. She stayed there for a long time talking and Mat could hear the women's voices rising and falling in a regular rhythm. He could hear odd phrases. 'Terrible, uhuh!'—'Is it no' awful?'—'Uhuh!'—'Uhuh!' The note of the women's voices was of that avid complacency, a mixture of smugness and fear with which people discuss other people's disasters. Although the sound of their monotonous voices humming on at the doorstep increased Mat's depression, the natural tone of pity was missing which would have prepared him for what his mother told him when she came back into the room.

'I just heard there, that wee Geordie's dead.'

Mat didn't answer his mother. He tried to think about it but he couldn't. He couldn't imagine Geordie dead. He couldn't feel anything except that he was miserable and cold. All this while his mother was clucking her tongue and commiserating with herself.

'Ma?' The sound of his voice startled even himself it was so desperate and cajoling. 'Can I go round to Faither's to stay the night?' By 'Faither' he meant his grandfather Devlin.

'All right,' his mother said, 'if you like, but you'd better get away before your father comes home or he'll not let you.'

Outside it had turned chilly and the street lamps were on. Mat's shadow flitted round him silently as he passed the street lamps and he felt afraid. The street was so still and he was frightened of his own loneliness and of his shadow and of the quiet street. Suddenly, while he was thinking about Geordie, he realised. All through the summer the girls had played singing games in the street. Mat could almost hear their sharp indifferent voices as they sang.

> Water, water, wallflowers,
> Growing up so high.
> We are all children,
> And we must all die.

As he remembered the girls' song the night became empty and alien. As he looked up the sky seemed nothing but a vast black windy space. He fled through the street and ran up the stairs to his grandfather's house knocking desperately at the door until it was opened; then he hurried into the warm bright room with its clutter of dishes, remnants, string, screwnails, pipes, people, knobs, newspapers and its smell of tobacco and women and people; he rushed up to the fireplace and sat down on the fender with his back to the oven door.

From *The Dear Green Place* by Archie Hind

NOTES

'Street Songs': both of Molly Weir's books about her Glasgow childhood, *Shoes were for Sunday* and *Best Foot Forward* (Hutchinson), are full of fascinating material, as are the early chapters of Clifford Hanley's *Dancing in the Streets* (Ur Books) and Evelyn Cowan's *Spring Remembered* (Southside).

'Scottish Literature in the Secondary School' (HMSO, 1976) lists some useful audio material. Adam McNaughtan's recording *The Glasgow that I Used to Know* (Caley), is recommended.

The great unfailing source for this theme is the monumental achievement of I. and P. Opie in providing a comprehensive record of children's lore in their books *The Lore and Language of School Children*, *Children's Games in Street and Playground* and *The Oxford Book of Nursery Rhymes* (OUP).

'The Big Sui and the Lucky Middens': Billy Connolly's recordings *Solo Concert* and *Cop Yer Whack for This* (Transatlantic) include hilarious reminiscences of his Glasgow childhood, scabrous but authentic.

4

MAN AND BEAST

The Six Travellers

Somewhere beyond the dark huddle of the Grampians Ronald Macdonald scraped a living. The land was poor and so was Ronald but he had a proud and plump ewe.

In the weeks before Christmas he said to his wife: 'The sheep will have to go. If we kill her we'll have our Christmas dinner and meat in the barrel for the rest of the winter. And we could do with the wool. We could make enough cloth for ourselves and sell the rest. With the sheep gone we'll manage through February. Otherwise I have my doubts.'

February was the month of fevers.

The ewe overheard their conversation and, while she was willing to help them through the winter, she wanted to see her knock-kneed lambs dancing. So that night she left the field and crossed the valley. It was slow progress and the fear of getting lost was never far away.

She had not gone far when she came across the black shape, red eyes and gruff voice of a bull. Animals have their own dialects, but there is a common farmyard language. She had spoken with bulls before.

'And what brings you to the road on a night like this?' asked the sheep. Her soft accent belonged to the Cheviots.

'It's a sair trauchle Ah've hid this mony a day,' said the bull, who was Aberdonian. 'Aye, Ah thocht it wis fine owerbye; jist masel and a hale field o gress tae chow oan. The fairmer wis a kindly chiel, tho there wir times he lookit at me kinna weary-like.

'How-an-ever, jist the day he brocht this ither chiel Ah'd nevir set een oan, an he says, "Aye, there's guid beef there, Geordie"—that wis the fairmer's name, like—an they stairtit talkin about prices. The wey o't wis, Ah'd tae get kill't fur the Yuletide fairins. Losh, Ah thocht, Ah cannae hae this! So here Ah um.'

'Me too,' said the sheep. 'If you like we could walk together.'

'Aye, fairly lass, fairly. It'll be company if nuthin else.'

The night was now darker but less lonely. The bull trudged a path through the snow and the sheep trotted behind him. When the bull stopped she ran up to see what was wrong.

'Aye, min?' demanded the bull. Skulking by a dyke was a black and white collie with his tail between his legs.

'Och, it's not a night to be out in at all, at all,' he said. 'If they had toald me about thiss when I left the island, I neffer would haff come.'

When the bull shook his head, the dog continued hurriedly: 'I wass a sheep-dog, to let you know. I wass a good sheep-dog too. Neffer did I bark or touch the poor craturs. It was chust a chob, you understand, and all I wass trained for. It seemed to come naturally to me.'

'Aye; a guid dog's hard tae find,' said the bull. The sheep was silent.

'My trouble started when they brought thiss young pup, and now he duss all the running. I suppose I'm no use to them any more. My eyesight's not what it wass and I'm too old for the running. So I thought I'd chust leave them to it.'

Now there were three. The dog ambled behind the sheep and smiled softly when she looked back warily.

'Michty me!' said the bull after a few more miles. 'Whit wid yon be?' A pair of green eyes glinted five feet above the snow. They approached a round shape at the top of a gate.

'Och, it's chust a cat. Is it lost you are?' enquired the dog kindly.

'Naw, Ah widnae say loast. Well, aye, mebbe Ah um loast.'

His grizzled fur rose and he spat half-heartedly into the snow. His guttural tones were hard to make out: 'Ye see, it's like this. When Ah was a wee kitten, they taen us in a boax and drapp't us aff at this fairm. It took us a wee while tae get yased tae the place; but Ah knew aw aboot divin aifter they rats an at, so the big fairmer kepp us. Ah did aaright fur thaim tae. Know whit Ah mean?

'Tae let ye unnerstaun. A rat oan a fairm does aboot a hunner quids worth o damage a year, an Ah caught aboot a hunner o thaim every year, so Ah masel, personally speakin, Ah saved thaim a right few bob, didn't Ah? An it wisnae jist the rats. Aw naw, there wis rabbits tae. They're aye intae they cabbages. An lettuce! Ye couldnae keep a rabbit in lettuce; ne'er ye could but.

'Then the auld dear that runs the place said Ah wis hoachin wi fleas and she wis gonnae droon us. If Ah'd a quid fur every rabbit, rat an Goad-knows-whit-aw Ah've caught Ah widnae be here, Ah kin tell yese. But instead o a wee pension, Ah wis tae get droont! Tae hell wi this fur a caper, Ah thought; Ah'm off.

'Ye widnae huv a wee bite tae eat on ye, wid ye missus?'

'We are just like yourself,' said the sheep, 'with stories the same as your own.'

'An where ur yese gaun?'

'Well, we hadn't altogether decided that,' said the dog. 'But I dare say we'll know when we get there.'

'Any chance o a lift, big yin?'

'Ye kin walk wi us if ye like. But it's yer ain fower feet ye'll yase, an no mine.'

'Nae hairm in askin son.'

The pewter sky was streaked with brass and snow crystals glistened in the morning light. The four travellers were wet and weary of the road. The dog and cat spoke of long evenings in front of a fire, while a sturdy byre would have suited the other two. At the moment there was little prospect of either.

Then a new voice split the morning air. 'I say! Anyone know where a chap could get a peck of gwain?'

A weary, plumed cock sat on a drystane dyke some way off the path. A walking breakfast thought the cat as he strutted towards them, wet but elegant.

'Sowwy to twouble you chaps—I say; is that cat safe? Oh good. No offence, old boy. How do you doodle doo?

'Thing is, I've nowhere to stay, don't you know. I was on a farm but they took me away from the hens—dashed poor show that was— and stuck me in a coop, which wasn't too bad at first ectually. Plenty to eat and that sort of thing.

'The farmer, a fwightfully decent old boy, happened to let it slip that it was near Chwistmas and that the hens would be needed for the eggs; so one morning I looked out, and there was this young cockewel fellow stwutting about as if he owned the place.

'Well, weally; that was the last stwaw. What with the extwa gwain I was getting and Chwistmas not far away I put two and two together and knew I was in a pwetty pickle. Best not to hang about here, I thought. So I made a dash for it and here I am. What are you cwowd up to then?'

The sheep patiently explained why they were there and where they were going.

'Hah lovely!' shouted the cock. 'Dashed good fun, I should think. I say, would anyone mind if I tagged along, so to speak?'

There was silence. 'Naw, ye kin come,' said the cat. 'But gonnae cut oot that shoutin? Gie's a break, eh pal. Wid ye?'

They were about to move off again when there was a squabbling noise from behind the dyke.

'Uno momento—jeest a wee meeneet, eh!'

A goose came half-waddling, half-running through the grass. At times she completely disappeared among the undergrowth but was soon panting in front of them.

'Oh here! Mamma! Helpa! Helpa! Ah dida no see da pussy cat. Noo you come-ah near me an Ah'll...'

'Hold on, old bird. He's all wight, weally. Quite a decent chap, ectually. Bit of a wuff diamond, but all wight once you get to know him.'

'Okay den, okay. As long as he no start ah funny beesness, eh? Well, ah tell youse whit it's aw aboot, okay?'

'Ma mudder she wees Italian an ma faidder he wees Italian tae. Dey come here tae Scotlan an dees where Ah wis born. So dat make ah me a Scotch wumman, okay? Well, oan da fairm we lay some eggs an get oan fine. De udder animals no bodder us aifter a wee whilie. At first der wees a wee bit o a schamozzle when da hens say we were taking da food oota deir mooths, so we keep oorsels tae oorsels an no bodder naebody.

'Da family we get split up aifter a while and der wis jist me an a brudder and seester. Ma seester wis kilt at Easter. An ma brudder he wis kilt fur a wedding at da fairm. So wi da Chreestmas time no faur away, it no take much to know who's tae be finito next, eh?

'Ma poor brudder, he wis a beautiful seenger. An ma seester. She wis as bonnie a wee lassie as ever you see. But da beeg black fairmer— he keel dem!'

She started crying loud, long sobs.

'Och, here noo. There's nae need tae tak on like that,' said the bull. 'That's jist a thing we aa hae tae live wi. Come oan wi us, an we'll get oan fine enough.'

'Let's get tae hell oot o here afore any mair bampots turn up,' said the cat.

They walked through the murky day, talking to keep their spirits up. By nightfall they had found nothing to eat and had seen no one.

'We'll jist gang ower tae the ither side o this hill,' said the bull. 'Then we'll meybe get a bit o rest mmh?'

Over the hilltop was a small square of light. They followed their noses till they heard voices.

'Dive up oan the big yin's shooders an tell us whit's in there,' suggested the cat.

The cock perched himself up on the bull's back and the two of them crept towards the light. They weren't gone long.

'Whit's the score?' asked the cat.

'Six chaps in there! Counting money onto a table! But there's a cracking good fire and bags of food.'

'Okay then,' said the cat. 'We waant tae get in there, but tae dae that we've got tae get thaim oot, right? Noo, there's only wan way we're gonnae dae that, an that's tae gie thaim a right good fright. So we'll creep up tae the windae an let oot a big roar. Okay? We'll try it; see whit happens.'

The snow carpeted their noise as they huddled together underneath the window. The cat whispered: 'Right then! Efter three. Wan... two... two-an-a-hauf... THREE!'

'Lin-tin-addie, toor-in-addie!' roared the bull.

'But I wish the cauldest winds would never blaw,' sang the sheep.

'O-o-ochone a-a-areee!' howled the dog.

'Ger-intae-thum!' screamed the cat.

'I say, I say, I say' crowed the cock.

'O sole mio!' hissed the goose.

Immediately the light went out, the back door opened and the gangsters didn't stop till they reached a wood some way from the house. The damp grass was cold and they'd brought nothing to eat. Then there was the problem of the money they'd left.

They spoke of going back to have a look. It could have been anything—a Scotch wind, bagpipes, or maybe it was Hogmanay already.

One of them volunteered to go. He approached the house, then stopped to listen. The lights were out and nothing stirred in the darkness. The door opened easily enough and he groped his way towards the fire. But then he tripped over the sheep and, when he fell, the cat sprang and sunk his claws into the sprawling face. He scrambled to his feet, stood straight on the dog's tail and got teeth marks on his arms, legs and thighs. Demons were in his mind as he rushed for the door. Before he reached it the cock attacked with his claws and beak. Then the sheep butted him into the path of the bull, who tossed him out the door where the goose set about him with her wings.

He came to, bruised and battered, on the dung heap; then dragged one foot after another back to where the rest were waiting with heavy whispers: 'That was some dust-up! What's the low-down, Bugsy?'

'I guess there musta been a heavy kinda Highlander guy in there an he musta tripped me or somethin. Ah got as far as the fire and his ol' lady was waitin for me with a stiletto. Now she spits like crazy and that ain't good for my complexion! Ah gets away from her an' then the big Highlander really gives me the woiks. I get to him okay cos he squeals some, but he don't give up easy. Some other guy in this clan dived on me and they kicked n' battered me twice around the joint.

Gee, did they play it rough! One guy had the brass knuckles in my guts and his buddy's whippin me round the ankles with a chain — barkin like a dog, fer Chrissake! Then when I fell out the door there was another guy firin a bazooka! They're some mob, this Highland gang. If any of you guys want the dough you can go git it yourselves. Ah'm goin straight or somethin, but Ah sure ain't goin near that dive again as long as there's brains in ma head!'

'Say Bugsy. If we take the top road outta here, there's a few farmers' shacks along the way. We might get somethin outta them, uh?'

The animals watched them go and re-entered the house in triumph. They closed the shutters, lit the candles, ate and drank, then lay down carelessly to sleep: the bull leaned against the door, the sheep stretched out in the middle of the floor, the dog and cat curled up by the fire, the cock perched in the rafters and the goose settled herself in the midden just beyond the door.

When the sun rose it folded the house in a fresh day's light.

From *A Scent of Water* by Carl MacDougall

Ayrshire Farm

Every new year's morning the farmers
Would meet at 'Harelaw' with their guns
For the shoot. Mungo red in the face,
Matthew hale as a tree, John huge
In old leather. The others in dribs
And drabs, shotguns over their shoulders,
Bags flopping at their sides, collars up.

We'd set out across the north park,
The glaur on our leggings freezing
As we left the shelter of the knowes.
No dogs. Even the ferrets on this day
Of days were left squealing behind
Their wire. We'd fan out, taking
The slope at a steady tramp.

Mungo always aimed first, blasting away
At nothing. Hugh cursed under his breath;
The rest of us kept going. Suddenly
The hares would rise from the bracken-clumps
And go looping downhill. I remember
The banks alive with scuts, the dead
Gorse-tufts splattered with shot.

One by one the haversacks filled,
The blood dripping from them, staining
The snow. Matthew still in front,
Directing the others; the sun red
Behind its dyke, the wind rising.
And myself bringing up the rear,
Pretending I was lost, become the quarry.

Three blasts on a whistle, the second
Time round. And, in from the sleet,
We would settle on bales with bottles
And flasks, to divide the spoils. The bodies
Slit, and hung on hooks to drip. The dogs
Scrabbling on their chains. Todd's stallion

Rearing at the reek of blood. Then in
To the fire and a roaring new year:
Old Martha and Mima scuffling to and fro,
Our men's bellies filling, hands
Slowly thawing. And for me, off to bed,
A pig in the sheets, the oil lamp
Throwing shadows of rabbits on the wall.

Stewart Conn

The Rabbits

Funny, even Alec, his best pal, was against the rabbits, said they were
only silly pets for wee boys. Sometimes he thought Alec was right, but
once the door was locked nobody knew the silly things he said to the
rabbits.

He climbed up inside and slipped the bolt behind him. He put the
bicycle lamp on the tea-chest so that it shone along the netting fronts
of the hutches. The light made the rabbits thump and scurry. The
buck's eye shone red as it stared at him, head to one side.

'It's only me, me bonny beasties,' he said. This was his place, his
and his only. He'd built the hutches from old boxes and crates, some
knocked from a joiner's yard, some from Laidlaw's vegetable shop.
The door was shut behind him and he was the boss. Only he knew
what went on in here. First he fed the nursing doe, a three-year-old
bought from Findlay the big Chinchilla expert at Bridge of
Kilmorchan, Findlay o' the Brig. He'd been three or four when a man
called Murdoch or Murtagh or something like that had kept a few
black and white rabbits at the back of the tenement. One day his

daddy had taken him down to Murdoch or Murtagh's hutches and showed him a pair of young rabbits in an orange-box hutch.

'They're for you,' his daddy had said. 'Mister Murdoch says you can keep them here, but you've got to feed them and clean them out or he'll take them back.'

Of course he'd been too young. And then one day, he went down to feed them and he saw what looked like wee mice lying about on the straw, one of them was bleeding. He'd run to tell his father, and then had to stand by and watch while Murdoch or Murtagh and his father pulled out the babies and put them in the bin, Murdoch saying the father rabbit always killed the wee ones if you didn't get him out quick enough. Imagine keeping a buck in with a litter! They'd said he couldn't have them after that, they were too much bother, he remembered crying.

He'd almost forgotten those rabbits until one Saturday he'd gone with Alec on the train from Ayr to Glasgow, to see the Dairy Show and then Rangers and Hibs in the semi-final of the League Cup. They'd gone to Kelvin Hall in the morning, sitting in the upstairs front compartment of a tramcar, out past the Art Galleries. They had proper rabbits at the Dairy Show and as soon as he saw them he thought of Murdoch and the dead babies. He'd hung about until a man started speaking to him and told him the different breeds. Chinchillas were the best, a sort of bluey-grey with thick fur, solid, sensible somehow. This man gave him a book with breeders' names and addresses and it was there he'd found out about Findlay, whose rabbits won championships. About that time old McAllister died and next thing he was building hutches (using the old man's tools) and going out, rather nervously, to Findlay's. Fifteen bob for a mated doe! He'd brought the money (eleven and six in his biscuit tin and the rest from selling his football pictures to boys in the class) the next Saturday and Findlay gave him the big doe in a cardboard box. By the time he'd walked over the braes from Findlay's smallholding, which was at the back of beyond, to the Brig bus stop the doe had wet the bottom of the box and fallen out on the grass. He'd carried her under his arm, the people staring at him in the bus, the scheme kids following him as he walked down from the High Street.

Now he had that doe and three other full-grown does kept from her first litter, plus the buck (also bought from Findlay, for eleven and sixpence) and two half-grown does kept from Doe One's last summer litter. He'd only been at it a couple of years, Findlay said he wasn't producing show standards yet, but he could take all the young ones he produced to Ayr (in his mother's leather shopping bag) to sell to the pet stores for half a crown each. Findlay (a funny sort of man who liked to make a bit of mystery about rabbits) said that if he bred one with the correct fur density and markings he would help him to show it. Proper feeding, that was it, hay for bulk, corn for nourishment, a pinch of wheat for fur-gloss, just enough cauliflower leaves for liquid, water only for nursing does. Dandelion leaves!

He fed them corn from National Dried Milk tins and hay from the tea-chest. On Sunday he'd clean them out, good dry manure (if you fed them right the droppings were like soft, dry marbles) which Laidlaw the vegetable man dug into his allotments. At least it gave him something to do on Sundays, when you weren't allowed to play football on the Corporation pitches, or even listen to the Light Programme on the wireless. Imagine not being allowed to listen to comedies because your mother thought they were sinful on the Sabbath. Stupid old Dickens's serials were all right though!

When they were all fed he opened the door of the old doe's nesting compartment, while she munched corn from her thick clay Woolworth's dish, husks dribbling from her mouth. Placing his hand gently on the warm mound of downy white hair torn from her belly, he parted the nest and shone the lamp on the litter. They were the colour of a Gillette razor blade, blind little piggies with tiny furled ears and blunt snouts, fat little bodies already tinged with whitish hair. He moved them with his fingers, counting eleven. One was white-skinned, a throw-back to the beginning of the Chinchilla breed when Angoras were crossed in to give the grey rabbits a thick coat. The whitey could go for a start. Four was plenty for a winter litter— Findlay didn't believe in winter litters at all, but the mating and counting the thirty-one days' gestation and watching the wee ones develop was the best part of it. It didn't do any harm, as long as she was fed right.

Two runts. They could go. The bucks were supposed to have square, blunt heads. He decided to keep one buck and three does. The other seven went into the cleaning-out pail. Before he'd left school he'd knocked two thick science books to use for breeding records, weight graphs and income and· expenditure. You had to do it scientifically, grandfather and granddaughter but never brother and sister, grandmother and grandson, interbreeding the way they did with race-horses, to develop your own strain. It was something, Findlay said, you could only learn by years of experience, books were no good.

He shut the nesting compartment and took the pail to the far end of the hut. Once he had two or three does littering together he could kill all the poor ones and foster the remainder equally among the mothers, a delicate operation but nothing to a bright laddie with the right knack (and the knowledge that it's the smell that they notice, the secret being to rub your hands in the foster-mother's dirt pile before giving her the new babies).

'You see, you're all thinking this is cruelty,' he said, out loud, thinking of his mother and the cripple woman and the girl friend he didn't have, 'but it's just sensible stockmanship. Farmers can't afford all this sentimental blether, animals are only animals, these wee brutes don't even know they're alive yet. Women just don't understand what it's all about.'

He knocked their heads on the rim of the pail, one at a time, their warm, delicate bodies giving one long last pull against his palm, then going limp as the life went out of them. When they were all growing cold he shoved them down among the dirty straw in the pail. Laidlaw might get a shock—if he found he was digging in a heap of wee corpses! By now old Charlie would be lubricating trains, no doubt.

Only once in his life had he killed something for the hell of it, he'd never forget it, a dirty brute of a tomcat that kept hanging about their landing, yowling for their she-cat to come out, he'd got sick of that tom, especially one day he was in the house himself, in the afternoon, doing homework, they must have been let out early from school, anyway, the bastarding tomcat was up on their landing yowling like a demented creature, he'd been about twelve at the time, his father had a hammer which he used to cobble their shoes, he'd stood behind the door with the hammer and let the tomcat into the lobby, slamming the door behind it, grabbing it by the tail and thumping its nut with the hammer, it'd gone out after two hits, but it wasn't dead, so he'd taken it downstairs to the lavvy on the landing and locked himself in and shoved the dirty great brute down the seat, head first, holding its head under the water by the scruff of its neck, it'd come round and tried to scrabble backwards up the seat, he'd had to belt it again with the hammer and hold it under, Christ it'd taken *hours*. He must have been dead callous then, he couldn't do anything like that now. You had to have a good reason to kill—even wee blind rabbits.

Before he left he gave them all a small hunk of turnip, something to chew on, to stop the ever-growing teeth from coming out and round in a circle, back into their own brains.

'Right then, now for the happy home.'

One day he'd have a big shed and keep enough Chinchillas to live off them, some for fur coats and gloves, some for showing, some for eating, some for selling to the young breeders who'd come around his place, aye, ye cannae dae better'n buy frae Logan, finest strain o' Chinchillas in Scotland . . .

From *From Scenes Like These* by Gordon Williams

Todd

My father's white uncle became
Arthritic and testamental in
Lyrical stages. He held cardinal sin
Was misuse of horses, then any game

Won on the sabbath. A Clydesdale
To him was not bells and sugar or declension
From paddock, but primal extension
Of rock and soil. Thundered nail

Turned to sacred bolt. And each night
In the stable he would slaver and slave
At cracked hooves, or else save
Bowls of porridge for just the right

Beast. I remember I lied
To him once, about oats: then I felt
The brand of his loving tongue, the belt
Of his own horsey breath. But he died,

When the mechanised tractor came to pass.
Now I think of him neighing to some saint
In a simple heaven or, beyond complaint,
Leaning across a fence and munching grass.

Stewart Conn

Lion Tamer

So, the hot breath, the ring round me
Of haunch and mane, the eye always on me.
Strop of muscular shoulder, the easy
Stride, tail switching the sawdust up.
The jaws foremost in my mind—which take
Flesh, drip flame: could at no notice
A man's sinews snap, like a clown
Draw me tattered through a paper hoop.

Not skill, but knowledge. Of the fiery
Bowl, the fierce flower that's lion.
Attention caught. The soft paw. Giant
Cat. Who's met, who's held, who's master.
The one danger (and lion can sense it)
That the mind slip from its ring
To where the crowd sits, tier upon tier,
Its breath fetid, hungering for the killing.

Stewart Conn

NOTES

The available literature on this theme is, of course, vast. A particularly good
anthology is *Creatures Moving* ('Penguin English Project Stage One'), which

contains some interesting Edwin Morgan poems, including 'Hyena' (also in *From Glasgow to Saturn*, Carcanet Press), 'The Third Day of the Wolf', 'Heron' and a concrete poem, 'The Chaffinch Map of Scotland'.

Alasdair Maclean's fine collection, *From the Wilderness* (Gollancz), provides a veritable Scottish bestiary with 'Eagles', 'Hen Dying', 'Crow', 'Our Bull', 'The Old Dog' and 'Rams'. The obvious comparison with Ted Hughes' animal poems is illuminating and not necessarily entirely to Maclean's disadvantage.

'The Six Travellers' is a delightful piece for the young of all ages. Seemingly so simple, it has thematic depths worth exploring. The marvellous use of dialogue makes the story a painless introduction to questions of accent and dialect.

Orwell's *Animal Farm* (Secker & Warburg) is a possible companion piece.

'Ayrshire Farm': D. H. Lawrence's poem 'Mountain Lion' also deals with the hunting of animals. Other good Lawrence poems, such as 'Snake', 'Kangaroo' and 'Bat', analyse the relationship between man and beast.

'Todd' can be compared with the same writer's 'Strange Seraph' (*Stoats in the Sunlight*, Hutchinson) and Edwin Muir's 'Horses'.

5

HAPPY DAYS

Hallowe'en

When I was a wee girl in Glasgow, Hallowe'en was celebrated by all of us with keenest enjoyment. The weather always seemed clear and frosty, the skies filled with stars, and there was the exhilaration of dressing up in strange garments, with the added tension and nervousness of a performance about to begin. I usually wore Grannie's old hat, when it had got beyond the stage when a bunch of cherries or a spray of flowers could rejuvenate it, and I sat it on top of my head at a rakish angle, over my blackened face. A long skirt of my mother's, and Grannie's tartan shawl completed the disguise, but I wasn't able to round off the effect with my mother's high-heeled shoes because I couldn't even hobble in them, so my long-legged boots and black woollen stockings just had to be worn, even though they were completely out of character. This was a terrible disappointment, for I longed to prance about in elegant high heels, but for running out and in closes and up and down dozens of stairs sure footing was vital, and boots it had to be.

There was much giggling and mutual admiration when we all met after tea, and set out on the rounds of all the neighbours' houses. Sometimes, greatly daring, we went beyond our own district, and we shivered with excitement, and a little dread at the thought of knocking at such strange doors. We were very critical of the brasses, and surprised to find that in some posh closes the name-plates weren't a patch on the glittering gold polish our own mothers managed. We each carried a little bag, home-made from an old petticoat or blouse, with a draw-string top, to hold the expected apples and nuts and sweets we hoped we would collect, and we prepared our acts as we raced along from close to close. We never expected to be handed our Hallowe'en gifts just for knocking on a door and chanting, 'Please gi'e us wur Hallowe'en!' We knew we were expected to do a turn to entertain our benefactors.

We would be invited into the house, and the family would sit round in lively anticipation as we went into our performances. I usually sang the latest popular song, and I particularly liked one requiring the use of my hostess's fluebrush, which I stuck over my shoulder and used as a bayonet. Very dashing I thought this, and so did my audience! There were recitations and ballads, and we generally finished with all of us doing a Highland Fling. We received our applause with flushed and happy faces, and we opened our draw-string bags to receive the apples, and the nuts, with maybe a piece of puff candy or some home-made tablet. Tablet was a great treat and so tempting that it was devoured on the spot, and seldom rested in the bag for a second. A turnip lantern lit our way and we went bobbing through the darkness like glow-worms. The preparation of those magic lanterns was a great ploy. We hollowed out swede turnips skilfully, made two slits for the eyes and a perpendicular line for the nose. A curved slit made a smiling mouth. A little hollow in the bottom held our candle, and the complete effect was golden and delightful. I may say everybody in our district ate mashed swedes for days afterwards, using up the discarded insides of our lanterns.

A party was a great excitement at Hallowe'en, and everyone went in fancy dress. Home-made, of course, for these were unsophisticated as well as hard-up days, and only 'toffs' would have known about hiring clothes. Angels and fairies, their wings fashioned from cardboard boxes coaxed from the Cooperative, and covered with coloured crinkled paper, were ten a penny, for the girls. The boys favoured pirates and cowboys, which were easily fashioned from old hats, and their father's leather belts, and toy guns. All this helped to break down the shyness we would have felt in ordinary clothes, although Hallowe'en fun was so different from any other form of merriment there was never a minute of sitting still wondering what you were expected to do. After the tea, with its salmon sandwiches if we were lucky, or corn mutton if money was tight, followed by the jellies, the games started. The big zinc bath was pulled from under the bed and filled with cold water, then rosy-cheeked apples were tumbled in in a colourful shower. A chair was placed with its back to the bath, the apples and water given a vigorous stir to send them bobbing as wildly as possible and make a difficult target, and we would each kneel, one at a time, on the chair, head sticking out over the top edge just as though we were about to be guillotined. A fork was held between clenched teeth, and we'd gaze at the bobbing fruit below us, waiting for the moment when the biggest and reddest apple was exactly placed for our aim, then *plonk*, down went the fork, usually to slither off between the bouncing apples. There would be howls of glee from the onlookers, and gulping disappointment from the unlucky contestant as he or she climbed down from the chair to go to the end of the queue again. Not till everybody had speared an apple would the next game start, and, of course, it became harder and harder to succeed as the numbers of apples grew fewer and fewer with each win, and the final apple had the whole room shouting opposite advice. 'Drap yer fork noo. *Noo*, Wullie. Ach missed it', 'Gi'e the watter a steer, it's easier when it's movin'', or 'Don't steer it noo, gi'e 'im a chance seein' there's only wan'. And from the faint-hearted, or those who wanted to go on to another game, 'Ach just gi'e 'im it, and let's get on wi' the party.'

There was a lovely game, unpopular with parents but beloved by us children, where a huge home-baked soda scone was covered in treacle and suspended on a string from the centre gas bracket, or hung from a string stretched across the room. It was sent spinning by the leader, and then, with hands clasped behind our backs, we would leap into the air and try to snatch a bite. What a glorious mess we were in at the end of the caper, hair, eyes, cheeks and neck covered in treacle. Mothers and aunties and uncles urged us instantly towards the kitchen sink, 'Go and dicht yer faces noo, we don't want treacle a' ower the hoose,' and what a splashing there was under the cold tap, and a battle for the solitary towel as we removed the mess.

And, of course, we loved the trinkets which were buried in a mound of creamy mashed potatoes. Even the poorest family could afford tatties, so everybody could enjoy this traditional bit of fun. The quantities of potato we consumed in search of our favourite ring or threepenny piece must have saved many an anxious hostess from worrying how she was to fill us up.

The older girls were full of romantic notions concerning apples. They'd try to take off the peel in one continuous strand, which they threw over their left shoulder, and whichever initial it formed was supposed to be that of the lad they would marry. Oh the teasing and the blushing if by chance the initial formed was that of their current heart-throb. The boys pretended they had no interest in this performance, but there was plenty of jeering and pushing when the initial fitted, and a casual pairing off when the game had finished. Especially if the next game was the one where an apple was placed on the top edge of a door, with a chair placed on either side, a boy on one chair and a girl on the other. They each ate towards the core, and the winners were the couple who reached the core—and a kiss—in the shortest possible time.

We children thought the swinging apple game was far better, and it was funnier too. There were up to six contestants at a time required for this game, which made it rare and noisy and exciting. They had to stand in line, in front of six apples suspended on cords from a string stretched across the room. The apples were set swinging, and the point of the game was that, without using hands to help, the contestants had to bite the fruit right down to the core. The winner, of course, was the one who finished first. The apple could be manoeuvred on to one shoulder only *once* during the game to assist the eating, but otherwise everybody leaped and bit like hungry birds, and a most comical sight it was for the onlookers. It was especially funny when the grown-ups took their turn, and we held our sides with laughter when specs slithered down perspiring noses, when braces parted from buttons, and when false teeth were dislodged on hitting an apple too suddenly. We could have played this game all night, but all at once the apples were finished, and it was time to go home, this time without lanterns to light our way, for, of course, we didn't take them to parties, only when we went out chanting 'Please gi'e us wur Hallowe'en'.

From *Best Foot Forward* by Molly Weir

Trio

Coming up Buchanan Street, quickly, on a sharp winter
    evening
a young man and two girls, under the Christmas lights—
The young man carries a new guitar in his arms,
the girl on the inside carries a very young baby,
and the girl on the outside carries a chihuahua.
And the three of them are laughing, their breath rises
in a cloud of happiness, and as they pass
the boy says, 'Wait till he sees this but!'
The chihuahua has a tiny Royal Stewart tartan coat like a
    teapot-holder,
the baby in its white shawl is all bright eyes and mouth like
    favours in a fresh sweet cake,
the guitar swells out under its milky plastic cover, tied at
    the neck with silver tinsel tape and a brisk sprig of
    mistletoe.

Orphean sprig! Melting baby! Warm chihuahua!
The vale of tears is powerless before you.
Whether Christ is born, or is not born, you
put paid to fate, it abdicates

                                under the Christmas lights.
Monsters of the year
go blank, are scattered back,
can't bear this march of three.

—And the three have passed, vanished in the crowd
(yet not vanished, for in their arms they wind
the life of men and beasts, and music,
laughter ringing them round like a guard)
at the end of this winter's day.

Edwin Morgan

Tinsel

The swing-doors of the steamie had windows in them but even when
he stood on tiptoe he couldn't reach up to see out. If he held the doors
open, the people queuing complained about the cold and anyway the
strain would make his arms ache. So he had to be content to peer out
through the narrow slit between the doors, pressing his forehead
against the brass handplate. He could see part of the street and the
grey buildings opposite, everything covered in snow. He tried to see
more by moving a little sideways, but the gap wasn't wide enough. He
could smell the wood and paint of the door and the clean bleachy smell
from the washhouse. His eye began to sting from the draught so he
closed it tight and put his other eye to the slit, but he had to jump
back quickly as a woman with a pramful of washing crashed open the
doors. When the doors had stopped swinging and settled back into
place he noticed that the brass plate was covered with fingermarks. He
wanted to see it smooth and shiny so he breathed up on it, clouding it
with his breath, and rubbed it with his sleeve. But he only managed to
smear the greasy marks across the plate leaving it streaky and there
was still a cluster of prints near the top that he couldn't reach at all.

He went over and sat down on the long wooden bench against the
wall. His feet didn't quite reach the ground and he sat swinging his
legs. It felt as if his mother had been in the washhouse for hours.

Waiting.

People passed in and out. The queue was just opposite the bench.
They queued to come in and wash their clothes or to have a hot bath
or a swim. The way to the swimming baths was through an iron

turnstile, like the ones at Ibrox Park. When his father took him to the match he lifted him over the turnstile so he didn't have to pay.

Unfastening his trenchcoat, he rummaged about in his trouser pocket and brought out a toy Red Indian without a head, a pencil rubber, a badge with a racing car, a yellow wax crayon and a foreign coin. He pinned the badge on to his lapel and spread the other things out on the bench. The crayon was broken in the middle but because the paper cover wasn't torn the two ends hadn't come apart. It felt wobbly. He bent it in half, tearing the paper. Now he had two short crayons instead of one long one. There was nothing to draw on except the green-tiled wall so he put the pieces back in his pocket.

The coin was an old one, from Palestine, and it had a hole in the middle. He'd been given it by his uncle Andy who had been a soldier there. Now he was a policeman in Malaya. He would be home next week for Christmas. Jesus's birthday. Everybody gave presents then so that Jesus would come one day and take them to heaven. That was where he lived now, but he came from Palestine. Uncle Andy had been to see his house in Bethlehem. At school they sang hymns about it. Come all ye faithful. Little star of Bethlehem.

He scraped at the surface of the bench with his coin, watching the brown paint flake and powder, blowing the flakings away to see the mark he'd made.

The woman at the pay-desk shouted at him.

'Heh! Is that how ye treat the furniture at hame? Jist chuck it!'

He sat down again.

Two boys and two girls aged about fifteen came laughing and jostling out of the baths, red faced, their hair still damp. One of the boys was flicking his wet towel at the girls who skipped clear, just out of reach. They clattered out into the street, leaving the doors swinging behind them. He heard their laughter fade, out of his hearing. For the moment again he was alone.

He stood his headless Indian on the bench. If he could find the head he'd be able to fix it back on again with a matchstick. He pushed the Indian's upraised arm through the hole in the coin, thinking it would make a good shield, but it was too heavy and made the Indian fall over.

He shoved his things back into his pocket and went over to the doorway of the washhouse. The place was painted a grubby cream and light green and the stone floor was wet.

Clouds of steam swishing up from faraway metaltub machines. Lids banging shut. Women shouting above the throbbing noise.

He couldn't see his mother.

He went back and climbed on to the bench, teetering, almost falling, as he stood carefully up.

A woman came in with a little girl about his own age. He was glad he was standing on the bench and he knew she was watching him.

He ignored her and pretended to fight his way along the bench, hacking aside an army of unseen cut-throats, hurling them over the immense drop from the perilous bench-top ridge. He kept looking round to make sure she was still watching him, not looking directly at her but just glancing in her direction then looking past her to the pay-box and staring at that with fixed interest and without seeing it at all.

The woman had taken her bundle into the washhouse and the little girl sat down on the far end of the bench, away from him.

His mother came out of the washhouse pushing her pram. He jumped down noisily and ran to her. As they left he turned and over his shoulder stuck out his tongue at the girl.

Once outside, his mother started fussing over him, buttoning his coat, straightening his belt, tucking in his scarf.

'There yar then, ah wasn't long, was ah?' Gentle voice. Her breath was wheezy.

She was wearing the turban she wore to work in the bakery. Today was Saturday and she only worked in the morning, coming home at dinnertime with cakes and pies. He'd gone with her to the steamie because his father was out at the doctor's and he couldn't find any of his friends. They'd probably gone to the pictures.

He had to walk very quickly, sometimes trotting, to keep up with the pram. The snow under his feet made noises like a catspurr at every step. The pram-wheels creaked. In the pram was a tin tub full of damp washing which was already starting to stiffen in the cold. It was the same pram he'd been carried in when he was a baby. His mother's two other babies had been carried in it too. They would have been his big brothers but they'd both died. They would be in Heaven. He wondered if they were older than him now or if they were still babies. He was six years and two weeks old. His wellington boots were folded down at the top like pirate boots. His socks didn't reach up quite far enough and the rims of the boots had rubbed red stinging chafe-marks round his legs.

They rounded the corner into their own street and stopped outside the Dairy.

'You wait here son. Ah'll no be a minnit.'

Waiting again.

Out of a close came a big loping longhaired dog. The hair on its legs looked like a cowboy's baggy trousers. Some boys were chasing it and laughing. All its fur was clogged with dirt and mud.

His mother came out of the shop with a bottle of milk.

There was a picture of the same kind of dog in his Wonder Book of the World. It was called an Afghan Hound. But the one in the book looked different. Again the steady creak of the pram. The trampled snow underfoot was already grey and slushy.

They reached their close and he ran on up ahead. They lived on the top landing and he was out of breath when he reached the door. He leaned over the banister. Down below he could hear his mother bumping the pram up the stairs. Maybe his father was home from the doctor's.

He kicked the door.

'O-pen. O-pen.'

His father opened the door and picked him up.

'H'Hay! Where's yer mammy?'

'She's jist comin up.'

His father put him down and went to help her with the pram.

He went into the kitchen and sat down by the fire.

Dusty, their cat, jumped down from the sink and slid quietly under the bed. The bed was in a recess opposite the window and the three of them slept there in winter. Although they had a room, the kitchen was easier to keep warm. The room was bigger and was very cold and damp. His father said it would cost too much to keep both the room and the kitchen heated.

He warmed his hands till they almost hurt. He heard his mother and father coming in. They left the pram in the lobby. His father was talking about the doctor.

'Aye, e gave me a prescription fur another jar a that ointment.' He had to put the ointment all over his body because his skin was red and flaky and he had scabby patches on his arms and legs. That was why he didn't have a job. He'd had to give up his trade in the shipyards because it was a dirty job and made his skin disease worse.

'An ah got your pills as well, when ah wis in the Chemist's.'

His mother had to take pills to help her breathing. At night she had to lie on her back, propped up with pillows.

'Never mind hen. When ah win the pools . . .'

'Whit'll ye get ME daddy?' This was one of their favourite conversations.

'Anythin ye like sun.'

'Wull ye get me a pony, daddy? Lik an Indian.'

'Ah'll get ye TWO ponies.' Laughing. 'An a wigwan as well!'

He could see it. He'd ride up to school, right up the stairs and into the classroom and he'd scalp Miss Heather before she could reach for her belt.

He'd keep the other pony for Annie. She was his friend. She wasn't his girlfriend. That was soft. She was three weeks older than him and she lived just round the corner. They were in the same class at school. She had long shiny black hair and she always wore bright clean colours. (One night in her back close—showing bums—giggling— they didn't hear the leerie coming in to light the gas-lamp—deep loud voice somewhere above them—sneering laugh—Annie pulling up her knickers and pulling down her dress in the same movement— scramble into the back—both frightened to go home in case the leerie had told, but he hadn't.)

The memory of it made him blush. He ripped off a piece of

70

newspaper and reached up for the toilet key from the nail behind the door where it hung.

'Jist goin t' the lavvy.'

From the lobby he heard the toilet being flushed so he waited in the dark until he heard the slam of the toilet door then the flop of Mrs Dolan's feet on the stairs. The Dolans lived in the single end, the middle door of the three on their landing. The third house, another room and kitchen, was empty for the moment because the Andersons had emigrated to Canada.

When he heard Mrs Dolan closing the door he stepped out on to the landing and slid down the banister to the stairhead. In the toilet there was only one small window very high up, and he left the door slightly open to let light seep in from the stairhead.

A pigeon landed on the window-ledge and sat there gurgling and hooing, its feathers ruffled up into a ball. To pull the plug he climbed up on to the seat and swung on the chain, squawking out a Tarzan-call. The pigeon flurried off, scared by the noise, and he dropped from his creeperchain, six inches to the floor.

He looked out through the stairhead window. Late afternoon. Out across the back and a patch of wasteground, over factory roofs and across a railway line stood Ibrox Stadium. He could see a patch of terracing and the roof of the stand. The pressbox on top looked like a little castle. When Rangers were playing at home you could count the goals and near misses just by listening to the roars. Today there was only a reserve game and the noise could hardly be heard. Soon it would be dark and they'd have to put on the floodlights.

*   *   *

For tea they had sausages and egg and fried bread. After they'd eaten he sat down in his own chair at the fire with his Wonder Book of the World. The chair was wooden and painted bright blue.

His father switched on the wireless to listen to the football results and check his pools.

The picture of the Afghan Hound had been taken in a garden on a sunny day. The dog was running and its coat shone in the sun.

'Four draws,' said his father. 'Ach well, maybe next week . . .'

'There's that dog, mammy.' He held up the book.

'So it is.'

'Funny tae find a dog lik that in Govan,' said his father.

'Right enough,' said his mother. 'Expect some'dy knocked it.'

Nothing in the book looked like anything he had ever seen. There were pictures of cats but none of them looked like Dusty. They were either black and white or striped and they all looked clean and sleek. Dusty was a grubby grey colour and he spat and scratched if anyone tried to pet him. His mother said he'd been kept too long in the house. There was a section of the book about the weather with pictures of snow crystals that looked like flowers and stars. He thought he'd like to go out and play in the snow and he asked his mother if he could.

'Oh well, jist for a wee while then. Ah'll tell ye what. If ye come up early enough we kin put up the decorations before ye go tae bed.'

He'd forgotten about the decorations. It was good to have something special like that to come home for. It was the kind of thing he'd forget about while he was actually playing, then there would be moments when he'd remember, and feel warm and comforted by the thought.

He decided he'd get Joe and Jim and Annie and they'd build a snowman as big as a midden.

*　　*　　*

Joe was having his tea and Jim felt like staying in and Annie's mother wouldn't let her out.

He stood on the pavement outside the paper-shop, peering in through the lighted window at the Christmas annuals and selection boxes. The queue for the evening papers reached right to the door of the shop. The snow on the pavement was packed hard and grey-brown, yellow in places under the streetlamps. He scraped at the snow with the inside of his boot, trying to rake up enough to make a snowball, but it was too powdery and it clung to the fingers of his woollen gloves, making his hands feel clogged and uncomfortable. He took off his gloves and scooped up some slush from the side of the road but the cold made his bare fingers sting, red. It felt as if he'd just been belted by Miss Heather.

Annie's big brother Tommy was clattering his way across the road, trailing behind him a sack full of empty bottles. He'd gathered them on the terracing at Ibrox and he was heading for the Family Department of the pub to cash in as many as he could. Every time the pub door opened the noise and light seeped out. It was a bit like pressing your hands over your ears then easing off then pressing again. If you did that again and again people's voices sounded like mwah . . . mwah . . . mwah . . . mwah . . .

He looked closely at the snow still clogging his gloves. It didn't look at all like the crystals in his book. Disgusted, he slouched towards his close.

Going up the stairs at night he always scurried or charged past each closet for fear of what might be lurking there ready to leap out at him. Keeping up his boldness, he whistled loudly. Little Star of Bethlehem. He was almost at the top when he remembered the decorations.

*　　*　　*

The kitchen was very bright after the dimness of the landing with its sputtering gas light.

'Nob'dy wis comin out tae play,' he explained.

His mother wiped her hands. 'Right! What about these decorations!'

The decorations left over from last year were in a cardboard box under the bed. He didn't like it under there. It was dark and dirty, piled with old rubbish—books, clothes, boxes, tins. Once he'd crawled under looking for a comic, dust choking him, and he'd scuttled back in horror from bugs and darting silverfish. Since then he'd had bad dreams about the bed swarming with insects that got into his mouth when he tried to breathe.

His father rummaged in the sideboard drawer for a packet of tin tacks and his mother brought out the box.

Streamers and a few balloons and miracles of coloured paper that opened out into balls or long concertina snakes. On the table his mother spread out some empty cake boxes she'd brought home from work and cut them into shapes like Christmas trees and bells, and he got out his painting box and a saucerful of water and he coloured each one and left it to dry—green for the trees and yellow for the bells, the nearest he could get to gold.

His father had bought something special.

'Jist a wee surprise. It wis only a coupla coppers in Woollies.'

From a cellophane bag he brought out a length of shimmering rustling silver.

'What dis that say daddy?' He pointed at the label.

'It says UNTARNISHABLE TINSEL GARLAND.'

'What dis that mean?'

'Well that's what it is. It's a tinsel garland. Tinsel's the silvery stuff it's made a. An a garland's jist a big long sorta decoration, for hangin up. An untarnishable means . . . well . . . how wid ye explain it hen?'

'Well,' said his mother, 'it jist means it canny get wasted. It always steys nice an shiny.'

'Aw Jesus!' said his father. 'Ther's only three tacks left!'

'Maybe the paper-shop'll be open.'

'It wis open a wee minnit ago!'

'Ah'll go an see,' said his father, putting on his coat and scarf.

'Shouldnae be very long.'

*   *   *

The painted cut-out trees and bells had long since dried and still his father hadn't come back. His mother had blown up the balloons and she'd used the three tacks to put up some streamers. Then she remembered they had a roll of sticky tape. It was more awkward to use than the tacks so the job took a little longer. But gradually the room was transformed, brightened; magical colours strung across the ceiling. A game he liked to play was lying on his back looking up at the ceiling and trying to imagine it was actually the floor and the whole room was upside down. When he did it now it looked like a toy garden full of swaying paper plants.

73

Round the lampshade in the centre of the room his mother was hanging the tinsel coil, standing on a chair to reach up. When she'd fixed it in place she climbed down and stood back and they watched the swinging lamp come slowly to rest. Then they looked at each other and laughed.

When they heard his father's key in the door his mother shooshed and put out the light. They were going to surprise him. He came in and fumbled for the switch. They were laughing and when he saw the decorations he smiled but he looked bewildered and a bit sad.

He put the box of tacks on the table.

'So ye managed, eh,' he said. He smiled again, his eyes still sad. 'Ah'm sorry ah wis so long. The paper-shop wis shut an ah had tae go down nearly tae Govan Road.'

Then they understood. He was sad because they'd done it all without him. Because they hadn't waited. They said nothing. His mother filled the kettle. His father took off his coat.

'Time you were in bed malad!' he said.

'Aw bit daddy, themorra's Sunday!'

'Bed!'

'Och!'

He could see it was useless to argue so he washed his hands and face and put on the old shirt he slept in.

'Mammy, ah need a pee.'

Rather than make him get dressed again to go out and down the stairs, she said he could use the sink. She turned on the tap and lifted him up to kneel on the ledge.

When he pressed his face up close to the window he could see the back court lit here and there by the light from a window, shining out on to the yellow snow from the dark bulk of the tenements. There were even one or two Christmas trees and, up above, columns of palegrey smoke, rising from chimneys. When he leaned back he could see the reflection of their own kitchen. He imagined it was another room jutting out beyond the window, out into the dark. He could see the furniture, the curtain across the bed, his mother and father, the decorations and through it all, vaguely, the buildings, the night. And hung there, shimmering, in that room he could never enter, the tinsel garland that would never ever tarnish.

From *Its Colours they are Fine* by Alan Spence

NOTES

'Hallowe'en': Clifford Hanley's *The Taste of Too Much* (Hutchinson) includes an amusing but sharply-observed account of a Glasgow New Year party (Chapter 6), which might well serve as a contrast.

Two short stories which deal with celebrations are Edward Gaitens' 'A Wee Nip' (*Scottish Short Stories*, edited by Fred Urquhart, Faber) and Alan Spence's nostalgic 'For Auld Lang Syne' (*Its Colours they are Fine*, Collins).

'Trio': Liz Lochhead's cool account of Glasgow's annual Kelvin Hall fun-fair, 'Carnival' (*Memo for Spring*, Reprographia), and Hugh MacDiarmid's gloriously joyful 'With the Herring Fishers' (*Selected Poems*, Penguin), are suggested companion pieces for Edwin Morgan's successful piece of poetic anthropology.

'Tinsel': this fine story concludes with an unforgettable image, the Joycean epiphany of 'that room he could never enter, the tinsel garland that would never ever tarnish'.

'The Rain Dance' (*Its Colours they are Fine*), by the same writer, which describes a Glasgow registry office wedding, captures the eternal ritualistic quality of the great occasions in human life, yet remains local and authentic.

Dylan Thomas's autobiographical piece, 'Memories of Christmas' (*Quite Early One Morning*, Dent), has some features in common with 'Tinsel'.

6

THE PITY OF IT

Accident Report

A man with a crumpled chest, a woman gone with child,
and a boy of five, neck broken, scarcely breathing,
cool in their own blood. From a flurry of bells
two men leap down and begin efficiently heaving

the stretchered bodies into the ambulance,
and box its doors on the worst of the whole affair.
It rocks and sways through blue and white alarm
three people past all hope of human repair

to the hospital it makes its sallies from.
Meanwhile, a policeman blots their blood with sawdust;
another stoops to measure suddenness,
as if from twenty screaming yards the law must

somehow exact an answer that restores
normality. Two cars, crouched in the shape
of fixed obscenities, drain like burst animals.
Edging cautiously past, the rest of us gape,

are fascinated; smell the moment of strike
that—Christ!—how narrowly missed us, yet happened far
enough away to blame on luck or carelessness,
and exorcise the raw decline we are.

Maurice Lindsay

The Blind Reading

My father, two uncles and an aunt in Canada, all in two years. Two had died within four days of each other. My grandmother said we never were a lucky family: someone had put a curse on us.

Everywhere life is full of heroism. I learned when someone went into a room alone, it was best to leave them. Our busy times lapsed into a silent semi-circle staring at the fire. Sobbing. Strangers sat in their heavy coats, swallowing a stream of tea. Some old buddy would sigh, sigh and stare at me, shake her head, bite her lower lip, then mutter into her cup, 'Aye he's like his father.' I knew what it caused.

'Go out and play, son.' But I wasn't to play with Toe Blair or the foul-mouthed Jackie Carson. Anyway, they wanted to be soldiers or cowboys. I didn't like pretending to be dead and was too soft for football. You'll get kicked, my grannie had told me, and I knew she was right. Books helped me escape, but there was a hard reality. Everyone looked wild, red-eyed and miserable. I believed the dead would never be left in peace.

Every Sunday, after lunch, we took the tram to Lambhill Cemetery. The afternoons were warm and clammy in uncomfortable clothes. Black was the colour. We walked from the terminus and there were always crowds of people.

Up the hill and round the bend an old lady read aloud from a Braille Bible. She sat on a wooden kitchen chair and whispered parables into her grey clothes. Her pepper-and-salt hair was tied in a bun at the back of her neck; stubby fingers read the pages, horizontally translating to lips that hardly moved. She was undisturbed by the chink of money in a shoe-box at her feet. I was fascinated and could have watched for hours. It's rude to stare, I was told. But I thought she didn't know I was staring.

There was talk. Some said she lived in a mansion and a car collected her at night. Others maintained she wasn't blind at all, or had memorized one passage and repeated it over and over again.

I was an impatient gravetender, anxious to be back at the Bible. One time she wasn't there on our way home. After that I made sure we left early. When I saw a car I looked to see if she was in it, even if there was only the driver. She burgled my dreams. A blind voice read from the Bible and the darkness was no longer my friend.

On a summer Sunday, Toe, Carsie and I were bored. We kicked cans and lay up the park pretending to be explorers.

'If you want to be real explorers, I know where we can go,' I said.

We got money from bottles hidden for such an emergency and sang, laughing, on the tram. At the terminus we were quiet and alone.

'Where'll we go now?' said Carsie.

'C'mon back,' said Toe.

'I know where to go,' I said.

They trailed up the hill after me, kicking stones.

Round the corner I saw her and smiled at the discovery.

'It's just a woman,' someone said.

'She's blind and reads the Bible.'

'So what?'

I stood snared.

'He's daft,' said Toe. 'C'mon back.'

'. . . and taught them, saying, Blessed are the poor in spirit: for theirs is the kingdom of heaven. Blessed are they that mourn: for they shall be comforted. Blessed . . .'

Time was words and fingers and money. When the people were gone she closed the book, picked up the shoe-box and turned her yellow and white eyes to the day. I wanted to talk, but there was a racing pulse and a heavy throat.

'What are you doing here, son?'

I turned and saw the voice in a police car.

'Nothing.'

'Where do you stay?'

'Keppochhill Road.'

'Are you lost?'

Lost.

'You're a bit out of the way for a wee boy. We'll give you a lift. Get in the back.'

From the car I saw sightless eyes, staring, alone, a Bible and a shoe-box full of money on her lap.

The policeman dropped me off at the foot of the road.

'You can make your own way home. We don't want to give your mother a fright do we?'

Archie Wallace saw me first.

'Here he is. The daft explorer. Imagine going to see a daft old woman reading the Bible.'

The laughter was forced, loud and followed me, landing at the pit of my stomach.

That was the end. I did not know it, but time healed and memories darkened. A grey salve stopped us going to the cemetery. I never saw her again.

Carl MacDougall

78

In the Snack-bar

A cup capsizes along the formica,
slithering with a dull clatter.
A few heads turn in the crowded evening snack-bar.
An old man is trying to get to his feet
from the low round stool fixed to the floor.
Slowly he levers himself up, his hands have no power.
He is up as far as he can get. The dismal hump
looming over him forces his head down.
He stands in his stained beltless gaberdine
like a monstrous animal caught in a tent
in some story. He sways slightly,
the face not seen, bent down
in shadow under his cap.
Even on his feet he is staring at the floor
or would be, if he could see.
I notice now his stick, once painted white
but scuffed and muddy, hanging from his right arm.
Long blind, hunchback born, half-paralysed
he stands
fumbling with the stick
and speaks:
'I want—to go to the—toilet.'

It is down two flights of stairs, but we go.
I take his arm. 'Give me—your arm—it's better,' he says.
Inch by inch we drift towards the stairs.
A few yards of floor are like a landscape
to be negotiated, in the slow setting out
time has almost stopped. I concentrate
my life to his: crunch of spilt sugar,
slidy puddle from the night's umbrellas,
table edges, people's feet,
hiss of the coffee-machine, voices and laughter,
smell of a cigar, hamburgers, wet coats steaming,
and the slow dangerous inches to the stairs.
I put his right hand on the rail
and take his stick. He clings to me. The stick
is in his left hand, probing the treads.
I guide his arm and tell him the steps.
And slowly we go down. And slowly we go down.
White tiles and mirrors at last. He shambles
uncouth into the clinical gleam.
I set him in position, stand behind him
and wait with his stick.

His brooding reflection darkens the mirror
but the trickle of his water is thin and slow,
an old man's apology for living.
Painful ages to close his trousers and coat—
I do up the last buttons for him.
He asks doubtfully, 'Can I—wash my hands?'
I fill the basin, clasp his soft fingers round the soap.
He washes, feebly, patiently. There is no towel.
I press the pedal of the drier, draw his hands
gently into the roar of the hot air.
But he cannot rub them together,
drags out a handkerchief to finish.
He is glad to leave the contraption, and face the stairs.
He climbs, and steadily enough.
He climbs, we climb. He climbs
with many pauses but with that one
persisting patience of the undefeated
which is the nature of man when all is said.
And slowly we go up. And slowly we go up.
The faltering, unfaltering steps
take him at last to the door
across that endless, yet not endless waste of floor.
I watch him helped on a bus. It shudders off in the rain.
The conductor bends to hear where he wants to go.

Wherever he could go it would be dark
and yet he must trust men.
Without embarrassment or shame
he must announce his most pitiful needs
in a public place. No one sees his face.
Does he know how frightening he is in his strangeness
under his mountainous coat, his hands like wet leaves
stuck to the half-white stick?
His life depends on many who would evade him.
But he cannot reckon up the chances,
having one thing to do,
to haul his blind hump through these rains of August.
Dear Christ, to be born for this!

Edwin Morgan

Fifty Pence

The old woman opened her eyelids when the gas-light flickered, but
soon closed them again. With the newspaper raised nearer his eyes the
boy squinted at the football news on the back page, trying to find

something new to read. He let the paper fall onto his lap and lifted the tongs. He released the catch and wangled the points round a large coal lying in the shovel and carefully placed in on the spare fire in the grate. The old woman regarded him gravely for a moment. When he smiled back her forehead wrinkled in a taut kindly expression. Her eyes roamed upwards to the clock then the lids closed over.

He glanced at the clock; 8.40. He should have been home by now. The poker lay near his foot inside the fire-surround. He wanted to rake among the ashes to see if anything red remained. Perhaps there would be enough to kindle the lump and save the fire, perhaps the new lump was too big to catch light. The rustle as he turned a page of the paper seemed to reverberate around the narrow, high-ceilinged kitchen. There was nothing to keep him. His parents would be annoyed. The bus journey home took nearly an hour and during the long winter nights they liked him to be in bed by ten. They would guess he was here.

He got to his feet, stretched. The movement roused the old woman; she muttered vaguely about apples being in the cupboard. He drank a mouthful of water straight from the brass tap then returned to his chair.

The fire looked dead. Lifting the poker suddenly he dug right into the ashes. The old woman bent forward and took the poker from him without comment. Gripping it with her right hand she moved her left deftly in and out the coals. Finally she balanced the new lump on smaller pieces, her thin fingers indifferent to any heat which may have remained. The poker was put back in position; handle on the floor with its sooty point projected in the air, lying angled against the fender. Wiping her fingertips on her apron she walked to the door and through to the parlour.

Neither spoke when she came back. She sat on her wooden chair and stared into the fire. Cloying black smoke drifted from the new lump. It crackled.

A little after 9.45 she looked up on hearing the light rap on the outside door. The boy stirred from his doze. He made to rise and answer but relaxed when she indicated he should remain where he was. The outside door opened and closed, and muttering as the footsteps approached. She came in first and he followed, he appeared to be limping slightly. Mumbling incoherently and did not notice his grandson. She moved across to the sink and filled the kettle and set it on the oven gas to make a pot of tea. The boy wondered if she knew what his grandfather was saying to her. He called a greeting. The old man turned slowly and stared at him. The boy grinned but the old man turned back and resumed the muttering. His grandmother seemed to notice nothing odd about it. As the old man spoke he was scratching his head. There was no bunnet. The bunnet was not on his head.

81

The muttering stopped, the old man stared at the woman then at the boy. The boy looked helplessly at her but she watched the man. The expression on her face gave nothing away. Her usual face. Again the boy called a greeting but the old man turned to her and continued his muttering. The tone of his voice had altered now; it was angry. She looked away from him. When her gaze fell on him the boy tried to smile. He was aware that if he blinked, tears would appear in his eyes. He smiled at her.

Ten shillings I'm telling you, said the voice.

The boy and his grandmother looked quickly at the old man.

Ten shillings, Frances, he said. The anger had gone from his voice.

As if noticing the boy for the first time he looked straight at him. For several seconds he stood watching the boy then he turned sharply back to face his wife: Ach, he grunted.

She was standing holding the apron bunched in her fists. Shaking his head the man attempted a step towards her but fell backwards to the floor. He sat there for a moment then fell sideways. The boy ran across crying it was okay — it was okay.

His grandmother spoke as he bent down over the old man.

He fell down, she said. He fell down.

She knelt by him on the floor and together they tried to raise him to his feet but it was difficult; he was heavy. The boy dragged over a chair and they managed to get him up onto it. He slumped there, his head lolling, his chin touching his chest.

He lost money, said the old woman, he said he lost money. That was what kept him. He went looking the streets for it and lost his bunnet.

It's okay, Grannie, the boy said.

It kept him late, she said.

The boy asked if they should try and get him changed and into bed but she did not reply. He asked again, urgently.

I'll get him, son, she said eventually. You can get away home now.

He looked at her in surprise.

Your mum and dad will be wondering where you've got to, she added.

It was pointless saying anything else. He could tell that by her face. Crossing to the bed in the recess he lifted his coat and slipped it on. He opened the door. When he glanced back his grandmother nodded. She was grasping her husband by the shoulders, propping him up. He could see the old man looking at her. He could see the big bald patch on the head. His grandmother nodded once more. He left then.

James Kelman

Afternoon Visit

It is a gusty April afternoon.
    The wrestling is on television,
Punctuated by adverts. Her walking, even
    This past week, has slowed down

Perceptibly, her leg grown stiffer.
    At one point, getting up
To adjust the set, she overbalances. Before
    Either of us can intervene, a cup

And saucer fall to the floor.
    Neither breaks. What does snap,
Surprisingly, is her composure.
    Taking her grandchild on her lap

She strokes his head over and again,
    Not noticing the tears
Flow. 'Love is the main
    Thing. Yet let Nature take its course.

Children are their own. Time must come,
    It cannot be helped.' And strokes
That helpless head. I remember at home
    Sitting on her lap, surrounded by books

And ornaments bought over the years,
    Most of them to be chipped, at least,
By ourselves as children. 'There's
    No evading it . . .' Some fearful beast

Within me refuses to listen; would smash
    Down the walls, the watercolours
In their frames; the precious trash
    Of a lifetime. I am no longer hers.

She is saying—not knowing it
    But speaking simply, without grievance,
From the heart. How can I be fit
    To raise children, I wonder; tense

With foreboding on their behalf and my own,
    Who am already a father before
Having learned to be a son.
    The child slips lightly to the floor

And plays there. Her eyes mist
    Over. I concentrate on the faded green
Of an apron. What will become of us, at the last?
    Men fight through blizzards, on the tv screen.

Stewart Conn

Incident

'Watch yer caur fur a tanner, mister.' Strange
As hieroglyphs the words froze in his breath.
His eyes rifled the passing faces deftly, trained
To pick each moment's pockets of small change.
Thin body in its trousers of frail cloth,
Elbowless jersey, cracking shoes, attained
An emblematic stance, defying pity.
Like a confidential file his starved face read
'Congenital case of backstreets of a city'
While Glasgow suppurated round his head.

The man looked down, feeling his well made suit
Grow luxuriously heavy. That raw face
Formed in his glance a chance cast of bleak bones
(Life throws them casually before our feet)
Where the future had already taken place.
While the dark street bled infection from its stones.
His thumb traced on a coin his indecision.
Drop a sixpence in a scummy wishing-well?
His wife's voice—sacrificial, cold precision:
'Tell the little brat to go to Hell.'

They wandered in a maze of ideal homes,
Kitchen units, cookers, and hi-fis.
Welfare Wonderland had come to Kelvin Hall.
Racked by the cost of carpeting two rooms,
His wife struggled with their stern economies.
(Necessity makes martyrs of us all.)
But tasting dishes, testing heaters, he
Astigmatically saw one clenched grey face
Superimposed on chair, wood fireplace.
And all it said relentlessly was 'Me'.

That night he dreamed a different exhibition—
Stands where children advertised the sores
Of other people's failure. Bargain schemes
In which injustice was the prime condition.
Mock rooms with plush indifference on their floors.
Comfort that was fuelled on warm dreams
Of everything's vague rightness. And he heard
Coming from places that he could not see
Insistent as canned music, the soft words:
'Nothing can be real that counts out me.'

But routine brings us to serenity.
Next morning he ate well, washed down the car
And paused, shocked to see scraped across his boot
With stone or knife a brief obscenity,
Blemishing his wellbeing like a scar
Of violence that was to come. He took
A tube of matching paint, healed it but could
Feel malice mounting still like a thrombosis
Unseen, implicit with tomorrow's blood.
Aloes on nails do not cure a neurosis.

William McIlvanney

NOTES

'Accident Report': some of Maurice Lindsay's best poetry is concerned with
the sudden moment of hurt or violence which lurks beneath the deceptively
placid surface of normality, as in 'Accident Report'. Other examples are
'Aged Four', 'At the Mouth of the Ardyne' and 'Glasgow Nocturne', all from
This Business of Living (Akros), his best collection to date.

James Copeland's well-known Glasgow dialect poem 'Black Friday' forms a
good comparison and contrast with 'Accident Report'.

'In the Snack-bar' has attained a well-deserved popularity. A fine example of
Edwin Morgan's wide-ranging compassion, it can be compared with his
'Glasgow Green' and 'Death in Duke Street'.

For further exploration of this theme Orwell is recommended, particularly
'A Hanging', 'Shooting an Elephant' and 'Marrakech' (*Collected Essays Volume
1*, Penguin). All of these are fairly accessible in various anthologies.

Bill Naughton's 'Spit Nolan' (*The Goalkeeper's Revenge*, Heinemann
Educational) is a powerful short story which is relevant.

'Afternoon Visit' comes from Stewart Conn's collection *Under the Ice*
(Hutchinson). Other interesting poems in this volume are 'To the Bear Park'
and 'Balancing Act'.

7

A SENSE OF PLACE

The Dear Green Place

He was standing on the bridge looking over the parapet into the dirty water, at the very spot where Boswell had stood and looked at the widest streets in the whole of Europe. Gles Chu! Glasgow! The dear green place! Now a vehicular sclerosis, a congestion of activity! He felt for a cigarette in his pocket and the match which he lit flared bitterly in the cold air. The city about him seemed so real, the buildings, the bridge, the trams, the buses, so separate and hard and discrete and other. He felt again a wave of nostalgia for another kind of existence—waxed fruit, sword sticks, snuff, tobacco, shining brass valves, steam pipes, jet ware, wag-at-the-wa's, horse-hair sofas, golf cleeks, cahootchie balls—all the symbols of confidence, possibility, energy, which had lived before this knotted, tight, seized-up reality which was around him had come to be.

He looked over towards where the obelisk in the park squatted, obscene. With its memories, Omdurman, Ypres, Tel-el-Kebir, screaming pipes, whisky, sweeping moustaches, regimental dinners, photographs in barbers' shops and boys with malacca canes. Brass button sticks and old medals in junk shops. The park looked grey like a plucked fowl with its stark leafless trees. He leaned on the smooth granite parapet of the bridge easing the weight on his legs. Glasgow! Gles Chu! The dear green place!

Just as the Clyde comes into Glasgow it takes its last big loop. On the inside of this last loop is the old common land, the Glasgow Green, with its public bleaching green, its play parks, its People's Museum. To the west of the Green is the old hub of the city where the old merchants once conducted their business and built some of their houses. From this spot, but slightly to the south of the modern commercial hub of the city, the river runs nearly straight on, under the bridges and railway viaducts to the docks and the famous Clyde shipyards at Govan. Mat turned away from the parapet and started to follow the river in this direction. He moved off the bridge to the north bank of the river and walked along past the fish market again. He went past the exodus of vehicles, past the long narrow streets with their shipping offices, sundriesmen, pubs, seamen's institutes, carriers' quarters, chandlers, whisky bonds and coopers' yards. He smelled the spice, rope, tallow, flour, butter, treacle, fish and beer. He could see the varnished tops of the ships' masts, their stays and rings and splices all whipped and white with paint. There were big red funnels and spidery derricks and cranes looming over the tops of warehouses. He was walking along an almost straight mile of river. To the north was the hub of Glasgow, a piled-up heap of buildings, offices, shops, theatres, cinemas. As he looked up the long telescopic streets the magnificent views and perspectives were all blocked by a tangle of wires and roofs and chimneys and gables. On the other side of the river he could see where Hutchesontown and Gorbals lay with their broad streets and their good sandstone houses all sordid with abuse and disrepair. Mat thought of the enthusiastic Victorian citizenry who had built all this—the city fathers, all waistcoated, befobbed and frock-coated—who had accumulated all this great heap of iron and glass and steel and stone, all these great blocks of sandstone and granite. Were they really slaking an aesthetic passion? Trying to understand them sympathetically Mat felt he could understand their counting house satisfaction in this great pile-up orgy of anal-erotic vigour.

A Calvinist, Protestant city. The influx of Roman Catholic Irish and Continental Jews had done nothing to change it, even if they had given to its slum quarters an air of spurious romance. Even they in the end became Calvinist. A city whose talents were all outward and acquisitive. Its huge mad Victorian megalomaniac art gallery full of acquired art, its literature dumb or in exile, its poetry a dull struggle in obscurity, its night life non-existent, its theatres unsupported, its Sundays sabbatarian, its secular life moderate and dull on the one hand and sordid, furtive and predatory on the other. Yet Mat had to admit that all this moved him in a way that art could only be secondary to; the foundries, steelworks, warehouses, railways, factories, ships, the great industrial and inventive exploits seemed to give it all a kind of charm, a feeling of energy and promise. He thought of its need for introspection which was traditionally satisfied by the Saturday night binge, when its hero, Homer, and apotheosis in a cloth bunnet would lull his maudlin soul to rest with the drunken hymn.

> When Ah get a couple of drinks on a Saturday,
> Glasgow belongs to me.

Belongs! Belongs! Mat could understand that, too. A dirty filthy city. But with a kind of ample vitality which has created fame for her slums and her industry and given her moral and spiritual existence a tight ingrown wealth, like a human character, limited, but with a direct brutish strength, almost warm. Glasgow! Gles Chu!

From *The Dear Green Place* by Archie Hind

Glasgow Sonnet i

A mean wind wanders through the backcourt trash.
Hackles on puddles rise, old mattresses
puff briefly and subside. Play-fortresses
of brick and bric-a-brac spill out some ash.
Four storeys have no windows left to smash,
but in the fifth a chipped sill buttresses
mother and daughter the last mistresses
of that black block condemned to stand, not crash.
Around them the cracks deepen, the rats crawl.
The kettle whimpers on a crazy hob.
Roses of mould grow from ceiling to wall.
The man lies late since he has lost his job,
smokes on one elbow, letting his coughs fall
thinly into an air too poor to rob.

Edwin Morgan

Glasgow Rehousing

It was a total change. A new house that was literally new and not merely new to us. My mother, always too inoffensive for her own good, had, all the same, browbeaten some Corporation official into recognizing what she saw as justice and handing over the magic key. The house was the end of a terrace, with a garden back, front and side. The front garden was small and consisted entirely of a steep little hill running from the front path to the pavement, and it was made of reddish clay that ran in coloured streams down the front steps each time it rained. There were no windows on the gable end, and we could play in the garden at the side without being seen from the house, a cherished form of secrecy. Three elders that were planted later, close together, made an impenetrable screen that hid the side strip entirely and left it dark, sunless and secret.

Jimmie, who *had* travelled on the flitting lorry and explored before I arrived, took me out of the front door and round to view the side and back garden, with all the pride of a tenth-generation squire. I was worried by another door that gave into our garden from the back of the building, and incredulous when he insisted that that door was ours too. He even claimed that hot water came out of the tap, but when I tried it, Flora rushed at me and turned it off and warned me that it was *her* hot water. Everybody, except Jackie and Jimmie and me, developed a passion for baths, but Flora most of all, and when we were fighting with her, which was reasonably often, we would wait till she had gone upstairs to the bathroom and then quickly turn on the hot taps downstairs to empty the hot tank before she could run her bath.

We were still in the pioneering days of Glasgow's massive rehousing operation. Sandyhills was a small, tidy district, but it still had unbuilt ground that was corrugated from the recent passage of a farmer's plough. I discovered that the move, in a way, was a return home for the Hanleys. Sandyhills lay between the old villages of Shettleston and Tollcross. My mother had been raised in Shettleston and had worked in Tollcross as a girl, and on learning this I first became preoccupied with the effects of time. I tried to picture the place when plough-horses walked over the ground our own house stood on, and when the stage-coaches clattered through Shettleston on their way to Edinburgh. It wasn't easy, for even the empty farm land around us was being cleared and built up all the time.

The place was so raw and virgin as a community that the back garden was littered with builders' debris—not just old slates and broken chimney pots, but one whole concrete doorstep and such-like chunks of masonry. A kindly neighbour admitted to us that as we were the last to move into the block, the people in the other houses had heaved the rubbish from their gardens into the empty one. Jimmie and I instantly heaved some of the smaller pieces of concrete back into the yard next door, but they returned on the following day, and we finally had to drag them, in the dark, into even newer gardens of other unoccupied houses. This clearance work was our own idea entirely.

My mother was shocked to learn that we had wished the stuff on other innocent people, but she didn't go to the length of telling us to bring it back.

By Gallowgate standards our new house was a vast and palatial affair and we were intensely proud of it.

One of the most obvious things about Glasgow today, a great thing in its way but a worrying thing too, is the way the Corporation housing programme has expanded. It's great because people shouldn't be living in dank old slums, crumbling and congested and insanitary, and the new houses have light and space and baths and the physical decencies of life that folk should have whether they have money or not. But the new housing schemes have spread so far and fast that something has been lost in the flitting, and I think it's the spiritual vitality of the old slum streets—the songs and the games and the social manners and the homely feeling of living in a place that has got used to people living in it, and is adjusted to people.

It's easy to say this from outside Gallowgate or Gorbals, when nobody in his senses would deliberately choose deliberately to live in Gallowgate or Gorbals if he didn't have to, and like all reminiscers, I would never expose my own children to the uncouth accents and rowdy adventures of my own childhood. But something has gone out of life in these great airy suburbs. A string has been broken and left the children rootless and starved of tradition, and tradition means a lot to children. They don't have the handed-down legends of the slum streets, and they don't have the different legends of children in country villages. The people in the enormous new suburbs know this very well in their hearts. There's an unease and an unrest in the biggest of the new districts, and television isn't a complete substitute for the feeling that has gone.

This unease isn't just a matter of not having the old neighbourly feelings. The suburbanites have plenty of neighbours. Sometimes they have too much of their neighbours, as most of the postwar houses in Glasgow are less soundproof than the persistent old stone tenements. Up a close in Gallowgate, in fact, a family could very well keep itself to itself if it didn't want to mix with the neighbours, and a lot of families did and do today. Maybe it's because the far-flung suburbs mean a complete separation of domestic life from work and all the other social activities.

In Sandyhills in the 'thirties, things hadn't developed that way. We arrived with our childhood traditions intact, and the place was so small, and so close to the old villages that merged into it on either side, that there was no break in the continuity of what you could call cultural life. Life was merely more hygienic and less dusty and had more open spaces for playing in.

From *Dancing in the Streets* by Clifford Hanley

On Top of the World

Matt Leishman and his family have just moved from a semi-detached corporation house into a flat in a multi-storey block.

He leaned over the bath, only a half-sized bath at that, and knocked on the wall—hardboard. He moved on his knees over the rubber tiles of the floor and tried another wall—hardboard again. He looked at the holes which the expansion bolts had already made in the narrow panel beside the sink, and cursed the jerry-built monstrosities. The women could gitter on about central heating, nice big kitchens and the like, but it was a hell of a house when a trained carpenter couldn't find a wall solid enough to bed a towel-rail screw. Wearily, he got up and measured the width of the door with his tape. He rapped his knuckles against the door—thin ply on a frame. He knew how long a heavy chrome rail would lie into that. The bathroom was like a fridge. He tried the handle of the metal door which opened on to the fire-escape catwalk along the front of the building. The metal was like ice to the touch; that, and the stupid big window was what let in the cold. No insulation upstairs. He could have designed a better place himself in half an hour. The handle of the door would not yield and he kicked it with his heel. Some fire-escape; if the place went up and them on the eleventh floor, they'd all be roasted to death before he could get the damned hatch open. He kicked it again and the handle bent. With his forearm on the metal and a screwdriver edged behind the handle he jemmied it straight, and, to his surprise, found that the door had opened in the process. Bending low, he stepped through on to the catwalk.

Laurencegrove and Haughburn seemed to be right at his feet, and nothing between him and the Gleniffer Braes, miles away. He liked a bit of a view right enough but this lot was too much for him. In his fancy way Douglas had summed it up that night when they came, as a family, to see the premises for the first time. Douglas looked through the opening at the top of the stairs. 'It's like Jesus tempted of the Devil,' Douglas said. 'You know what I mean?'

The boy had hit the nail fairly on the head, Matt decided. It was indeed like being up on a high mountain with the world and all its temptations spread out before you. On a fine bright day it would be a sight worth seeing. Even now, with the lights, it was grand enough— too grand by far for him, and too high as well. He put his hands on the rail, at the level of his navel, and, holding himself carefully, peeped over the edge. The side of the building dropped smoothly to the asphalt below. He could see the shine from a few lit windows on the wall beneath him, against the night air, but the windows themselves down the plumb wall were like thin pencil lines, or razor-cuts. The people below and the two or three cars in the square in front of the concrete garages were smaller even than toys, more like beetles, or flies, midges. Two islands, where if the kids gave them a chance, flowers might some day grow, were like threepenny bits. He had a good head for heights, trained on scaffolds and cranes as high as this, but even so . . . He peered along the catwalk. The kitchen windows of the houses on the floor below opened on to it. Only their house had a bathroom exit. He wondered if he could put a piece of baffle board across the fire-door to cut out noise and insulate it against the cold. It would need to be easily removed though, just in case there ever was a blaze. How concrete and breeze-blocks and asbestos-treated boards would ignite he could not figure out, though the whole place must be riddled with electric wires and that was never safe.

He came in from the catwalk and pulled the door tight behind him. Once more he thumped the wall over the bath. Six months with water finding its way down the seams and the wall would turn to pulp. He would have to seal it with Marley tiles. From the rule pocket of his overalls he took a folded notebook, and with the blunt stub of a pencil scribbled a reminder on a page already crammed with measurements and memos.

He removed the bulb from the light socket and clumped downstairs in the dark. A maisonnette was more than he had bargained for. When they said a flat he thought they meant a flat all on the one level. Waste of space; bad planning; jerry-built. The fierce anger at what he was sacrificing to come here welled up in him again. There was nothing personal in this mammoth warren. He was like a rabbit in the side of a hill; no, even less individual than a rabbit: a bee in a box hive, a bee in its cell. This is what they were all so anxious to jump out of their homes for, to keep in step with progress. In five years—he'd give it five years—the whole place would be falling round their ears like a slum. Downstairs, he went through to the kitchen and looked out of the window. A square balcony opened from it, but it was flush with the wall of the building and there was nothing nice about it. You couldn't sit out there of a night. He wondered how Bunty would like it when it came to the bit. Straining his eyes he deciphered the pattern of lights, and made out the curve of Paterson Drive above the dark vegetation of the park, packed now with tall bare buildings just like this one In three months they'd be surrounded like a leek in a field full of leeks.

Progress; he'd be as well with a number as a name once he came here. It would suit the modern world, he thought. Give them all a number. It would suit Alice's generation fine. Every day a big computer would put two numbers together and they would mate for the night. A different number every night, and the babies brought up by the government, the way they were in Russia.

From *Night Pillow* by Hugh C. Rae

Poem on a Day Trip

It's nice to go to Edinburgh.
Take the train in the opposite direction.
Passing through a hard land, a pitted
and pockmarked, slag-scarred, scraped land.
Coal. Colossus of pit-bings,
and the stubborn moors where Covenanters died.
Hartwood, Shotts, Fauldhouse, Breich—
Something stirs me here
where the green veneer is thin,
the black-gut and the quarried ash-red
show in the gashes.

But the land changes
Somewhere in the region of West and Mid Calder.
Greener and gentler, rolling Lothians,
Edinburgh. Your names are grander—
Waverley, Newington, Corstorphine,
never Cowcaddens, Hillhead or Partick.
No mean city,
but genteel, grey and clean city.
you diminish me—
make me feel my coat is cheap,
shabby, vulgar-coloured.
You make me aware of your architecture,
conscious of history and the way it has
of imposing itself upon people.
Princes Street.
I rush for Woolworths anonymous aisles.
I feel at home here
You could be anywhere—
even in Glasgow.

Liz Lochhead

Greenock at Night I Find You

As for you loud Greenock long ropeworking
Hide and seeking riveting town of my child
Hood, I know we think of us often mostly
At night. Have you ever desired me back
Into the set-in bed at the top of the land
In One Hope Street? I am myself lying
Half-asleep hearing the riveting yards
And smelling the bone-works with no home
Work done for Cartsburn School in the morning

At night. And here I am descending and
The welding lights in the shipyards flower blue
Under my hopeless eyelids as I lie
Sleeping conditioned to hide from happy.

So what did I do? I walked from Hope Street
Down Lyndoch Street between the night's words
To Cartsburn Street and got to the Cartsburn Vaults
With half an hour to go. See, I am back.

See, I am back. My father turned and I saw
He had the stick he cut in Sheelhill Glen.
Brigit was there and Hugh and double-breasted
Sam and Malcolm Mooney and Alastair Graham.
They all were there in the Cartsburn Vaults shining
To meet me but I was only remembered.

W. S. Graham

A Kilmarnock Childhood

I am not without credentials. I knew the rules for playing 'Mississippi
1 2 3' before I could spell it. I still toss a tolerable milk-top. I've
played 15-or-so-aside football in the muddy lee of Peeweep Hill
(before the bulldozers dismantled it), heard two newcomers allotted
sides by the expedient of being named 'a cock or a hen', and run
through alternate lathers of sweat and shivers of coolness until the ball
disappeared in dusk or a player walked off wearing one of the
goalposts. While someone relayed the latest dirty story like a bulletin
from the adult world, I've crouched in the long grass among my 14-
year-old contemporaries, and laughed when I didn't see the joke. I
have the recipe for home-brewing 'sugarally watter' below the bed. I
know Glasgow on Fair Friday when drunk men have been known to
address the world just after mid-day, with one arm round a com-
panionable lamp-post. I've been on a mystery tour that ended up at
Largs, seen service on the fronts of Troon, Prestwick and Ayr, where I
clumsily chatted up unsuspecting girls, been waterlogged in a tent in
Skye, and been a seasonal sophisticate in Arran where I danced with
my girlfriend into the early hours, suave in shirt, shorts, woolly socks
and sandshoes. I've fished for meenies and beardies with an old bleach
bottle, walked whuppets, sung 'Skibbereen' at Hogmanay, listened to
the chaff at the bookie's corner, had friends called Rab and Jimmock
and Shug. I know what a brooshie is. I think broth is always better the

second day but I don't like my chips back-het. I call a spade a shovel, the mantelpiece 'the brace', fire-grate 'the ribs', an acquaintance 'a friend'. And I don't like policemen.

In other words, I served my adolescence and graduated to what I take for manhood in the working class of the West of Scotland. I should imagine youth is pretty much a common currency in most places. But it is perhaps not too fanciful to suppose that special contour lines of experience invisibly demarcate certain regions from others or that the West of Scotland, where nature and industry contend along the seaboard, is one such region. Certainly, the towns there have always seemed to me to form a loose fraternity, to sport flora of matching colours and breed fauna of like habits.

My town is Kilmarnock. The population is given as around 50,000, which surprises me, since I always felt I knew most of them. I don't know what such guide-books as there may be of the town and district would say, but I'm fairly sure they wouldn't mention very many of the places that have mattered to me: The Twelve Steps, Nailer's Close, The Swinging Bridge, Moses' Well, Mason's Ragstore—names that make up a private mythology of childhood. It is obviously impossible in the rather stilted perspective of adult remembrance to translate that private experience into accessible terms without stylising the truth. So it might be as well to formulate my memory completely and quote from a poem I wrote a long time ago when I was trying to crystallise for myself what my environment had meant to me:

> I had the run of the day in the cobbled town,
> Was cock of the leafy walk and the drayman's yard,
> While the steeples kept my green and casual time
> And the lazy hours drifted like thistledown
> Past the square and the pub and the darkened arch
> Where the coopers hammered manhood into rhyme.
>
> I was fish to the water and fowl to the banking air,
> League-booted lord of a land where in castled mills
> Men wove out the sullen patterns of their mood,
> Was prince of the storied dust and the sun-laid streets
> Where women impassive in massive womanhood
> Were folded like Sphinxes on their windowsills.
>
> I galloped my heart's green length on the harnessed
>   hills.
>
> Ran with the kiting clouds, with the wind was one,
> Foundered in sounding grass where the breakers broke,
> Barrelled my metal finger and murdered the sun,
> Died at a dreaming wish and was born again,
> Slept long and was safe in my woman-wanted self,
> Dreaming a man till my waking, but always woke

Alone in the world with the mourning wind.

And all of the brewing and baking and shoemaking
    town
With the evening shawled on its shoulders and wearing
    cloud
Was calling my truant manhood to come down
Where the pubs burst with laughter, windows were
    lit and loud

And the men had come home from the day with the
    wagging dogs
Bundles of barking chained to their iron heels.

I followed that voice through the streets and the
    omened mills

Past the curtained cat and the woman chopping logs
And before me went the pied and piping town
Playing my shadow on walls and the arable park
That cropped with couples in summer love and prams,
Singing my body up and my boyhood down
And under the private hill of an early dark.

From *Growing Up in the West* by William McIlvanney

Harelaw

Ploughlands roll where limekilns lay
Seeping in craters. Where once dense
Fibres oozed against gatepost and fence
Till staples burst, firm wheatfields sway;
And where quarries reeked, intense

With honeysuckle, a truck dumps load
Upon load of earth, of ash and slag
For the raking. Spliced hawsers drag
Roots out and wrench the rabbit wood
Apart as though some cuckoo fugue

Had rioted. On this mossy slope
That raindrops used to drill and drum
Through dusk, no nightjar flits nor numb
Hawk hangs as listening foxes lope
And prowl; no lilac shadows thumb

The heavy air. This holt was mine
To siege and plunder; here I caged
Rare beasts or swayed royally on the aged
Backs of horses—here hacked my secret sign,
Strode, wallowed, ferreted, rampaged.

But acres crumple and the farm's new image
Spreads over the old. As I face
Its change, a truck tips litter; hens assess
Bright tins, then peck and squawk their rage.
The truck spurts flame and I have no redress.

Stewart Conn

The Bringan

'Trees talk' his Grandpa had once said. And around Conn lay a
countryside brimming with dangers, peopled by all races, mountained
wildly, amok with monsters.

Other people called it 'The Bringan'. Conn knew the name but had
frequently managed to forget it. It was applied to the stretch of
countryside lying north east of the town, between the Dean Estate on
the one hand and the Grassyards Road on the other. Built above the
Barren Red Coal Measures, Graithnock was an industrial town under
siege from farmland, so that Bringan was only one of many areas of
rich greenery, but to Conn it was what 'the country' meant.

Introduced to him by His Grandpa Docherty, it became more than
a place and assumed the importance of a relationship, establishing in
him a growing and shifting complex of responses which partly
measured and partly influenced his development. Seeing it first
through the druidical eyes of his Grandpa, he was frightened,
deliciously stirred. Trees were brooding presences, soughing incan-
tations. Every bush hid an invisible force, frequently malevolent. Just
to walk was to invade all sorts of jealously held terrains and you had to
avoid taboos and observe placative rites.

But it wasn't long before deliberate misdemeanours without retri-
bution undid the old man's enchantments, and Conn was able to
imbue the place with his own more enlightened and manageable
mythology. There was the Crawfurdland Estate, wooded with a
luxuriance unlike any other part of Bringan, in summer dark and
dense with undergrowth. Anyone with any knowledge of these things
could see that it was Africa.

The familiar part of the river where the land shelved down
dramatically towards it for fifty feet or so, balancing trees, was Indian

country. You had to move warily there, for—Indians will be Indians—they had that habit of whooping suddenly over the crest of the hill to sweep down on you among the trees. The trick was to keep your nerve until they were on you, crouch swiftly, and, straightening unexpectedly, catapult them on down the slope where they drowned in a huddle of broken bones.

Just beyond the main bridge on the other of the two rivers, which ran through the Bringan before converging in the Dean, the forest became fir. There, among the pine-cones, trappers moved, swaddled warmly in fur-lined jerseys, their bare feet defying the snow as they fought off the ravening wolves. Perhaps best known of all was the hill he had discovered by himself, coming on it suddenly round a bend in the river. It was uniquely ribbed, a huge semi-circle of grass like an eroded stairway. For whoever dared to climb, the rewards were great. Standing victorious on its summit, you could see the world spread out like a map twenty feet below.

Little by little, though, the forces of practicality reclaim their own. The man absorbed in trapping the passing seasons in his field is a persistent presence. It's all right if you can remain invisible to him so that he becomes unknowingly a part of whatever landscape you put him in. But seeing you some days, he tames the tumult, atomises all reivers with a look. The war-paint fades, the whoops of pursuit wane into sunlight, and you're left standing small beside a hedge, looking at a man ploughing, legginged in mud, who waves and laughs with a jauntiness that is no way to treat a warrior. At least the horse is beautiful.

It was a slow and patient process, by those who worked the land, lived on it, used it, this reclamation for ordinary purposes of country usurped by fantastic intruders. For Conn, some salutary moments, which measured his acceptance of reality rather than provoked it: being chased from the Crawfurdland Estate by the gamey, who, while Conn dodged among the trees, remained an invisible pursuer, enraged Zulu, but, seen from the safety of the road beyond the gate, emerged from the trees middle-aged and jacketed, and disappointingly out of breath. Falling into the river while defending a fort, so that he had to sit naked on the grass while his clothes 'dried' and Angus and some other boys engaged in wild battles. When he arrived home shivering in damp jersey and trousers, he was given a mustard bath by his mother, who kept muttering 'pneumonia'. Meeting poachers, whose preoccupied movements and bulbous jackets hinted at real adventures taking place around him which made his own imaginary ones seem silly.

Gradually, then, the Bringan became itself for him, no longer strange. Over several years, visiting it frequently, first with his Grandpa, then with others or alone, he made of it the opposite pole to his life from High Street. The Bringan was where he could escape from the arbitrary and frequently harsh identity which High Street impressed on him. It was more gentle, flexible, yielding easily to mood, and, in its timeless folds of field and aged conclaves of trees, it held places that could absorb any grief, soothe any hurt.

Two places in particular were special for him, drew his injuries to them like foxes hunted to their earths. One was the lake in Crawfurdland, the better for being forbidden—a big stagnancy of water, mocked frequently into small waves by the wind, haunted fitfully by wild ducks. Sedge made inroads into it, lilies drowned. Trees grew thickly, making colonnades of gloom along its edge.

The other was Moses' Well. He didn't know why it mattered so much to him, but its hold on him was potent as a shrine's. How many times he slid precariously down among the trees that overhung the river to reach the niche hollowed from the rock by the water— polished and slippery like green glass, damp and vapoury, largely screened by ferns and fronds of weed. The water didn't fall but hung, bright and still as an icicle which is melting from within, so that it seemed to shiver inwardly in a tremor of light. It was only at the base of the niche that you were aware of movement, as the water broke itself across a sycamore leaf (who kept renewing it?). The frozen length of water melted onto the leaf, delicately filming its intricately grained texture with the finest veneer until it channelled to the centre-tip, spouting into the air. That was where you drank.

But these places themselves, like the fantasies in which he had once clothed them, became residual. The lake and the well turned into the past, as if they contained sloughed selves. As he grew, the Bringan, which he thought he had used, had really been using him, had taken over a part of him. Always inclined to be withdrawn, he had allowed himself to become so addicted to the silences of Bringan, the shelter of its trees, the languor of its fields, that set against the demands which High Street made on his growing, it caused a conflict in him.

Holding him in a vice between them, Bringan and High Street squeezed him into puberty. In his emergence, what was left behind was what Bringan had meant to him. What stayed with him was High Street. Later, when he thought of his boyhood, it was Bringan he would remember. But, ageing towards work and responsibility within his family, his times in Bringan came more and more to seem like truancy from himself, the person he had to learn to be.

So, as time passed, returning in many dusks from Bringan, he was burying his boyhood, not once but again and again, as if it was a corpse which had to be disposed of gradually, limb by limb. And each time High Street took him to itself more firmly, claimed him as part of itself. Scattered throughout Bringan, buried several autumns deep like the traces of distant picnics, lay hopes of an impossibility such as only a boy's heart can encompass, preposterous ambitions, fragile dreams.

Instinctively, he had come to know that this was who he was. The geography of his future would be discovered among these things that greeted his return: the massive women folded like sphinxes on their window-sills; the pub that burst with laughter as he passed it; the dark archway where coopers hammered—the three men returning from the day, welcomed by a dog, a bundle of barking chained to their iron heels. One day he would be one of them. And he was glad.

From *Docherty* by William McIlvanney

Landscape and History

From reluctantly reciting 'To a Mouse' at school, I discovered Robert Burns' love poetry and began to be interested. I went on Saturday pilgrimages to the little stone cottage where he was born and lurked in the darkest corners waiting for a ghost which stubbornly refused to materialise. Even in winter when the place was empty of tourists I didn't hear so much as a hollow moan. However, I never lost heart, but wandered along ye banks and braes o' bonnie Doon (and there are none bonnier) or into the eerie churchyard where Tam o' Shanter had the temerity to yell out 'Weel done, cutty sark!' (Well done, short shirt!) to the most attractive member of a coven of witches, and just escaped with his life but left his horse's tail behind him. Seances with a tumbler and little bits of paper were a dismal failure, but even so, this total absorption in a landscape, and with a body of literature gave me a sharp awareness of atmosphere—a sense of place which I have vainly tried to recapture since. It is a thing of adolescence and is later glimpsed only briefly; never with that first heartbreaking clarity. We gather emotional skins until our hides are tough as trees.

The Ayrshire landscape had taken a fierce hold on me. My parents and I spent a lot of time in the countryside during those years and eventually lived there. Later summer was the best time with the sloping fields and corn stooks sharply defined by shadows, house martins clustering to set off south and disturbing, doomsday, blood-red sunsets behind the Isle of Arran. Never before or since has a landscape seethed with so many conjured phantoms for me. The place was enchanted. The lonely hills and moorlands were full of Celts in gold and leather—like the princes of Aeron who fought for the Eastern kingdom of Goddodin against the Saxons and returned. They were the lucky ones.

'There were three hundred, three score and three gold torqued warriors' the poem says. 'But after all the flowing mead, from those that went to war, only three by bravery in battle escaped—Aeron's two war hounds and brave Cynon.'

The kingdom of Goddodin, with its capital where Edinburgh now stands, was extensive and rich. But the Saxons were gaining in strength. The warriors went on a customary pre-battle drinking bout and were slaughtered by their stronger foes. The two young men from Ayrshire escaped. I found myself wondering who watched for them, with what delighted incredulity from what hill-top fortress?

I absorbed a hellish brew of Arthurian Mythology and the Golden Bough. It didn't seem to do me any harm. I ransacked the library for old histories and nineteenth-century archaeological reports of the area, written by ubiquitous, bicycle-equipped clergymen, inaccurate and readable. Then we went on hilarious weekend expeditions in search of ancient monuments where people fell in streams and my marvellous happy-go-lucky mother dried them out, sliced bread, fried frozen steaks in the rain and always forgot the sugar. Sawney Bean and his family lurked below Bennane Head, still waiting to cannibalise unwary travellers as they had done so many hundreds of years before. The southern hills were full of gypsies who at any moment might carry you off to a lonely cave. The wild Kennedy family had once inhabited a string of fortresses along the coast. They fought each other savagely, but united against all opposition. In my imagination, I heard the thunder of their hooves over old stone bridges, or the cries of the Abbot of Crossraguel being roasted in Dunure Castle—one of the less subtle forms of blackmail employed by the owner, a Kennedy, who wanted the rich Abbey lands signed over into his keeping.

Much to my appreciation, we moved into a house which possessed a real ghost. We had a flat in the oldest part of what had once been a coaching inn. A tall man in a brown cloak walked quickly past the kitchen window at intervals. I kept quiet about it until I found my mother looking suspiciously behind a rhodedendron bush one day. 'I could have sworn I saw somebody round here,' she said. The dog watched things that nobody else could see, glassy eyed. But he was a nice old ghost and frightened nobody—a bright, sunlit ghost who came only on hot summer afternoons.

Most of my friends were planning to go to Glasgow University or teacher training college and travel home at weekends. I wanted to go farther afield but I was still not ready to leave the shelter that Scotland had become. Edinburgh seemed, to a seventeen-year-old, to possess the required measure of glamour, apart from which it was, quite simply, a beautiful city. I was scared out of my wits at the idea of leaving home but we all knew that I had better make the break. And that made it easier. On our last school speech day I cried, as did so many of my friends, because we realised, in the panic of parting, the depths of our affection for each other, for many of our teachers, and for the school. How safe and secure the classrooms seemed!

Edinburgh lived up to expectations. If my move there did not exactly signify the end of childhood it was certainly the beginning of the end—the end of Scotland as my all in all. Edinburgh was full of intimations of another, wider world which I badly wanted to see. The grass isn't always greener on the other side of the fence but the different varieties are well worth inspection.

What I lacked then and still lack, is the mature regard which belongs to the place or person where or with whom one finally settles down—a certain contentment which I have not yet achieved. Nor, I have to admit, will I ever feel Scottish as I feel English in Yorkshire or Polish in Warsaw. That's something different again—a gut reaction, like family feeling. Now, with half my belongings on opposite sides of Europe, I am still looking for something I may well discover on my own doorstep, because I still find myself defending Scotland with a fierce loyalty when I am away, still remembering places, people, times with the occasional pang of homesickness, still coming back only to leave again. Maybe I'll never really be a Scottish writer: simply a writer with, among other things, a Scottish childhood.

From *A Sheltered Wilderness* by Catherine Lucy Czerkawska

Remote Country

The way goes snaking upward through the heat.
Out of the carving river's narrow space
Shaken with noise of water, black and white,
You climb at last into a scooped-out place
Where nothing moves but wind treading grass.

All cover's past. Below, the waterfalls
Dig out of sight, like memory. You stare up,
Strange in this trap ringed all about by hills,
To find the one way out, confined and steep,
Watched by whatever eyes look from the top.

When you have crossed the open, reached the height,
It is a brown plateau, cratered and bare,
Low, lumpy hills and black, eroded peat
Stretching as far as light can throw its glare,
No living thing in sight in sky or moor.

Mind finds its way to meet with solitude.
Bear this in mind: the image will not age
Of desert, light and always moving cloud.
It is a vision to exhaust all rage.
Calculate nothing. Leave an empty page.

Sydney Tremayne

The Very End of the World

In the spring of the year that his time was out as an apprentice to Cousin Alec, John Joe was excited by news which Duggie Milligan brought him. The story was going about that old Plunkett of Black Craig was giving up. It wasn't a new story, of course. The old man had been saying that he was done and ready for his place in the kirkyard for a long time, and the hills about the Black Water of Dee would know him no more; but the hills had known his shadow for a lifetime, man and boy, and his flock too, and if Black Craig was a lonely, desolate place, it was a place for a man bred to the country, used to loneliness and the heart-catching cry of the even more lonely creatures of the moor and the hill.

'Black Craig is worth nothing,' said Duggie. 'You could get in for no more than old Plunkett's paid this forty or fifty years past. Oh, it's a wild place, and you'd have a sore job keeping your sheep there in winter, but you'd be settled if they'll have you!'

John Joe stared out across the wooded land stretching all the way from Palnure to Creetown, and at the slopes beyond. North from there, in the wilderness beyond the hills, was Black Craig, the last corner of the earth, it seemed; a place beyond which no man ever seemed to have wanted to go, for there was nothing but the thin grass, the stone screes, the boulders and the crag that gave the place its name. Old Plunkett was hardly ever seen, except on rare occasions when he brought sheep to be sold. His family had emigrated, leaving him to a hermit's life when his wife died. Neighbours came to see him once in a while. They said he was failing, and now, hardly able to draw water from the well down at the side of the burn, he talked of selling his flock and going to New Galloway, where he had lived for a short time as a boy.

'He's like an old bird,' said Duggie. 'The feathers is falling out of him. He can neither scratch nor pick. Another lambing will be beyond him.'

John Joe made plans to go to Black Craig and talk to old Plunkett. He asked Duggie to meet him there on Sunday. It was a long ride, away up the Clattering Shaws road beyond Murray's Monument, but John Joe was anxious to visit the old man before someone else came to him, to discuss his going out and a possible recommendation to the agent who had the tenancy at his disposal.

The following Sunday, with a package of scone and cheese in his pocket, John Joe set out on his bicycle for the slopes of Cairnsmore, the meandering Black Water of Dee and the huddle of stone buildings known as Black Craig. It was a long and wearying ride on the rough road that wound its way from the outskirts of Newtown all the way to New Galloway. He met no one and expected to meet no one, but a fox stood on a green hillock above a burn and watched him as he painfully pedalled his old bicycle through the long hollow and over a little humped stone bridge.

From the bridge the road went steadily up to the skyline, a skyline of wild hills and rocks, mares' tails of water, black scars of eroded peat, banks of dead or burnt heather, rockfalls, tracts of heaving moss. All of it with the cold hand of winter still upon it, even though spring had come. Up here, John Joe told himself, he would live in a very private world. He had been born in such a place, but he had lived for three times as long in the rookery of the town with the sounds of the town in his ears, the creaking of doors, the muffled sound of voices in houses, the clatter of feet on cobbled paths, laughter and the almost rhythmic pattern of the barking of dogs and the crowing of cocks. Here, in the hills, the cascading water was a subdued sighing sound, and beyond all, the cry of a bird or the occasional bleating of a sheep, there was a hush, a silence, that made a man aware of his breathing, the pumping of his blood and above all, his insignificance.

For the rest of the way up the long slope he was afraid that he would never be able to realise his dream. There was nothing quite so vast as the great bowl of the wilderness, nothing quite so empty.

Duggie awaited him on the side of the road. They had made no appointment to meet on the road. The older man had simply sat down in a niche between great boulders so that he could watch the road. His dogs kept him company. They were all quite motionless, and John Joe was startled when Duggie hailed him. Only then did the collies rise and come to sniff round him and his battered bicycle, and he knew that Duggie had told them to lie still so that the surprise would be complete.

'You were watching me coming!' he said, smiling.

'All the way from below the old crow's nest yonder,' Duggie said, pointing back down the road.

John Joe lifted the bicycle and carried it over into the shelter of the peat bank.

'Where now?' he asked, for he had never been to Black Craig before. Duggie pointed the way. There was no road and there never had been. Like many places in the wilderness the road was wherever the ground happened to be hard, or where the sheep or cattle walked. All roads began as drover's roads, Duggie said. Where a beast walked, man walked, and this accounted for all the Devil's Elbows that were encountered in different places. The way to Black Craig had its own devil's elbow. He would see the rooftops of the little steading long before he reached it.

In due course John Joe got his first clear view of Black Craig across a long, boggy hollow. The route to the farmstead wound along one side of the hollow and back along the other. A few stunted trees marked the way. Black Craig itself was shaded by a gnarled tree that might have been an apple or a plum. It was a dying tree, Duggie said, and had probably carried very little fruit in its prime. The soil was poor, hardly enough to root a willow or sallow, enough for myrtle bushes and one or two spindly birches. On the strip of well-worn grass, above the farmhouse hugging the slope, a dozen hens were picking food. A trickle of smoke came from the chimney.

Old Plunkett wasn't to be seen, but his dogs were about for they barked warning and at length the old man came and stood in the space between the buildings and put his hand to shade his eyes. He was outlandishly clothed in long drawers, a flannel shirt and a cloth cap. When he had examined them from his look-out place he disappeared within the house. John Joe guessed he had gone to put on some trousers. The guess proved to be correct for presently old Plunkett reappeared, properly clothed. Duggie greeted him with a wave of his hand and the old man waved back.

'We've come,' said Duggie, 'because I heard tell that you are going out.'

'You've heard right,' said old Plunkett. 'The time has come. I can thole it no longer. I'll have to away out o' this or they'll bury me here.'

'A rest you deserve,' said Duggie. 'This is John Joe James. You kenned the father of him at Craigencalie.'

'John Jim,' said old Plunkett, 'and the father of him before that.'

He shook hands with John Joe and looked him in the eye. 'Ah boy,' he said, 'but you're not a herd like your father, eh?'

'I'm supposed to be a time-served shoemaker,' said John Joe, 'but I'm done with the shoemaking.'

He explained how he had gone to work for his mother's cousin, but left Duggie to explain about the sheep.

'Man o' man,' said old Plunkett. 'There's no accounting for the things a body will do. Forty year I've struggled and worked here and I've nothing, and this is what you'd want. Deed boy, I would be doing you no favour if I spoke for you. You would curse the day I did!'

Duggie cleared his throat but John Joe answered before his sponsor could speak:

'You're going out, and I want to come in. I've got the will to work and manage sheep. I want nothing else. I couldn't live the rest of my days in the town. I'll be somewhere like this if I'm not here. All I want is to get you to say a word for me.'

Old Plunkett looked at the slopes above the Black Water of Dee. 'Well, well, then. They'll ask if you can guarantee the rent, I expect. They'll want to know that if you get the lease you can make a show of it, and not fail, but I doubt that there will be anybody that wants to offer as much, or more, or anybody that wants to come here, for this is the very end of the world. You'll keep nothing but sheep here, not a wife nor a family, for this is where God finished his work and he was tired!'

From *The Galloway Shepherd* by Ian Niall

105

Renfrewshire Traveller

Home rain, an aerial night-Clyde,
Spray of recollection
And my only appropriate welcome.

Have I come back?
It was dark
Through Kilmarnock,

Johnny Walker blinked
Imperfectly; history
Is whisky, lacrimae rerum.

Have I come back?
I am Scots, a tartan tin box
Of shortbread in a delicatessen of cheddars

And southern specialities.
I am full of poison.
Each crumb of me is a death.

Someone you never see again
After funerals in the rain.
Men who return wearing black ties,

Men who return having looked for work—
Hear them, their Glasgow accents
In the night of high-rise

Skyward tenements, railway platforms,
The accents of rain and arguments.
What have I come to?

Not this. Not this
Slow afright over rails,
This ache in a buffet of empty beer-cans.

This wiping of windows to see a city
Rise from its brilliant lack,
Its fixtures in transparent butter.

Not this visitor
To a place of relatives,
A place of names.

Douglas Dunn

NOTES

'The Dear Green Place': this extract, from Archie Hind's novel of the same title, supplies the historical perspective so often missing in the cliche 'No Mean City' images of the City which often dominate mass media presentations of Glasgow. Vista of Glasgow have published an interesting series on the City's history, including *Glaswegiana* by W. W. Blair and *Simply Anderston* by J. N. Cooper.

'Glasgow Sonnet i': one of a sequence of ten 'Glasgow Sonnets' included in Morgan's collection *From Glasgow to Saturn* (Carcanet Press). Some of the others, in particular iii and vi, are relevant.

'Glasgow Re-housing': Adam McNaughtan's songs 'The Glasgow that I Used to Know' and 'They're Pullin' Doon the Building Next tae Oors', both included in his recording *The Glasgow that I Used to Know* (Caley Recording), are valuable companion pieces, as is Stephen Mulrine's poem 'Nostalgie' (*Scottish Poetry* 6, Edinburgh University Press).

'On Top of the World': Alan Spence's short story 'Greensleeves' (*Its Colours they are Fine*, Collins) deals with the problems of an old woman living in a tower block, while Adam McNaughtan's well-known song 'Skyscraper Wean' is a humorous treatment of children's difficulties in the same situation.

'Greenock at Night I Find You': the literature of Greenock is amazingly rich and varied with novelists John Galt, George Blake, Alan Sharp; dramatists Bill Bryden and Peter McDougall; and poets John Davidson and W. S. Graham. As James Alison has pointed out, similar clusters of good local material may remain to be discovered.

'A Kilmarnock Childhood': the content and style of William McIlvanney's piece of poetic juvenilia recall Dylan Thomas's 'Fern Hill'. It is also very interesting to find the material of this early poem being reworked in 'The Bringan', an extract from McIlvanney's mature novel *Docherty* (Allen & Unwin).

'Harelaw': Stewart Conn's first volume of poetry, *Stoats in the Sunlight* (Hutchinson), contains several good poems about the Ayrshire landscape of his boyhood. *Corgi Modern Poets in FOCUS 3* includes a selection and an interesting introductory essay.

'The Very End of the World': Ian Niall's books about the Galloway landscape and people, in particular *The Poacher's Handbook*, *A Galloway Childhood* and *The Galloway Shepherd*, all published by Heinemann, are in the great tradition of literature about country life. The poetry and fiction of the Orcadian, George Mackay Brown, form a natural comparison.

PART TWO

8

DAY-DREAMS

Sailmaker

It was a fine poem my father told me, a poem about a yacht.

> Ah had a *yacht*
> *Y'ought* tae see it
> Put it in the *canal*
> Ye *can all* see it

I thought he had written the poem himself, but he had learned it from his own father. He was simply passing it on.

The poem had a special meaning for me because I did have a yacht. As yet it had no mast, no rigging, no sails, but my father had promised to set that right.

My father was a Sailmaker. The fact that he was working as a credit-collector instead made no difference to that. To others he might be no more than The Tick Man, a knock at the door on a Friday night, someone to be avoided when money was short. But that was no part of my reality. He was My Father, and if anyone asked me what he did, I would tell them proudly that he was a Sailmaker, in much the same way I would have answered if he had been a Pirate or an Explorer. The word itself rang, in a way that 'Tick Man' never could. It echoed back across time. For as long as there had been ships there must have been Sailmakers.

My father had inherited a craft, an ancient art. His sail-making tools were kept in a canvas bag that he had made himself. There were marlinspikes, some of hard polished wood, and some, wooden-handled, of shining steel; there was a set of thick heavy needles, and for pushing them through, a leather palm with a hole for the thumb. Often I would play with them, wielding the spikes as dagger, sword and club, pretending the needles were arrowheads and the palm some primitive glove worn only by hunters or warriors. In quieter moods I might even pretend to be a Sailmaker myself.

I never played at being a Tick Man. That was a different kind of job altogether. Sailmaking was a trade, and to have a trade was something special. It was to be an initiate, a master of secrets and skills.

To be a Tick Man was to be up and down stairs all day, covering close after close, trying to collect payments on clothes and furniture bought long ago on credit, trying to sell more to keep the whole process going. The never-never.

There was nothing in my father's battered briefcase—a set of ledgers, some leaflets, a pen—to compare with those sailmaker's tools; except perhaps for his torch, heavy and balanced with a shiny metal barrel. My father needed it to find his way up some of the darker, more dismal closes where the stairhead lights were always smashed. And more than once he'd been grateful just for the weight of it when he'd been attacked for the money he was carrying, the little he'd managed to collect. So far he had been lucky, and the worst he had got out of it was a bloody nose. At one end of the torch was a dent where he'd connected with some thick skull in fighting his way clear.

I sometimes used the torch to help me explore the bedrecess in our room. That was where I had found the sail-making tools. The recess was a clutter of old junk, piled to the ceiling with furniture and clothes, cardboard boxes full of books and toys, the residue and jetsam of years. My mother called it the Glory Hole. I liked nothing better than to wriggle my way in through a tunnel of chairlegs to the very centre of the recess where there was space enough to stand upright. And from there I could climb and rummage and ransack, forever unearthing something new, or something old and long forgotten—an old comic I hadn't read in years, a toy I'd thought was lost. It was the one place that was mine. Once I'd burrowed in there I was safe, I was hidden. I could look out as from deep in the heart of a cave. The Glory Hole.

It was in the Glory Hole too that I found the yacht, wedged under a sideboard. Triumphant, I dragged it out into the light. It was just a hulk, three feet long with an iron keel. The varnished surface was chipped and scraped and scarred. But already I could see it, fresh-painted, with a new set of sails, scudding across the pond at Elder Park. I carried it carefully through to the kitchen, lovingly cleaned it with a wet rag.

'What ye doin wi that auld thing?' asked my mother.

'Ah'm gonnae get ma Daddy tae fix it up.'

'Then we can all sail away in it,' she said, laughing. 'Away tae Never Never Land!'

Never Never Land was where my father was going to take us when he won a lot of money, from the football pools, or from betting on horses and dogs. He had always been trying, as long as I could remember. 'Trying the Pools' was a magical game that in some mysterious way could make us rich. It had once conjured an image of my father fishing in deep pools of water. And although I had later been told that this had no reality, the image, at some level, had remained.

The other betting had less of a magic. Sometimes I would take my father's line to the back-close bookie. And the bookie scared me. His pitch was in a close that was dark and smelly, and there I would have to queue, everybody furtive, looking out for the police. In my young head, bookie was an echo of bogey. He was the back-close bogeyman, sinister and mean. And somehow this bogey could keep our money or give us back more. He had the power. For writing out his lines, my father used a secret name, a nom de plume, because the whole game was illegal. The name he used was Mainsail, carried over from his sailmaking days.

He still had faith that he would one day win a fortune. Then that mainsail would be set, and away we would sail.

There was a song I liked in those days; I used to hear it on the radio:

> Red sails in the sunset
> Way out on the sea...

That was the way I could see my yacht. Red sails.

When I asked my father to fix it up for me, he was tired after work. But he said he would rig it out whenever he had time and they could spare the money for materials. I asked him when that would be and he said 'Wait and see'.

My mother told me the yacht had belonged to my cousin Jacky. His family had emigrated to America years before and all the toys he couldn't take with him had been shared out among his cousins. The yacht had been passed on to me, only to lie forgotten until now.

Because the yacht had been Jacky's, I felt that now it was a link with America, where he had gone. And that pleased me. America was a fabled place, like Never Never Land, a place of cowboys and gangsters, prairies and canyons, skyscraper cities and giant cars. From America, at Christmas, I had been sent a parcel, a fat bundle of comics. They were all in colour, not black-and-white like the ones I could buy here. Superman and Blackhawk, Donald Duck and Mickey Mouse. America was colour.

One Saturday afternoon, my Uncle Billy was visiting and I had the yacht out on the floor. Overturned, with the deck face down, the hulk could be a submarine, or a hill for toy soldiers to climb, or a giant shark, the keel its back fin.

'Where d'ye get the boat?' asked Uncle Billy.

'Used tae be Jacky's,' I said.

'He dragged it out that Glory Hole,' said my mother.

'Ah'm gonnae fix it up,' said my father, 'when ah've got the time.'

'Ah could paint it if ye like,' said Uncle Billy. He worked as a painter's labourer.

He took it away with him that night and brought it back a week or so later. The hull was painted a pure shining white, the deck a light brown, the keel royal blue. I held it, amazed and unbelieving. It was like a whole new boat, unrecognizable, reborn.

After that I must have pestered my father, kept at him to get down to rigging out the yacht. I was aching to see it sail.

But always he was tired from work. Fixing the yacht, he said, was a difficult job. It would take time. Materials were expensive. He didn't have the right tools. But some-day he would do it.

'When'? I would ask.

'Wait and see.'

That went on for weeks. And months. And gradually I stopped asking. The yacht went back to being a hulk. A hill for toy soldiers, a submarine, a shark.

In the end I forgot about making it sail, and it found its way back into the Glory Hole.

The next time I saw the yacht was long years later.

It was a hard time then. My mother had died. My father had no job. A dark time. Across the road from us was a pub on the corner, and next door to that was a betting shop. The street bookie was no longer outlawed and had opened up a place of his own. Between the betting and the pub, my father passed most of his days. Afternoons in the shop, mornings and evenings in the pub. Often enough, though, he had no money for either.

This night I remember, the last of our coal had run out. My father's dole money wasn't due till the next day. It must have been January, the bleakest part of winter, miserable and dank, wind shaking the panes, a damp patch spreading on the ceiling.

And there we sat, freezing, wrapped up in coats and scarves, trying to keep warm. We had nothing much to say to each other in those days. He was a middle-aged man, unable to cope with the death of his wife. I was in the first wretched throes of adolescence. We might have come from different universes. We sat facing each other, separate, at either side of the empty hearth, letting the blare of the radio fill the silence between us.

Then my father had an idea. He thought we could dig out some of the old sticks of furniture packed away in the room, break it up and make a fire.

That meant going in again to the Glory Hole. I hadn't been in there in years. I had grown too big to crawl in and under and through. It was more chaotic than ever, darker, more crammed with junk. The dust had settled thicker. I took down the curtain that hung over the doorway and I eased my way in. The front of the recess was blocked with two old kitchen chairs. Piled on top of them were a few tatty cushions, a cardboard box and a stack of old magazines called *Enquire Within*. The chairs and the magazines would burn so I passed them out to my father. The cushions could be thrown out another time. The cardboard box I brought out, to investigate in the light.

My father had the fire going quickly. He tore up a few of the magazines, scrumpled up the pages in the grate. He smashed up the chairs with a cleaver, placed some splintered bits on top of the paper; then he lit it, and we watched it catch and flare and roar; and we grinned at each other as we warmed ourselves.

'That's more like it,' he said. 'That's the stuff!'

In the cardboard box were more old papers, a tartan biscuit-tin full of buttons and elastic bands, a few toy soldiers and cars, and my father's old torch. The surface of the torch was dull, had lost its shine. The button was stiff and it wouldn't light.

'Batteries'll be dead,' said my father.

'Pity,' I said, 'Could've used it tae see intae the recess.'

I unscrewed the end of the torch and looked in. The inside had rusted and the batteries were stuck, rotted, covered with pale stuff like green mould.

'What makes it go like that?' I asked.

'Don't know,' said my father. 'Just time. Just . . . time.'

The fire blazed and crackled, but the wood burned quick. So back I went into the recess to bring out more.

This time I took a candle, to see further in. I shifted a mattress and the dust stirred up made me choke and cough. I passed out a wooden stool, a bagatelle board and the headboard from a bed. And I brought back out with me a little canvas bag.

Again my father set to breaking the wood and stoking the fire.

In the canvas bag were his sailmaking tools, the marlinspikes, the needles, the palm. He looked at them long and he started reminiscing, going back. He had worked on the *Queen Mary*, made awnings and tarpaulins, made gun-covers for destroyers during the war. He told me of his apprenticeship when he was my age, how hard those days had been. He looked at the tools and it came back to him. Then he put the wooden marlinspikes on the fire. They were made from lignum vitae, the hardest wood. They were solid and they burned slow.

'Thae other tools can go in the midden sometime,' he said. I put them away and went back once more into the recess. Most of the space was taken up by a sideboard. I tried to shift it and managed to dislodge a mirror that shattered to pieces on the floor.

'Seven years' bad luck,' said my father, then 'Still. Cannae get much worse than it's been, eh!'

He took the frame from the broken mirror, shook the last bits of glass from it. 'This'll burn,' he said. Then together we struggled and heaved out the sideboard. It was too old to sell, he said, or to be of any use, so it might as well go in the fire with the rest.

. As he set to with the cleaver once more, chopping and splitting, he started again to remember back. The sideboard was all that was left of the furniture they'd bought when they were married.

'Got it in Galpern's,' he said. 'That's him that was the Lord Provost . . . Solid stuff it is too.'

He fingered the carved handle on a door, the fancy beading round the edge. 'Nobody takes the care any more,' he said. 'Nobody's interested in this old stuff.'

He was talking himself back into being sad.

'Seems a shame tae break it up,' he said. 'Still. It's a shame tae freeze as well, isn't it!' He split the door into strips, broke the strips in half to fit the fire.

'Ah remember when we bought this,' he said, his eyes glazing over as he watched it burn. His voice was growing maudlin again, drifting into sentimentality. I couldn't take it, and went back into the room.

All the wood was gone now from the recess. We had stripped it bare. But there on the floor, behind where the sideboard had been, was the hull of that old yacht. I picked it up and dusted it off, carried it through to the kitchen.

'Remember this?' I asked my father.

'Oh aye,' he said. 'Yer uncle Billy painted it.'

'You were always gonnae fix it up for me.' I said. 'Ah could always imagine it. Like that song. Red sails in the sunset.'

'Ah always meant to,' said my father. 'Just . . .'

'Just never did,' I said.

'Story a ma life,' he said.

Then I wedged the yacht into the grate. The flames licked round it. The paint began to blister and bubble. Then the wood of the hull caught and burned. And the yacht had a sail of flame. And it sailed in the fire, like a Viking longboat, out to sea in a blaze with the body of a dead chief. Off to Valhalla. Up Helly-A!

And the wood burned to embers, and the iron keel clattered on to
the hearth.

Alan Spence

Ships

When a ship passes at night on the Clyde,
The swans in the reeds picking the oil from their feathers
Look up at the lights, the noise of new waves,
Against hill-climbing houses, malefic cranes.

A fine rain attaches itself to the ship like skin.
The lascars play poker, the Scottish mate looks
At the last lights, that one is Ayrshire,
Others on lonely rocks, or clubfooted peninsulas.

They leave restless boys without work in the river towns.
In their houses are fading pictures of fathers ringed
Among ships' complements in wartime, model destroyers,
Souvenirs from uncles deep in distant engine rooms.

Then the boys go out, down streets that look on water.
They say, 'I could have gone with them,'
A thousand times to themselves in the glass cafes,
Over their American soft drinks, into their empty hands.

Douglas Dunn

Walking through Seaweed

Two girls are talking outside a cafe. The sound of a juke-box can be heard.

FIRST GIRL: I like dancing.
SECOND GIRL: So do I.
FIRST GIRL: I like rock-an'-roll and jiving.
SECOND GIRL: I like that too—it's lovely.
FIRST GIRL: Everyone goes jiving.
SECOND GIRL: Yep. (*Pause*) You got a boy friend?
FIRST GIRL: Yep. I got lots of them.
SECOND GIRL: You got lots of boy friends?
FIRST GIRL: Yep.
SECOND GIRL: What d'you do with them?

FIRST GIRL: Not much ... Go jiving.

SECOND GIRL: That all?

FIRST GIRL: Go to the pictures.

SECOND GIRL: That all?

FIRST GIRL: What else?—Go jiving, go to the pictures. Play the juke-box in a cafe. What else?

SECOND GIRL: I got a boy friend.

FIRST GIRL: Have you?

SECOND GIRL: Yep. I got a boy friend. And he's sort of special. I mean—I mean I've just the one special boy friend—and do you know what he and I do?

FIRST GIRL: No.

SECOND GIRL: Well, guess—go on. Remember about—about the seaweed, and ... Remember he's my one special boy friend ... Now you try and guess what he and I do ...

FIRST GIRL: Go to the pictures?

SECOND GIRL: No.

FIRST GIRL: Go jiving?

SECOND GIRL: No.

FIRST GIRL: If you had enough money, you could go jiving—or something—every night.

SECOND GIRL: Oh, he and I got plenty money. He and I are *loaded.*—But we don't go jiving.

FIRST GIRL: No? Can't he jive then?

SECOND GIRL: Yep. But he doesn't want to.—He ain't like an ordinary boy. He's special.

FIRST GIRL: All the boys nowadays go jiving.

SECOND GIRL: You're supposed to be guessing what he and I do ...

FIRST GIRL: No pictures. ... No jiving. ... I suppose you go in a cafe and play the juke-box ...

SECOND GIRL: No. We never play a juke-box.

FIRST GIRL: Sounds like your boy must be a square.

SECOND GIRL: No, he ain't a square.

FIRST GIRL: Well, what d'you do? You'll have to tell me.

SECOND GIRL: Me and my boy friend—I told you he's special—*we go walking through seaweed.*

FIRST GIRL: You don't!

SECOND GIRL: But we do.—We go—in his car—down to where the sea is, and then—we take off our shoes ... and we walk through the seaweed ... it's ever so lovely!

FIRST GIRL: You must be crackers—you and your boy friend.

SECOND GIRL: We are not crackers. He's a very nice boy. *(Pause)* And while we're walking along through the seaweed—he's ever such a nice boy—he takes hold of my hand ...

FIRST GIRL: What does he do?

SECOND GIRL: When we're walking?

FIRST GIRL: No, what does he *do*? What does he work at?

SECOND GIRL: He's—he's in advertising.

FIRST GIRL: What's his name?

SECOND GIRL: His first name's Paul.

FIRST GIRL: You ain't just making all of this up, are you?

SECOND GIRL: How'd I be making it up? I told you his name, didn't I—Paul. His name is Paul and he's ever so handsome.... He has nice dark hair and he's ... kind of smooth ...

FIRST GIRL: It doesn't sound to me like a nice, smooth, handsome boy that's in advertising—a kind of a boy like this Paul—would want to go walking through a lot of seaweed ...

SECOND GIRL: I beg your pardon, but he *does*. Let me tell you—he wouldn't *mind* getting bit by a crab. (*Pause*) The fact is, he's *fond* of crabs.

FIRST GIRL: Is he?

SECOND GIRL: And we never do get bit.

FIRST GIRL: What kind of seaweed is that seaweed?

SECOND GIRL: Well, I'll tell you.... We walk through every kind of seaweed—the liquorice stuff like all them straps there—and also the other poppy kind.... And as we walk, we hold hands.

FIRST GIRL: It sounds square to me.

SECOND GIRL: Well, it isn't.—We could take you along with us one day.... You could come along with me and Paul, and we could all three of us go walking in the seaweed ...

FIRST GIRL: I think your Paul must be bats.

SECOND GIRL: He is *not* bats. He's a very sensible boy. He only sometimes gets fed-up of being in—the office.... He gets tired of—the office—and on Saturdays—he wants a change.... He gets sick-fed-up-to-the-teeth with that old office.... So we go and walk through seaweed ...

FIRST GIRL: Where d'you work yourself?

SECOND GIRL: In a factory.

FIRST GIRL: How come you happened to meet this Paul fellow who's so handsome and works in advertising?

SECOND GIRL: You sound like you don't believe me.

FIRST GIRL: I'm only asking—how come you met him?

SECOND GIRL: We met ... at a dance. (*Pause*) You know—like me and you did. (*Pause*) I suppose you weren't seeing your boy friends that night?

FIRST GIRL: No.

SECOND GIRL: Sometimes ... you feel like being more on your own ... Yep ...

FIRST GIRL: I never met any handsome fellows—out of advertising—at a dance ...

SECOND GIRL: Well, maybe you will ...

FIRST GIRL: I never even *saw* any fellows who looked like that ...

SECOND GIRL: Well, it's just your luck.—And then Paul and I have the same tastes...

FIRST GIRL: Yep. You both like walking through that seaweed...

SECOND GIRL: Yep. That's our favourite thing. (*Pause*) Don't you ever get fed-up with going to the pictures? Don't you ever get sick-fed-up-to-the-teeth with just ordinary boys? And work? And all that...?

FIRST GIRL: I dunno. I don't think about it.

SECOND GIRL: Where d'you work?

FIRST GIRL: In a factory.

SECOND GIRL: Same as me.

FIRST GIRL: Yep. Same as you. But I never met—at a dance—any handsome fellow out of advertising. I *read* of them in magazines. I read of *lots* of them in that magazine my Mum gets....Tall, dark and smooth....And come to think of it, *their* name was Paul.

SECOND GIRL: Paul is a very common name in advertising.

FIRST GIRL: Yep. But I never met one *real* such fellow...

SECOND GIRL: Maybe you will, though...someday.

FIRST GIRL: Maybe. Yep (*Pause*) I only hope if I do he don't have a taste for walking through seaweed.... Seaweed—and eating toffee-apples—

SECOND GIRL: You have to walk through seaweed sometimes—if you want to get down to where the sea is...

FIRST GIRL: Who wants to get to the sea?

SECOND GIRL: I do sometimes. I like it. (*Pause*) It ain't like a factory—the sea. It's big—and it's deep, and—. Well, I dunno. But I like the sea.

FIRST GIRL: You're a queer one, you are.

SECOND GIRL: What's the name of *your* boy friend?

FIRST GIRL: I already told you—I ain't got just *one* boy friend. I got lots of boy friends. I got hundreds.

SECOND GIRL: Who?

FIRST GIRL: I can't remember their names off-hand...

SECOND GIRL: Are they Beats?

FIRST GIRL: No they ain't.

SECOND GIRL: Do you think I'm a Beat—a Beat girl?

FIRST GIRL: Yep. The things you say—you must be a Beat. Though—well, you ain't *dressed* like a Beat. But walking in seaweed—*that's* sort of a Beat thing...

SECOND GIRL: My Paul walks through seaweed. And he ain't a Beat—he's an advertising man.

FIRST GIRL: What do they do in them places?

SECOND GIRL: Advertising places?

FIRST GIRL: Yep. Advertising places. What do they do there?

SECOND GIRL: Well, I dunno...I suppose....Well, they sort of—advertise things...

FIRST GIRL: What does *he* do?

SECOND GIRL: Paul?

FIRST GIRL: Yep. What does Paul do in that advertising place?

SECOND GIRL: He.—Well, he never talks much about it. You don't think of—of work when you're walking in the seaweed, see? You feel *romantic*.

FIRST GIRL: All the same you must know what he *does*.

SECOND GIRL: Well, as a matter of fact I do know. What he does is—is—is go to conferences.

FIRST GIRL: Conferences?

SECOND GIRL: Yep.

FIRST GIRL: I read about them conferences in my Mum's magazine . . .

SECOND GIRL: Uh-huh.

FIRST GIRL: It seems like advertising's *all* conferences. There's this boy—the one called Paul, you know—the one who's sort of smooth, and dark, and handsome—and what he does is, go to conferences.

SECOND GIRL: Uh-huh. Well, that's like Paul. Paul goes to conferences.

FIRST GIRL: Then, after the conferences—when they've knocked off advertising—then this boy Paul—this handsome smoothy—he goes and meets his girl and they go to a rest-ur-ant. They sit and eat lobsters and and maybe he's *too* smooth.

SECOND GIRL: My Paul isn't too smooth.

FIRST GIRL: Maybe. But what about the other one?

SECOND GIRL: I ain't *got* another one.

FIRST GIRL: Oh ain't you? Come off it . . .

SECOND GIRL: But I *told* you—we're special.

FIRST GIRL: What about the one with ginger hair and a snub nose. The engineer.

SECOND GIRL: I don't *know* any engineers.

FIRST GIRL: I bet *he* wouldn't walk through seaweed though. I bet the ginger one with the snub nose spends *his* Saturdays at a football match.

SECOND GIRL: I don't love *him*. I love Paul.

FIRST GIRL: You don't care about the engineer, eh?

SECOND GIRL: No. If you want to know, I can't stand him.—All he *ever* wants to do is—go and jive.

FIRST GIRL: That's what I said. He does the same things like everyone else does.

SECOND GIRL: But Paul—he's different.

FIRST GIRL: Yep. He's different. You're telling me he is! Any boy who spends his Saturdays just walking through seaweed is different. He's a head-case. (*Pause*) Ain't you even *scared* of what might be in it? Ain't you scared of all them crabs and things?

SECOND GIRL: No. I'm more scared of every day.

FIRST GIRL: What?

SECOND GIRL: Every day. The factory, and all that.—Just working and—(*Pause*) You know, when we've walked all through the seaweed—that kind like liquorice and the other poppy kind—when we've walked all the way through the seaweed, hand in hand—

FIRST GIRL: You and him—walking in seaweed.—The pair of you standing, walking—right up over the ankles too—in all that seaweed.—All of them crabs ready to bite you—and you and him just standing there telling things . . .

SECOND GIRL: Well, I always feel like telling things there in the seaweed. (*Pause*) And then—like I was saying to you—when we've walked right through it—all through the seaweed—and us holding hands too—holding our hands and telling our secret things—

FIRST GIRL: What sort of secret things?

SECOND GIRL: Like you tell yourself in bed at night . . .

FIRST GIRL: When I'm in bed at night I go to sleep. If we had the telly I'd sit up later though. Everyone round us has the telly. Only *we* ain't. You feel right out of it.

SECOND GIRL: You can come round some night and see our telly.

FIRST GIRL: That ain't the same as if it was your *own* telly.

SECOND GIRL: No. . . . Well, I was saying—when we've walked all through the seaweed . . .

FIRST GIRL: Yep?

SECOND GIRL: Then me and Paul—he's a real smooth fellow—we come to where the sea is . . .

FIRST GIRL: Yep?

SECOND GIRL: Ain't you listening? We come to the sea.

FIRST GIRL: I'm listening. (*Pause*) I like those records too. . . . All we got at home's an old wireless. . . . My other sister—she's got a radiogram.

SECOND GIRL: We come to the sea and—it's ever so beautiful.

FIRST GIRL: Some of them's beautiful. I like the cheery ones.

SECOND GIRL: I ain't talking about those records on the old juke-box—I'm telling you about Paul and me: we come to the *sea*.

FIRST GIRL: Well, the sea ain't *much*—in my opinion. I don't care *that* much about the sea that I'd risk my life—and spoil my shoes maybe—just walking through a lot of seaweed, all full of crabs and things, to get to it. (*Pause*) You could get bit like that. It just ain't nice.

SECOND GIRL: What ain't nice?

FIRST GIRL: Ain't I telling you?—Seaweed ain't nice. And the sea ain't nice. And having no telly ain't. Eating toffee-apples ain't nice either. I wouldn't put a *toe* in that seaweed . . .

SECOND GIRL: But it's—beautiful—the sea.

FIRST GIRL: Yep. I seen it.

SECOND GIRL: Did you ever dream of it?

FIRST GIRL: I don't have dreams.—Only once I dreamed we'd a telly...

SECOND GIRL: Yep.

FIRST GIRL: A great big telly with a screen as big as the screen in a picture-house. Not one of them wee old-fashioned picture-houses screens.... A big screen, about a hundred yards across...

SECOND GIRL: Yep?

FIRST GIRL: With a plastic-plated cabinet.

SECOND GIRL: I ain't never dreamed of a telly set...

FIRST GIRL: Another time I had a dream of a radiogram—and once I dreamed I was married to a disc-jockey.

SECOND GIRL: Well, there you are. You *do* have dreams.

FIRST GIRL: Yep. Well....Maybe...

SECOND GIRL: I dreamed—I dreamed of the sea once.... It was all—kind of dark—and—it was all big and dark—and—. Well, it was—beautiful!

FIRST GIRL: It was a beautiful radiogram in my dream. It was kind of Hi-Fi Stereoscopic. Posh! You didn't even have to press the button. You just had to *think* and it went and switched itself on.

SECOND GIRL: Yep? You know what the sea was like in my dream?

FIRST GIRL: It was Hi-Fi Stereoscopic—with *five* extra loudspeakers.

SECOND GIRL: It was just kind of like *home*—it was just kind of like what a *real home* is...

FIRST GIRL: What?

SECOND GIRL: I said—the sea in my dream—it was all big and dark and—just like home!

FIRST GIRL: You talk like a funny picture I saw.

SECOND GIRL: I could have stayed there by it—forever!

FIRST GIRL: It made me want to giggle. *Everyone* giggled.

SECOND GIRL: But my Mum came and waked me up.

FIRST GIRL: What?

SECOND GIRL: I had to wake up—out of my dream.

FIRST GIRL: I wonder why I dreamed of a great big radiogram?

SECOND GIRL: I suppose you'd like to *have* a great big radiogram.

FIRST GIRL: Yep.

SECOND GIRL: Maybe you could come with us down to the sea. Or—well, if Paul had to work some Saturday—if he got asked to do overtime—at advertising—we could go there...just the two of us.

FIRST GIRL: And walk through the seaweed—!?

SECOND GIRL: I could hold your hand—like Paul holds my hand—.

FIRST GIRL: You ain't like a magazine fellow that would make me feel all right about the seaweed....

SECOND GIRL: I'd hold it tight.—Ever so tight. (*Pause*) You and I—we could hold hands—we could go walking—like dancers—like on a tight-rope—all down through all that seaweed—and we'd tell each other things—all our secret things.—Yep, you and me—we could walk through the seaweed—all the way—right to the sea! (*Pause*) You got to walk through seaweed or—or you don't get anywhere. And seaweed—it's full of crabs and things. . . . But you got to walk through it—hand in hand—with some other person— because it's lovely too—you got to walk—like a dancer—like two dancers—all through the seaweed—right to the sea . . . !

FIRST GIRL: All my life I kept out of seaweed. I stayed away from seaweed. It ain't well—nice stuff. You can go and walk in all that seaweed—you can go if you want to—but not with me!

SECOND GIRL: I like the look of them toffee-apples . . .

FIRST GIRL: They're just for kids. (*Pause*) Let's go in the cafe now. (*Pause*) I like that one that's on the juke-box. Though it's kind of sad. . . . Come on, let's go . . .

SECOND GIRL: Yep. Let's go in the cafe and play the juke-box.— Maybe some of all of them boy friends of yours will be in the cafe— perhaps.

(*The music from the cafe juke-box grows louder: a sentimental song of dreams.*)

Somewhere . . .

Beyond the sea . . .

(*The two girls saunter off as the music grows still louder—then slowly fades.*)

From *Walking through Seaweed* by Ian Hamilton Finlay

NOTES

'Sailmaker': the transitions in this story are managed with exquisite delicacy and precision.

Other relevant Scottish short stories are 'O'Shaughnessy' by the young Glasgow writer Thomas Healy (*Introduction 6*, Faber) and 'The Flying Machine' by Douglas Dunn (*Scottish Short Stories 1975*, Collins).

James Thurber's classic. *The Secret Life of Walter Mitty*, is a full-blooded treatment of the day-dream theme.

9

GROWTH PAINS

Do This—Don't Do That!

'You've been messing about with those rabbits, haven't you?' his mother said, accusingly, as he went into the kitchen, a brightly-lit room with pale blue wallpaper and shiny linoleum, with a brown rug in front of the black-range fireplace. She was at the kitchen sink, her stout back towards him, her apron strings tied tight into her green woollen cardigan, her brown skirt pulled up to show the backs of her knees, the way he always thought of her, bent over the sink, the back of a wet, red hand pushing away a loose strand of brown hair.

'Only for a wee while,' he said, 'we were late getting away.'

They'd get a bigger house in the scheme but for some reason his mother thought Shuttle Place was decent and Darroch wasn't. They needed a bigger house. As it was you could hardly turn round in the kitchen for furniture, his bed in the alcove, his chest of drawers, the heavy, dark sideboard, the sewing machine, another chest of drawers, the sink, the sink drying-board, the gas cooker, the big armchair where his father used to sit with his feet on the range fender, the small armchair with square wooden arms and slots for magazines and papers (the *Kilcaddie Advertiser*, the *Daily Record*, the Church of Scotland *Life and Work*, the *Women's Pictorial*, Senga's *Girls' Crystal*) the couch, brown rexine with antimacassar squares. He sat on the couch and turned to the *Record* football pages. For all he knew that there wasn't much she could do to him (just let her *try* to belt him!) and *nothing* that his father could do, he was still a bit scared of her. When they were alone, which was as seldom as he could help, his voice became hoarse and reluctant, short, gruff half-sentences dragging themselves out through awkward lips.

'Put on your slippers and don't sit about the house in your socks,' she said. 'It isn't nice.' Moving as slowly as he dared he pulled the worn cloth slippers from under the heavy sewing-machine pedal and pulled them over his thick, damp socks.

'Where's Senga?' he asked.

'She's away to Aunt Bessie's, she had to have her tea because you were messing about out there,' his mother replied, always the threat of irritable anger—or even tears—in her voice. In the kitchen press they had a cardboard shoe box full of old family pictures and in some of them she was young (hair short and bobbed, wearing a leather coat) and smiling. He'd hardly ever known her smile like that. Long ago he'd decided his father was a brute and that was why his mother was always snapping at him, but even now, when the old man was shut up in the bedroom, she was still the same. Not so much with Senga though, just him. He didn't know why they hated him so much. Bobby Evans was back for Celtic, he read. He didn't care, either, they could hang themselves for all he cared, soon as he was over eighteen he was off out of it, away to England or even Canada, maybe go with Donald Telfer, two of them working on big wheat farms, moving about the country, doing what they wanted without being told off, picking up big women—

'Give me over the matches,' she said, always the same, do this, don't do that, never give you a moment's peace in your own house, hated to see you sitting still for two seconds in case you were doing something *you* wanted to do, run about like a wee boy going for the messages. Blackie would have spat in the fire and said get the bastards yourself.

He got up slowly and looked along the mantelpiece, the china dog bought in Oban on *their* honeymoon, a chiming clock always kept half an hour fast because *she* said it gave her extra time in the morning, a brass tea-caddy embossed with a stag, never used for tea but kept on the mantelpiece as an ornament, holding matches and Kirbigrips and elastic bands and a spare hairnet and a thimble and needles and three French coins brought home from the First War by Grandpa Aitchison. He took out the matches and held them towards her, careful not to go close enough for them to touch each other.

'I wish you'd come in for your tea at the proper time,' she said, taking the matches, trying to fix him in the eyes. He looked at his feet and turned away.

'Any proper farmer feeds his beasts before he feeds himself,' he said, his voice falling away, knowing that nothing he said would make any impression on her. One day he would just tell her to shut her gob and get the bloody tea on the table.

'Farmer, farmer,' she hissed, 'it's a disgrace, you and your schooling, we worked hard to get you into the Academy, now look at you, wasting your whole life in that dead-end job.'

He stared at the picture of Bobby Evans, a burly guy, he wished he'd a chest like that.

'No more dead-end than getting your back broke in a stinking engineering shop,' he said. That would shake her up a bit.

'You're selfish through and through,' she said, eyes glaring, hands clenched at the side of her apron. He shrugged. 'Wash your face and hands, your tea's ready.'

From *From Scenes Like These* by Gordon Williams

Our Son—the Dustman

Harry and Edith discuss their son, Tom, who has not taken a regular job after completing his degree-course at university.

HARRY: Where's Tom going tonight?
EDITH: The Cosmo I think.
HARRY: I thought he might have stayed in, on your first night home.
EDITH: Maybe he will. Not that there's any need to.
HARRY: He's getting nowhere fast.
EDITH: Give the boy time, dear.
HARRY: Not time he needs, it's initiative.
EDITH: Isn't he waiting to hear from the television people?
HARRY: He's heard.
EDITH: Did they turn him down?
HARRY: He turned them down.

EDITH: Wasn't it good enough for him?

HARRY: Damn sight too good. He doesn't know which side his bread's buttered. He'll be a dustman for a couple of months, because they're the salt of the earth. But anything more permanent, anything commensurate with his ability, he turns up his nose at it.

EDITH: At least he has his degree up his sleeve.

HARRY: It'd do as much good up his backside. You talk about his degree, as if it were some sort of... talisman. Degrees are ten a penny. It's what you do with them that counts. He's throwing his down the drain. He has nothing to show for himself. He's a waster. A wishbone for a backbone. Think of it, a son of mine... (*He drinks.*)

EDITH: That's what riles you, isn't it?

HARRY: For crying out loud, he doesn't even go in for sport. Never put a toe in the water, that I can remember. Says he abhors the competitive element.

EDITH: Maybe he has something. There's been far too much competition... phoney competitiveness... forced on children Tom's age.

HARRY: He isn't a child now. That's what you keep forgetting.

EDITH: When he was a child. All through school. Prizes for this, prizes for that. Then the Bursary Comp. Instead of each pupil, each student, being of value for himself. It was each one against his neighbour. Thank heaven, young people today seem to resist it. The rat race we've imposed on them. They simply opt out.

HARRY: Look at them! You can smell them a mile away...

EDITH: You're generalising.

HARRY: You're romanticising.

EDITH: In any case, Tom doesn't seem to feel obliged to identify with them... any more than with us. That's one thing I admire him for. He's level-headed, Harry. He's never been one for extremes.

(HARRY *has finished his drink.*)

HARRY: Extremes of idleness.

EDITH: Harry... every father wants to express himself... to fulfil himself, through his son. Nothing wrong with that. But Tom has a personality of his own. You can't hold sway over him, Harry. Not any longer. You must let him... lead his own life...

(HARRY *pours another drink.*)

HARRY: If I thought he would fulfil himself... I want him to succeed. To make something of himself. In the world.

EDITH: To make up for you? To compensate?

HARRY: I wasn't born with a silver spoon in my mouth. But at his age, I'd made a start. I had my foot on the ladder. Even if it was the bottom rung. I know I didn't make the top. And I'm damned glad I didn't. But I'd made a start. It's cut-throat at the top. Accountancy, advertising, anywhere you like. I cut my cloth. I refused to kow-tow, when the secretaryships were being doled out. My face didn't fit. So they squeezed me out.

EDITH: So you want Tom to get up the ladder you never got up.

HARRY: At least I want him to *succeed*. You sound as if you'd prefer him to *fail*.

EDITH: Why would I want that?

HARRY: Because your own career was interrupted. By the state of . . . holy matrimony . . . being inflicted on you.

EDITH: You know perfectly well I was only nursing because of the War.

HARRY: I mean teaching. You never got back to teacher training college.

EDITH: I was never cut out to be a teacher.

HARRY: None the less, you're still trying . . . because of that . . . to take it out on the boy.

EDITH: On Tom!

HARRY: On Tom, on me. I mean, there was a time I was promising . . . and see how I've ended up. Tom isn't even promising!

EDITH: He's full of ideas.

HARRY: They never come to anything. They're like . . . flies buzzing about inside a Toshie lantern.

EDITH: Perhaps we haven't given him enough encouragement.

HARRY: Who's fed and clothed him? Seen him through university? Who's still subsidising him?

EDITH: Enough stimulus, then? I mean . . . were we always there, when he needed us?

HARRY: I was there. The trouble was, I could never get near him. For you. You mollycoddled him, made a mummy's boy of him.

EDITH: You washed your hands of him.

HARRY: You turned him against me.

EDITH: You opted out. From the start.

HARRY: I'm his father, and entitled to his respect. It's high time he recognised that.

EDITH: You cannot command respect. You have to earn it.

HARRY: As his father. And mark my words, I'll have it. If I have to whip it out of him.

EDITH: You'll only make a laughing-stock of yourself.

(*He drinks.*)

HARRY: You think I haven't noticed? The two of you? Sniggering behind my back, every chance you get? That business of the sherry . . . you used that . . . The two of you ganging up . . .

EDITH: You're sidestepping the issue.

HARRY: I'm getting to the heart of it.

EDITH: You're setting up a smokescreen.

HARRY: Always the same. You egg me on, make out you approve of what I do, then turn your back and withdraw your sanction . . . so that you can store it, harbour it, against me. (*He drinks, crosses the room.*) He's careful, I grant you. He goads me. But he always manages to stop, short of the limit. But one of these days he'll over-step the mark. He'll sail too close to the wind. And by God I'll have him, if it's the last thing I do.

EDITH: You say that ... with such relish ...

(*Pause.*)

HARRY: He has no values.

EDITH: That's not true. He may have examined ours, and found them wanting. That doesn't entitle you to dismiss his.

HARRY: You're blaming me, again?

EDITH: If anyone's to blame, we both are. We're equally responsible for him.

HARRY: Responsible?

EDITH: Morally responsible.

From Act I Scene 1 of *The Aquarium* by Stewart Conn

The Dropout

scrimpt nscraipt furryi
urryi grateful
no wan bit

speylt useless yi urr
twistid izza coarkscrew
cawz rowz inan empty hooss

yir fathir nivirid yoor chance
pick n choozyir joab
a steady pey

well jiss take a lookit yirsell
naithur wurk nur wahnt
aw aye

yir clivir
damm clivir
but yi huvny a clue whutyir dayn

Tom Leonard

Freedom

Your father took you out to lunch and let you choose what you wanted from the menu. You asked him what were rissoles and he said something sort of Italian and he didn't fancy them but it was absolutely up to you. They were delicious.

All your childhood they told you this, at school, at home. Freedom. The Protestant Ethic and etcetera. One's own conscience face to face with god. Free will. Why then the guilt when what you have wanted has seemed to be different from what they wanted you to want?

That is how it was with Art. It was Art which caused the rift between you and your schooling. Before that the report cards glowed.

I was fifteen. I had chosen my course for the Highers, English and French, Geography, Latin and Greek. I had only just begun Greek. There were three of us in the class only, two of the cleverest pupils of the year, a pair who would go on and get in the First Hundred of the Bursary Comp. no bother. And me. I did not like to be bottom, even of three. I did not find Greek so congenial as Latin. One day from the bus I saw Jim Lindsay who had left school the year before. He was walking down Newarthill main street, he had a huge piece of hardboard under his arm. He looked free. He was at Art School.

I decided I wanted to go to Art School. I would drop this stupid Greek, do Higher Art.

It wasn't that easy. The Art teacher said yes if you've got permission from your parents and the Rector. My parents were not keen. But if that was what I wanted. The Rector said no, it would be a waste, said Higher Art was given absolutely no credit for University Entrance. I said I wanted to go to Art School, was sure, decided absolutely. He said I ought to do English at University and besides some of the people who had gone on to Art School had been awkward types, caused trouble, worn white socks, been lax about the uniform, thought they were somebody special.

After my third visit to his office he said all right, washed his hands of me, said it was my own look out.

In the Art class we got absolutely no instruction. But perfect peace to do what we wanted. My friend Irene and I spent our spare time in Motherwell Public Library borrowing books on Impressionism, Post Impressionism, German Expressionism. By the time we were filling in our last months at school we had flirted with Surrealism, even Dada. We thought Cubism too cold, too formal, too mathematical, altogether felt more of an emotional empathy with the line which followed Matisse out of Impressionism, rather than the one which sprang from Cézanne. But we hated the mess of American Abstract Expressionism—what had Jackson Pollock been playing at? Scribbles. Dribbles. And yet to think that only a year ago we'd thought gooey pink Renoirs were the greatest thing ever painted, so who knew we might end up Pollock fans yet. Friday nights we listened to the Record Library Recording of *Under Milk Wood* with Richard Burton, we tried in vain to develop a taste for Jazz, we talked about Art School, what we'd wear, we looked at *Honey* magazines and imagined ourselves with asymmetrical haircuts and kinky boots. It was the mid sixties and things were just about to swing. Especially for us. We dreamed of beautiful bearded men who'd rescue us from the boredom and humiliation of staying in on Saturday nights. I gazed into the mirror and made self-portrait after self-portrait of myself in my version of the style of Modigliani, whom I was keen on at the time.

I dyed my hair a startling blonde with some spray on concoction that lightened as it brightened as it set, grew my fringe to nosetip level, peered through it with eyes fashionably ringed with the burnt cork effect of black eye pencil and lashbuilder mascara, asked my mother did she think I looked like Marianne Faithful at all? Irene and I took to black stockings and elastic-sided suede bootees, were engaged in a lot of tiresome arguments with the lady adviser about uniform and maintaining standards. It was grey skirts only and if that was supposed to be charcoal then it was so dark a charcoal as to be practically black. We were going downhill fast. We got into trouble for laughing while a lady from Army Recruiting was giving us a Careers Talk. We couldn't wait to leave.

It dragged itself on and on, that last year. Until finally the last day, the day I'd been longing for when I could tell all those teachers exactly what I thought of them. But of course it was easy in the relief to let half-maudlin nostalgia take over before you'd even left the place, sitting in Motherwell Town Hall at the last Prizegiving Day looking at the rows of teachers in Academic gowns and the rows of parents in flowery hats; singing 'Who would true valour see'; sniggering for the last time up the sleeves of our Banner blue-blouses at the bad grammar of the local councillor convenor. (Seventeen and snobbish, we could swallow a platitude any time and not bat an eyelid—but one thing our education had done was provide us, we thought, with a litmus for the glaringly ungrammatical, and without any sympathy for the feelings of those we regarded as less fortunate than ourselves either.)

So I shook hands with my teachers on the way out, thanked them even if I mumbled it and contented myself with throwing away my school tie under the cars at Motherwell Cross.

Freedom. And if I'd any complaints about the next bit, the Art School, then I'd only myself to blame. It was my own choice.

From *A Protestant Girlhood* by Liz Lochhead

Changes

It was a lonely time, out of touch with old friends, never seeing any new friends outside of school, since they lived too far away. There was a stage when I grew nervous and morose, often cried for no reason. I retreated more and more into the comfort and refuge of a fantasy-world, of books, of pop music from the radio.

Reason and doubt too were developing. I had lost the simple faith of my earlier years. Sweet Jesus, and even Mother Mary, meant little to me. God was the stern father of the Old Testament, the grim righteousness of the kirk, something to be feared, and rejected.

New pictures went up on my wall; girl singers and actresses, Susan Maughan and Hayley Mills; rock-and-roll bands, the Shadows, the Tornadoes.

Often life was unbearably serious! I remember during the Cuban missile crisis I was sure the war was on us at last. I stayed away from school, wallowing a little in despair. I went walking in the park, quietly preparing myself for the end. But it didn't end. Things went on as before. I was almost disappointed. There was another stage when I became obsessed, still in a very romantic way, with Russia and China and the idea of revolution. I became aware of the inadequacies of our own social system. (From Govan they were not hard to see.) And up on my wall went Lenin and Marx.

Through all these changes, I had one close friend. We both did well at our schoolwork, picked up prizes every year. But we felt stifled by the outer constraints that the school imposed. The living image of all that we hated and feared was the headmaster. Black-cloaked, he would swoop round the school, stilling an unruly queue by his very presence, pulling people up for being rowdy, or untidy, or showing some slight discrepancy in their uniform—brown shoes instead of black, no cap, the wrong colour of pullover. He would frequently lecture classes, or sometimes the whole school, on some aspect of discipline. To the pupils he was known simply as 'The Boss'.

I can see now that the man had a certain dignity, stood by standards he had to uphold. He once moved me deeply, on the morning after President Kennedy's assassination, when he made a speech to the whole school, saying what he felt about it. 'Take care in your own lives,' he said, 'lest you murder not men but principles.'

But from where we stood then, 'The Boss' had to be fought.

As early as first year, my friend and I decided we would one day be beatniks. Another time we called ourselves pagans, and at yet another stage, we wanted to become Druids, which we decided was our true religion. In all this was a strange prefiguring of changes we would go through in later years, in the late sixties, when we would become drop-outs, call ourselves 'hippies', search for meaning in any and every religious tradition, and in none. But all that was still to come.

Our schooldays spanned the years when rock music was becoming a force, an influence on a whole generation. The Beatles and the Rolling Stones went up on my wall. So did the young Bob Dylan. We wanted, now simultaneously, now alternately, to be mods and rockers. We were learning about our world, not from school, but from television and radio, records and films.

At school we had a running battle with the headmaster. We cultivated scruffiness, wore coloured shirts and waistcoats, grew our hair long. A strange flowering in grey Glasgow. The headmaster gave us lines, belted us, threatened us with expulsion. We played a strange kind of hide-and-seek, keeping out of his way. The Who were singing about 'My Generation'.

> People try to p-put us down
> J-just because we g-get around
> Things they do look awful cold
> Hope I die before I get old!

And yet in all our bravado, there was a certain paradoxical innocence, for we were still doing our schoolwork, passing our exams, collecting prizes; we were still, at one level, being good little boys, still following a well-marked route towards jobs, success, respectability.

At the end of fifth year we took our Highers, the next rung. My friend decided to leave then and get a job. I stayed on for a sixth year in a state of total confusion about my future. Swayed by some sense of 'practicality', I had taken science instead of art, but I didn't want to go on studying it. What I really wanted now was to be a writer, and I knew no course of study could lead me to that. I had started writing poetry, after reading Dylan Thomas. My first poems were about Govan, the environment I knew and my childhood there.

During the free space I had in sixth year, I read more poetry. I discovered Allen Ginsberg and the other American Beat poets. Freedom was beckoning. I still kept contact with my friend. He had a regular girlfriend now and was talking of getting married. I had lost my tortured shyness of girls, but retained a certain awe of them that had me writing abysmally bad love-poems. Then, led on by the influence of the Beat poets, I began to read a little about Eastern religions. And I felt for what I read a joyful recognition.

Down came all the pictures from my wall, and instead I drew with a felt-tip pen, directly on to the wall, a life-size seated figure of the Buddha.

And this was an early sign of the direction I was to move in, towards an inner search. It was 1966. Within a year or two my friend and I had both dropped out, he from his job and I from university. We set off on a journey to London, moving out from the narrow confines of childhood and adolescence.

We would have to break and throw aside all those values we had received, if only to rediscover them for ourselves.

Much was still to be broken down in us. The journey we had started on was to lead us in separate ways, forever moving towards our own fulfilment, towards knowing who we are. I was to open myself once more to that gentle presence I had known as a child. In moving towards a new wholeness, I was to see the fragmentation of those years as just stages in a process, an endless process of becoming.

From *Boom Baby* by Alan Spence

Funny Ideas

What was it about guys like Blackie? Kilcaddie was full of them, tetchy bastards with hair-trigger tempers, guys who'd put a broken bottle in your face just for looking at them, guys who went to dances hoping for fights, guys who went on to a football pitch ready to break somebody's leg. He'd been a bit of a fighting cock himself, when he was younger. Once, when Shuttle Place had a lot more houses than it did now, they'd been playing football in the street with a composite-rubber imitation cricket ball and some guys from the scheme had run away with it. Guys? None of them could have been much more than five or six, including himself. The Shuttle Street boys had chased the Darroch scheme boys the length of Dalmount Drive before the scheme boys had stopped running. He could still feel the temper he was in at that moment when he grabbed one of them and dragged him to the pavement and sat on his chest and grabbed his hair and banged his head on the asphalt, banging and shouting, trying to kill him. Six years old! A man had dragged him off the other boy, a man in a boiler suit with dirty hands. He said he was going to get the police. They'd all run away and hidden in the coal yard, going home, eventually, in dread of a belting, only to find that the man hadn't called the bobbies and nobody knew anything about it.

So why had *he* stopped being like that? Was it because he'd gone to the Academy where, as his mother said, he mixed with a decent class of boy? Softies, to be exact. No, he'd had fights at the Academy. Was it the summer he'd been evacuated to Portpatrick, just after the Clydebank blitz when everybody thought the Germans were going to bomb the whole Glasgow area to smithereens? He'd gone to a village school there for a term. The country boys were bigger, they wore tackety boots, they had red faces ... no, he couldn't remember having any fights down there. Was it because he was a coward? How did you know if you were a coward—it was natural to feel a bit scared before you went into a fight, that was half of the reason you tried to kill the other guy, in case he turned out to be stronger than you were.

Why, then? One part of him would have jumped like a shot at the chance of parting McCann's hair with a fifty-six pound weight, maybe he would have to some time, but the part of him that *considered* things found the idea disgusting. He didn't mind roughing up guys in a game of football, that was natural, the harder a player you were the more respect you got. But not fighting. Maybe it was from the same daftness that gave him his funny ideas? At school he could not remember any occasion when he'd been in agreement with the rest of the class. When everybody else wanted to be a Cavalier he'd found himself liking the idea of Cromwell and the Roundheads, because they seemed more like ordinary people. When they'd reached the '45 Rebellion he was on the side of the Lowlanders who'd more or less ignored Prince Charlie's army. Funny about that, he didn't care all that much for the Jacobites when he read about them operating in Scotland, but as soon as they were over the border into England he found himself wishing they'd gone on south from Derby and taken London. It was the same with football. He'd never really *liked* Rangers, although he was a Protestant. Celtic had always seemed more friendly, somehow. Look at Charlie Tully. Rangers went in for strength, like granite. Charlie Tully had bowly legs and was bald and didn't look strong enough to beat carpets yet he had more personality in his little finger than Rangers had in their whole team. Charlie Tully would jink towards the Rangers defence—you'd need guts to take on big George Young and Willie Woodburn and Sammy Cox and Jock Tiger Shaw—and when they came at him, ready to hammer him into the ground, he'd bamboozle them, pointing the way he pretended to pass the ball, sending them chasing in the wrong direction, or running on without the ball but still pretending to dribble so cleverly they'd follow him, trying to make a tackle.

Yet despite all that, as soon as Scotland played England he thought of Waddell and Young and Woodburn as heroes—because they were Scottish then, not Rangers. Instead of being giants from Ibrox Park they became part of your own country taking on the might of England. That was the greatest thing he could imagine in the whole world, being picked against England—he'd *die* for Scotland.

It was just a pity that the Scottish selectors were blinded by Glasgow Rangers. Great players with small clubs didn't stand a chance of being picked for Scotland if there was some six-foot Tarzan at Ibrox Park. Rangers didn't even play like real Scots yet they dominated the whole game because they had the big money. Hibs played like Scots, tricky, clever, artistic—yet Gordon Smith, the great Gay Gordon who could do *anything* with a ball, hardly ever got capped for Scotland. Willie McNaught was the classiest left-back in the game, but because he played for Raith Rovers he never got a look in. Jimmy Mason of Third Lanark, small and round-shouldered and insignificant till he got on the ball, had helped Scotland beat England three-one at Wembley—but how many caps did he get after that?

So, he was chronically on the side of the small guy against the big guy. So what had that to do with not liking, or understanding, nature's hard cases? Was it just another of his silly-boy imaginings that he sometimes wondered if he belonged to a completely different race? Maybe aye, maybe hooch aye, as Grandpa Logan used to say. There was a man from another race, all right. According to his father, Grandpa Logan was such a nutcase he'd registered as a conchie in the First World War—knowing full bloody well they didn't take men whose right hands were carved out of wood and hidden under black leather gloves. Maybe he was a nutcase throwback to Grandpa Logan? That wasn't a very cheery prospect, all he wanted was to be like everybody else.

From *From Scenes Like These* by Gordon Williams

The Choosing

We were first equal Mary and I
with the same coloured ribbons in mouse-coloured hair
and with equal shyness,
we curtseyed to the lady councillor
for copies of Collins' Children's Classics.
First equal, equally proud.

Best friends too Mary and I
a common bond in being cleverest (equal)
in our small school's small class.
I remember
the competition for top desk
or to read aloud the lesson
at school service.
And my terrible fear
of her superiority at sums.

I remember the housing scheme
where we both stayed.
The same houses, different homes,
where the choices were made.

I don't know exactly why they moved,
but anyway they went.
Something about a three-apartment
and a cheaper rent.
But from the top deck of the high-school bus
I'd glimpse among the others on the corner
Mary's father, mufflered, contrasting strangely
with the elegant greyhounds by his side,
He didn't believe in high school education,
especially for girls,
or in forking out for uniforms.

Ten years later on a Saturday—
I am coming from the library—
sitting near me on the bus,
Mary
with a husband who is tall,
curly haired, has eyes
for no one else but Mary.
Her arms are round the full-shaped vase
that is her body.
Oh, you can see where the attraction lies
in Mary's life—
not that I envy her, really.

And I am coming from the library
with my arms full of books.
I think of those prizes that were ours for the taking
and wonder when the choices got made
we don't remember making.

Liz Lochhead

Possibilities

Any young man is a bundle of possibilities, and the world which is
before him is like a city seen at night with its lights shining and its gay
noise; this world is a beckoning, tempting thing. You can become
anything—Mat could remember the great marathon runner whom he
had seen as a child at a sports meeting, and he could remember the
cheers and the glory, the great wave of sound which followed the
athlete after he had plodded in agony into the running track; he could
remember the tiny figure of the famous centre forward running out
from beneath the stand at Ibrox Park, out into the middle of the
stadium and how as he stood enrapt on tip-toe his throat choked as the
voices of the fans rose into a magnificent roar.

And there had been moments like this which he had shared himself,
watching the oval ball's queer stuttering movement like a bat against
the sun, taking it from an awkward bounce and twisting and dodging
and finally being slammed down by a fourteen-stone scrum half, the
ball in his outstretched hands just six inches beyond the line and bang
between the sticks. And afterwards coughing and gasping, his wind
gone and the tears streaming from his eyes as the team pummelled and
thumped him with joy and the team supporters shouting and his
Commanding Officer running on to the field to shake him by the
hand.

He could remember the excitement of his last exams at school when he had sat reading the test papers and was aware that what he knew was more than what was really required and he had sat writing, thinking only of perfection, striving to probe, not just a passable result, but a hundred per cent mastery of his subject.

Footballer, sprinter, scientist, artist, scholar. All the possibilities of mastery and skill. All these possibilities which glitter before you like a set of lights. Not just a set of bewildering choices, but a rich flowering and opening out—girls, riches, glory, ease, skill—all the rich glowing life of adult freedom and responsibility.

Yet shades of the prison house! He had read only recently that a sprinter is past his best at the age of twenty-one, and he had thought with an irony that reflected a hidden discomfort that that was one possibility to be scored off the list. And with this formal acknowledgement which he made that it was now too late for something went another more subtle change in the consciousness itself. That dew-dropped leaf seen fresh and new with only its greenness and wet is now seen through a haze of memory and association. The physical world comes to us again and again until we become tired of it and for moments become just a little bored and satiated. The adult, of course, responds to this change by going further afield. His desires become more complex, richer; and it is here that he is often drawn up short, feels the violent tug of the curb, when all this theoretical latency becomes circumscribed by the bald, brutal facts of his own individual existence.

From *The Dear Green Place* by Archie Hind

NOTES

Some novels which examine the male adolescent experience in the west of Scotland are William McIlvanney's *Docherty* (Allen & Unwin), Clifford Hanley's *The Taste of Too Much* (Hutchinson) and Gordon Williams' *From Scenes Like These* (Secker). Perhaps significantly, there is no comparable examination of female adolescence in a major novel.

From Scenes Like These is one of the key post-war west of Scotland novels, a brutally frank exposure of the pressures attendant on a boy's struggle towards manhood. The book's pessimism contrasts notably with Clifford Hanley's treatment of the same theme.

Docherty, which is set in the second decade of this century, traces the growth of Conn Docherty and, just as importantly, is a moving and convincing portrait of Conn's father, Tam Docherty.

Keith Waterhouse's *Billy Liar* (Penguin) and J. D. Salinger's *The Catcher in the Rye* (Hamish Hamilton) are good companion texts for *The Taste of Too Much*.

Iain Crichton Smith's *The Last Summer* (Gollancz) is a sensitive and honest evocation of a highland adolescence.

'Our Son—the Dustman': Keith Waterhouse's play *Billy Liar* (based on his own novel) has some features in common with this extract and with Tom Leonard's 'The Dropout'.

'Freedom': the essays in *Jock Tamson's Bairns* (see notes on 'To Be a Child') contain a good deal of interesting and relevant material.

'The Choosing': Liz Lochhead's collection *Memo for Spring* (Reprographia) contains other suitable poems, in particular 'Revelation'.

10

WORK

The First Trip is the Hardest

Paddy is determined to go to sea

That long empty horizon between the south end of Arran and the
Heads of Ayr broken only by Paddy's Milestone somewhere in the
middle. Twenty-five to eight. Keep your eye on it a smudge then a
train of smoke appearing. The shape of the ship gradually forming.
Here she comes. The M.V. *Lairds Isle*. They say she is the fastest cross-
channel ship in Britain. Bow like a knife. Two funnels. Oil burner.

Standing on the Cannon Hill watching for her. Be down on Montgomerie Pier when she docks at eight o'clock. See if there are any bags to carry. Then nip on board when you can get up the gangway and ask the Second Steward if there are any jobs going. You never miss her every night when she comes in. The answer always no, they've got a full crew. But you have to keep trying. That's the only way you can get to sea. Keep trying. Go on board all the ships in the harbour and see the Chief Steward. Your first trip is the hardest to get. *Have you been to sea before?* Nobody wants a first-tripper.

You watched the *Lairds Isle* lying up in the old dock all winter. Nobody on board but a watchman. Paint all faded. Abandoned looking. You saw it beginning to come alive in the late spring getting ready for the season. Fresh paint appearing everywhere. The funnels red and black with a thin blue stripe. New manilla ropes. Then the big day when the Catering Superintendent comes down from Glasgow to sign on his crowd for the season. You go along to try your luck. All the regulars there. Gudge McGurk sails on it every year. He'll sign on a tanker in the winter. One that will pay off before the *Lairds Isle* starts her run. Billy Biggar runs the tea bar on the saloon deck. The same Billy Biggar that gave you a black eye down the Bath Rocks. But that was a long time ago when you were just daft wee craythurs. He makes enough in the season to keep him all winter. Lining up for the dole money in his flash Fifty Robert Taylor suits. The Fifty Bob Tailor. All winter between the den and the bookie like one of Lord Inverclyde's sons.

But no luck. All the regulars signed on again and some new ones paid off the Anchor Line. Harry McKechnie comes off a White Star liner on the New York run and signs on as a cabin steward. But nothing for you. We're not signing any first-trippers. Your luck is dead out. You would even have taken the job as chocolate-boy but that goes to Joe Townsley.

The first trip is the hardest trip to get. Frank McCourt got his first trip as a cabin boy on a Baron boat. Frank McCourt. He dived off the big crane in the Old Dock when he was twelve. One of the best swimmers in the town. Great fella as well. Would never see you skint. If you were standing at the corner when he paid off a ship you would be sure of a good drink. From being a cabin boy he got on deck. Now he is going in for his A.B.'s ticket. Round half the world while still in his teens.

But keep trying. Every night when she docks, ask if they need anybody. Somebody might get sick. Somebody might fall overboard.

Once you get a trip on a coasting vessel and get your paper discharge you will have a chance of going deep-sea. Think of your first deep-sea trip. Where will it be. Anywhere. Some of the tankers sailing from here go across the Western. Tampico. Curacao. Galveston, Texas. Some go the other way to the Persian Gulf. Tramp ships go anywhere. Japan. New York. Shanghai. Up the Saint Lawrence. Port Said. Down to Rio. The *Nascopie* will take you to Hudson Bay and the Frozen North. The Sea Wolf. Jack London. The Call of the Wild.

You sent letters. You wrote to the Anchor Line. The White Star Line. Cunard. Shaw, Savill and Albion. The Isle of Man Steam Packet Company. The Burns and Laird Line. MacBraynes Steamers. The Firth of Clyde Steam Packet Company Limited. Hogarths. The Blue Funnel Line. You even wrote to Kelly's Coasters.

None of them sent a telegram asking you to report immediately to the Tail of the Bank with your gear and join their new ship. In spite of what it said in the boys' magazines or *Everybody's Weekly*. *You can go to sea on an ocean liner*. Send for free details enclosing a postal order for two and six.

After your first deep-sea trip you got your seaman's book when you paid off. That made you a real seaman. Then every trip you made after that was entered in the book with the name of the ship and signed by the captain. Yes, when you got a ship. When would that be?

You haunted the harbour. When a new ship appeared you wheedled yourself on board. You asked the mate if he needed a Deck Boy. You hung around the galley helping the cook so that if he liked your face you might get the Galley Boy's job when the ship signed on again. But you usually had about four rivals hanging around along with you, some of them trying to work their way up from Clyde puffers. And your last ship was McLauchlin's motor boat. And your last trip, to the Horse Island.

The *Lairds Isle* taking shape now as she bore down all out on the port for the last lap. Time to get down to the pier. The rocky path past the Drill Hall. Cut across the top of Hill Street through Kernahan's close into Glasgow Street. Then into Montgomerie Street, slide through a gap in the palings and you are in the big dock. Duke under rows and rows of wagons, watching that you don't lose a leg through a sudden shunt and work your way round.

Standing on the windy end of Montgomerie Pier waiting and watching with the railway porters and the harbourmen who will sling a rope on board and haul in the big manilla to tie her up. It is always a good time, a big moment. Her black smoke above the old dock sea wall then herself edging in between the tower at the end and the breakwater. She has a heavy list to starboard because, as usual, all the passengers have lined up at that side of the dock to be early down the gangway. She ties up as nice as ninepence.

I even give up the chance of carrying a few bags to be up that gangway as soon as I can wriggle my way through the crowds pouring down and along to the Second Steward's cabin to stand outside and wait for him to show up. As most of the crew know me I get on board easy.

A long time after the decks have emptied and the crowds have dwindled away and the trains have puffed out packed to the doors, along comes the Second Steward, very busy looking. I wait my chance to duke into his cabin.

'D'you need anybody, sir?'

He looks at me very sadly. I can see he is sorry for me and I know what he is going to say.

'We've got a full crew, son, and there's a waiting list forbye.'

'D'ye not need anybody in the galley. Or a tea-boy?'

'No . . .'

'Nobody sick?'

'A lot of them are sick of the sea and they can't wait till the end of the season. But they need the job.'

'Eh . . . So you don't need anybody, then?'

'No. I'm sorry, son. But keep trying. You never know.'

'Aye, aye, sir.'

I don't know what made me say that. It's no, no, five times a week with one night off and a rest on Sundays. And even then, down in the evening if there is a cruise to Portrush in case somebody has been marooned on an iceberg or something. Miss a night and you could bet your tackety boots that night there would be a mutiny.

*　　*　　*

After I had finished my banquet and dreamed at the green waters of the old dock for a while, I took a stroll in the direction of the tramp due for sailing, making my way under the big coal hoist that takes the wagons up, rails and all on a lift, cants them over and empties the coal into the ships' bunkers.

All the bustle of departure was around the tramp—S.S. *Palmira*. Stores on the quay waiting to be hoisted on board, sailors hosing down the docks, the engineers busy getting steam up.

I approached right under the bows to watch. A voice shouted.

'Hi, Connor! Hi, Pat!'

I looked up. It was George Hall, who was now a rope-runner for the harbour, leaning over the rail and hailing me.

'Who, me?'

'Aye. You want to go to sea, do you not? Come up here on deck.'

'What ye getting at?'

'Don't be daft. Get up here on board, quick.'

Without stopping to think or question any more, I made my way up the gangway and on to the ship. George was standing outside the saloon door with the Chief Steward and the Union man. The Chief Steward looked me up and down as if he was buying me on a stall and calculating how many helpings of curried boy I would make for supper. The Union man, a Highlander, began to speak.

'Now, here's a good lhad who wants to go to sea. He's a ghood clean lhad and a ghood worker. He was on the Arran bhoat for a while in the summer and he's no stranger to the sea. I know his fhamily well. All his fhamily went to sea, so they did, every one of them. And his ghrandfather was at the Battle of Jhutland and lost a leg in His Majesty's Rhoyal Nhavy.'

All this was news to me.

'You couldn't get a bhetter or more honest lhad. And, if he's wee, well, he's wiry so he is and he'll whork well for you. A right, whilling lhad . . .'

The Chief Steward made a sign and pulled him by the arm into the saloon alleyway where they talked together in whispers.

I had been trying to look all the things the Union man said I was— good, clean, honest, wiry, willing—and now said to George out of the corner of my mouth, 'What's going on?'

'The cabin boy didn't turn up from the Shipping Federation in Glasgow and they haven't got time to send up for another one so there's a chance of signing a local fella.'

The Chief Steward and the Union man came back out of the alleyway. The Chief looked at me and said, 'Do you want to go to sea, son?'

'I want nothing more.'

'Can you be on board with your gear at seven o'clock, ready to sail at eight?'

'Aye, aye, sir!'

They laughed at each other then the Chief said, 'Come on into the saloon, son, and sign articles.'

The Union man said, 'I've ghot you a berth as cabin bhoy and you'll sign the articles and be a ghood lhad. You'll need a white jacket, or two would be even better. And you'll ghet an advance note. Ask for four phounds and don't forget the hUnion, I'll have your bhook ready and pay up your dues in advance like a ghood lhad. I always try to lhook after my lhads.'

I thanked George and he laughed and said now I'd done it and went away to get on with his work. I went into the saloon a bit shaky and scared inside myself and signed the ship's articles in front of the Captain and the Mate. There was no turning back once I signed the articles and after I had arranged to see the Union man all right and been shown the cabin which I was to share with the galley boy, I made my way home at a run, my heart in my mouth, to tell the news.

* * *

Up the wooden stairs to the attic, two at a time, my advance note cashed by Beef Donnelly who had given me three pounds ten for it. An advance note is not supposed to be cashed until after the ship sails. So what happens is you get somebody who trades in advance notes to cash it for you for ten bob less. He cashes it with the shipping company after the ship sails, making ten shillings on the deal. But he takes a chance on you missing the ship.

I had squared the Union man, stopped at Tuohy's the ship chandlers to buy a white steward's jacket and a second-hand seaman's bag and now clutched these under my arm as I ran up the stairs.

As I opened the door, the smell of wintergreen met me, bringing black shadows which were trying to remind me of something, what was it, beside the set-in bed on which the oldfella lay stretched out, his jaws a bit clapped-in looking, while m'mother stood in the middle of the floor looking out of the window with a sad faraway dream in her eyes.

But Dan's face broke into a crinkly smile as he saw me, chasing the shadows away.

'Hullo, sonny mick.'

'Hullo, daddy.'

Maggie's face also lost the faraway look and the lines of sadness became fainter as she said:

'What have you got there?'

I said, 'Wait till I tell ye. Wait till I tell ye this . . .'

I stopped to let it sink in. Maggie said, 'Well, what is it you're going to tell us. We're waiting to hear.'

'I've got a job!'

M'mother said, 'A job. Glory be to God. What are you doing?'

'I've signed on a ship. We're sailing the night.'

She put her hand up to her mouth: 'Oh, Jesus, Mary and Saint Joseph!'

'Cabin boy. I was lucky. I was just on the spot when this fella hadn't turned up from the Federation. George Hall put in a word for me.'

'Oh son, you haven't signed on yet? Stay . . . Would you not stay here with us? And your father here not well?'

Dan raised himself up in the bed and said, 'I wouldn't stop him going for that.'

'It's too good a chance to miss, mammy. My first trip.'

'Where's this it's going?' continued m'father.

'I don't know. It could be anywhere. But we're sailing for Liverpool first for orders.'

'What's the name of it and what's your cargo?'

'The S.S. *Palmira*. I think it's general cargo.'

'Have you signed what they call the articles?'

'Aye, and I got my advance note. D'ye see my seaman's bag? I got it in Tuohy's. And there's my white jacket. I'll be wearing a white jacket when I go into the saloon.'

M'mother sat down with a long sigh.

'Dear God . . . Son . . . Do you know what you're doing?'

'I'm going to see the world—the only way I can.'

'Oh, sonny dear . . . Here . . . Look . . . Come over you here to me.'

I went over to her. She took my hand in both of hers. The sadness had come back and she was struggling for words.

'There's something on the side of your face. Something . . . Here. Come over here to the light of the window.'

She took me by the hand and we went over to the window behind the dresser. She pretended to be wiping something off my face. She began to whisper to me.

'Your father's quare and bad, you know. It's serious. I know it in my bones.'

'Ach, mammy, he'll be all right. You can't keep him down. You said that before and he was back up on his feet in no time.'

'He's bad. He's bad this time . . . Son . . . I'm telling you this . . .'

She was struggling for words again. Then she looked deep into my eyes and whispered slowly and clearly, 'If you go on that boat . . . your father won't be here when you come back. May God forgive me.'

Yes. May God forgive her for saying a terrible thing like that. Something I wouldn't even give space in my mind to.

'What do you want me to do—stay here on the dole and waste my life away? Up and down to the Burroo School or watching for the polis at the pontoon school?'

'I'm sure you would get a wee job.'

'A wee job. Some hopes. With queues a mile long for the dole.'

'At least you would be beside us and your father on his sick bed.'

'Ah, he won't be there long. He'll be up looking for his pint and you wait to you see his face when I bring him home some cigars. Cigars. I've always wanted to do that. And he'll be as right as rain.'

'Will you not take the warning. Is it not enough—one wandering the world?'

'John . . . Aye, but maybe I'll find John somewhere, mammy!'

Standing in the *Ship Bar* with Jim Neilson and Eesky Dan, my sea-bag by my side. A full-blown deep-sea sailor I know enough to buy the drinks when I have just signed on. What's left of the advance note had to be got through before sailing time, that's the drill. What's the time now? Getting on. The barman worked with Annie in the Kilwinning Eglinton Arms so he doesn't question my age. Eesky wants to be pals again even though I still have his scar on my lip. Oh well. I don't feel like fighting tonight. Buy him one for old times sake. He went to school with me, didn't he?

> *Drink to Paddy-across-the-water,*
> *Saint Mary's in our hearts always!*

Puddles of drink on the bar every time I look on the top I'm double-banked, two pints in front of me instead of one. Shove up the halfs, you must shove up the whiskies. You're the one that's signed on. Buy drinks. You get waves from all round the bar. Big Man. I hear you've signed on, Pat. Dan Watt. Give him a drink. Wish Charlie was here to drink my advance note with me. Frank McCourt's at sea as well. All the boys. A bunch of the boys. A bunch of the boys were whooping it up. In a marmalade saloon. Here I am. I'm at the bar. My horse is tied up outside. I've arrived. The Cook Aff The Tanker. Away across the ocean blue. Down they come, head two. Away down Ry-o. Where will she dock.

All the lights on the bottles but my mother's sad face. *What was that wee song John and you used to sing, son?* Yes. But lift the glass and drink deep. *Come draw a drap wi' the best o' it yet, go seek for pleasure where you will but here I never missed it yet.* Where did I hear that? Jim Neilson's face. Eesky Dan's face. A ship blowing from the harbour. That's your ship blowing, Pat. That's the *Palmira*. What's the time? It's after seven. Come on, Pat. You were to be turned to on board at seven. I want to sing a song before I go. Come on, Pat. You'll miss your ship. She's blowing again. Jim Neilson on one arm, Eesky on the other. Linked arms. Held up. Eesky carries my sea-bag. Out the bar. The street looks funny. The light is different. Past the corner. They're all looking. I'm the star of this picture.

All the fellas at the corner stand like statues. Bagwash McBain. The Fighting Scot. Monkey Nuttall. Kee-Kee Tam. Rab Walker. Dublin Dan. Moon McMullin. Gudge McGurk. They're frozen. They don't move. I've got a good send-off.

Past the corner around by the jail. Come on Paddy, you'll have to hurry. We'll see you on board, don't worry. Good fellas. Good mates. Shipmates forever for all that. They keep me from tripping over the railway lines, from falling over the hawsers. Come on Paddy, you'll make it.

Christ, my mother's at the ship. Standing by the gangway. Crying bitter tears. The last appeal. Don't go, Patrick. Oh, son, don't go. They're taking the gangway up. Paddy, come on. Eesky takes my bag on board and dumps it on the deck. She's waiting to sail.

I'm on the deck. The gangway's up. My bag stowed away. Slack away. There's a new angle. Where's the dock? Arran swinging into view. There's the North Shore. Away up there, Annie in her hotel in her apron. Go around the starboard side. She's under weigh.

Figures on the dock. Jim and Eesky holding each other up. Laughing. Your mother's wee stricken figure. She's growing smaller. A wee grey cr'atur'. And smaller. *What was that wee song John and you used to sing, son?*

'Camerad-o,
Camerad-o-o-o-o,'
fainter and fainter tailing away . . .

Aye, and here's Paddy off to box the compass and poghle the stars!

From *In a Marmalade Saloon* by Patrick O'Connor

The Miner's-Helmet

My father wore it working coal at Shotts
When I was one. My mother stirred his broth
And rocked my cradle with her shivering hands
While his black helmet's long-lost miner's-lamp
Showed him the road home. Through miles of coal
His fragile skull, filled even then with pit-props,
Lay in a shell, the brain's blue-printed future
Warm in its womb. From sheaves of saved brown paper,
Baring an oval into weeks of dust,
I pull it down: its laced straps move to admit
My larger brows; like an abdicated king's
Gold crown of thirty years ago, I touch it
With royal fingers, feel its image firm—
Hands grown to kings' hands calloused on the pick,
Feet slow like kings' feet on the throneward gradient
Up to the coal-face—but the image blurs
Before it settles: there were no crusades.
My father dies a draughtsman, drawing plans
In an airy well-lit office above the ground
Beneath which his usurpers, other kings,
Reigned by the fallen helmet he resigned
Which I inherit as a concrete husk.
I hand it back to gather dust on the shelf.

George MacBeth

First Day at Work

Norrie has just started work as an apprentice beveller, in a workshop where glass is cut and shaped for mirrors. A few minutes before this scene he was delighted to find an old newspaper in which there was an item about his old school.

NORRIE: Did you think the mornin went past quick, Bob?

BOB: Past quick? It vanished, disappeared. How d'you no?

NORRIE: It seemed quite long tae me. In school you've got different periods. Time goes quick.

BOB: Back at school again are ye? Take ma advice, son. Put it behind ye, unless you're thinkin o gaun back there, are ye?

NORRIE: Naw, nae chance.

BOB: Got tae make the break sometime. So stick in. You might think this is a rough trade and rough folk in it. But that's jist because we havenae broke away fae the oul' days—no a'thegither anyway. Ye cannae wipe oot years o' hard men an hard graft jist because the machinery changes a wee bit. No that it's a' that different, mind you. The wheels are a wee bit different here an' there, like the carborundum stone. That used to be the ould mill wi the hopper feeder and a sand-drip. That's when boys younger than you really grafted. Cairryin pailfuls o' saun an' sievin it in the trough beside the mill. They still use them in wan or two places yet, an' if somethin' had tae go wrong at Peter's end we might have tae use it yet, but it's no likely. As ah said, there wis a lot o Irishmen in this game at wan time. Haill families o them. It was wan o the few trades open tae them. The Rouger's oul' man wis a beveller. You think he's twistit. Ye want tae have seen his oul' man. They worked on piece work, each man seein his job through fae start tae finish, an' they had tae shift. The Rouger's faither wis a beaster. He'd collect his ain wages at the end o the week an' take the Rouger's tae. That wis the last they'd see o him tae the pubs shut on Setturday night. They were lucky if he had enough left tae get them pigs' feet fur the rest o the week. So maybe it's no surprisin that he's a wee bit rough. Course they wurnae a' like that, the oul' yins. Some o them could cut a design wi a wheel that wis merr like somethin' ye'd see in the Art Galleries. Ah wis never a' that good at figure-work masel'. But some o them raised families an' even put them tae the University. Ah see some lawyers' names aboot the toon an' ah can mind their faithers. Bevellers. Hard men, but good bliddy men, some o them. Aye, aye, Ye find the time long, then?

NORRIE: Jist keep glancin up at the clock a lot. Disnae seem tae move much.

BOB: Ah well, it's no much o a clock. Whit kinna stuff did they learn ye at school?

NORRIE: Usual. Bit o maths, science, techy-drawin, composition an' that.

BOB: Whit were ye good at?

NORRIE: English.

BOB: English?

NORRIE: Aye. Might no talk it very good, but ah wis a'right when it came tae writin it doon.

BOB: Wisnae exactly ma best subject. Mebbie you're wan o these fullas wi the itch.

NORRIE: Eh?

BOB: Ah've noticed. There's roughly three kinds o blokes get loose efter school. Wan's like me. Plods along, learns a trade and disnae see much further than a week's work an' his wages at the end o it. A wee bit o security tae keep the wife happy. Other kind's the wan wi a bit o education. They run businesses, buy a hoose, an' never seem tae be short o a few nicker. They might be dumplins, but that bit o education makes the difference. They're usually solid. Third kind's the wans wi the itch. An don't mean scratchin theirsel's or anythin' like that. A kind o internal itch. They'd come in an' look at a job like this an' say, 'Bugger that—ah'm off!' They might cast aboot fur a while before anythin' turns up, but it usually happens. They might be the kind that tries tae knock aff a couple o wage-vans an' get seven year fur their bother, but they're no exactly the really itchy wans. Naw, the fullas ah'm talking aboot don't seem tae need whit the rest o us need. They've a kinna instinct an' it gets them through. Some o them turn intae bookies, some do well at the buyin an' sellin, but occasionally ye get wan an' he really makes a name. Nae real start in life, but he's got the itch. We had a fulla like that in oor class at school. He wis good at composition, tae.

NORRIE: Ah don't feel very itchy now.

BOB: Ah well, we'll see. You're feedin up better. (*The bell goes.*) Stiff me, that's Leslie again. He's got the itch, but ah widnae like tae tell him where it is.

(BOB *goes off upstairs. The* ROUGER *and* JOE *start to talk together, hatching something.*)

ROUGER: Hey Norrie! Ye really fancy that bike, eh?

NORRIE: How, ye giein it away?

ROUGER: Naw, but ye could always have a gander at it.

NORRIE: Much'll it cost us?

ROUGER: Jist thought ye might be interested tae have a look. See these gears here, many permutations ye think's in the cogs therr?

NORRIE: You tell us.

ROUGER: Twelve. A dozen choices when you're nickin along. Hills, flats, corners, take yur pick.

(NORRIE *moves towards the bike and becomes absorbed.* JOE *snatches the old newspaper.*)

NORRIE: Whit kinna frame is it?

ROUGER: Continental. Top stylin. The lightest frame on the road.

NORRIE: Much it cost ye?

ROUGER: Best part o fifty quid for the frame itsel'. Wheels, gears, brakes, extra. Worth a hundred nicker as it stands.

NORRIE: That's no a bike, that's a space-ship.

ROUGER: Feel the position.

NORRIE: Position?

ROUGER: The relationship between the saddle, the rider, and the haunle-bars.

NORRIE: Whit's that got tae dae wi it? Ye no jist get on an' shove?

ROUGER: That's gringo talk. You see a rider wi his position right, ye know he's a pedaller. Ye see a bloke wi his arse in the air, ye know he's a plunk, a Joseph. Ye can always spot the pedallers weighin thursel's up in shop windaes as they pass.

NORRIE: Ah widnae mind whit ah looked like if ah had that thing under me.

ROUGER: Ye'd get the knock before ye reached Old Kilpatrick.

NORRIE: Ah've shoved a bike before this.

ROUGER: Ye'd get fire in yur gut. Jist like that fire behind ye.

(NORRIE *turns around and sees a small blaze on the floor.*)

NORRIE: Whit's that fur?

ROUGER: Ye no feel it cauld?

NORRIE: No me.

JOE: Ould papers make very good burnin.

NORRIE: Ye no feart ye set fire tae that straw?

JOE: No chance.

ROUGER: Don't think ye heard him right. Ould papers make good fires. Nice and dry.

NORRIE: (*looking towards his bench*) 'S 'at that paper that came oot the mirror?

ROUGER: You're gettin warm. But no so warm as that crap aboot yur oul' school.

(NORRIE *tries to kick out the fire and rescue the paper but it's too late.*)

NORRIE: Whit ye want tae dae that fur?

ROUGER: Jist a wee game. New boy—first day. Ye've got tae gee him up a bit.

NORRIE: Ah don't mind ye takin the rise, but the paper wis sometin' else. D'ye burn the lot o it?

ROUGER: Mebbe no.

(JOE *holds up the rest of the paper.* NORRIE *dives for it. The* ROUGER *collars him, while* JOE *puts the rest on the fire.*)

NORRIE: You're a coupla animals. Liberty-takers. Yez knew ah wanted that paper.

ROUGER: Teacher's pet. Gallopin back tae get a pat on the heid fur bein a good boy.

NORRIE: Ah thought you wur gaun tae be ma mate in here, Joe.

JOE: No chance, Mac.

NORRIE: Lousy bastards.

(BOB *comes down the stairs.*)

BOB: Whit's that burnin?

ROUGER: Gaun, tell him. Tell the teacher. The big bad boys set fire tae his paper.

BOB: You get some water on that at wance, Joe, or I'll land ye a severe kick on the arse. Rouger, ye're a louse-bag plain and simple. It wis daein he nae herm tae let the boy hiv the paper, but ye couldnae leave it, could ye? Ah knew yer oul' man. Ah widnae hiv crossed him, but he wis straight in his ain wey. You! When they bury you, they'll use a twisted coffin.

ROUGER: Ma oul' man wis a pig, an' when he got tae the age when he wis past it, ah let him know it, too.

BOB: Aye, don't tell us. Ah mind o his last days at the job. Ye used tae thump him on the chest an' say, 'Gaun, ya dirty oul' pig, ye.'

ROUGER: Mebbie he'll no be the last oul' man tae feel that.

BOB: If that's me you're talkin' aboot, ah'll tell ye somethin'. Ye wernae bred fur it. Ah'd cut ye fae yur heid tae yur arse, or ah'd find them that wid dae it fur me. Joe, don't let me catch you at that caper again.

JOE: Only a bit o kiddin, Bob.

BOB: Ye might've burnt the shop doon. Aw right, Norrie, don't staun therr like a stumor. Mix some merr pomas or somethin', but stir yur ideas—the lot o ye. Peter, Charlie. C'mere, ah want yez. We're gettin that big mirror-plate through right now. Leslie says we've tae try an' get it started by two o'clock this efternoon, so gie's your efforts, an' we'll get it through against the sterr therr.

JOE: You want me, Bob?

BOB: When ah want you, ah'll ask ye. Any oul' gloves aboot the place?

CHARLIE: Ah've got a couple ower therr.

BOB: See's wan. The right haun.

CHARLIE: They're baith fur the right haun.

BOB: Like the rest o the stuff in here. Two o everythin'—bugger all o nothin'.

ROUGER: Ah hivnae got wan.

BOB: Good. Mebbie ye'll do wan o yur arteries in.

(BOB, PETER and CHARLIE *move through to the side of the shop.*)

JOE: You've got me in bad wi the gaffer.

NORRIE: Ah got ye in bad? Ah didnae dae anythin'.

JOE: You and yur manky oul' paper.

NORRIE: Well, ye knew ah wanted tae keep it cause it wis ould.

JOE: Ould papers oot o ould mirrors are ten a penny in this job.

NORRIE: Ah didnae know that. Yez didnae need tae burn it anyway.

JOE: Ach, get bottled.

From Act I of *The Bevellers* by Roddy McMillan

The New Office

The new office was bewilderingly different from anything I had known. I was attached to the export department on the third floor, and the men and women worked strictly separately, apart from the actual time taken for dictation. The men worked at desks in a large open-plan room, and the typists were placed in a long narrow room leading off this main office. It was panelled up to eye-level, and had glass above this height, so that one could see into the main office when one stood up. Two typists were allocated to each section, and whoever was free answered the summoning bell. In case of emergency, or extra pressure of work, we all worked for anyone. There were about ten of us in each typing room, and the combined clatter of the machines in that narrow space was terrible. I'd never worked in such close proximity with other machines, and wondered if I would ever get used to the din. The head typist handed me a list of branch offices, and foreign offices, and details of the category of letter which would require three carbon copies, or four carbon copies or even six carbon copies, and I had to learn these by heart so that I would know at once how many copies were required. I could ask at first, of course, until I got used to things. I was shown where to get supplies of paper, and carbons, and ribbons, and pencils and rubbers. It was like a wee shop. It even had a lady in charge, who handed you out the materials you needed, and for which you signed a chit. Fancy an office doing so much work that there was a constant job just handing out materials! And office girls were kept busy all day long, emptying our baskets of finished work and taking them to the section heads for signing and dispatch. Commissionaires dealt with them at this stage, and they were in constant touch with the postal department. I was fascinated. All the jobs Patsy and I used to do between us were handled by separate departments in this office, and some of those grand typists with whom I now worked had never filed a letter or done a trial balance. They knew nothing but their own little cog in this vast machine. I began to realize what a splendid experience a small office was, when you just had to know how to do everything if the wheels were to turn smoothly. In spite of their poshness, I comforted myself that I knew a whole lot more about office routine than those fashionable typists. And I began to feel it was just possible that I was even worth my two pounds a week. I didn't let on, of course, that that was what I was earning, and I took my place as the most junior of junior typists, for I was by far the youngest in the typing room. Although I had been told to ask anything I wished to know for the first few weeks, I soon realized that those elegant young ladies didn't mean a word of it. Each time I queried a foreign market, or an Asiatic spelling, eyes would be cast heavenwards, and a voice dripping sweet-sour tones would say, 'You don't mind asking a great many questions, do you, Miss Weir?' I didn't recognize the sarcasm at first and replied innocently, 'Oh no, for you told me to ask.' But after I'd intercepted a few amused glances I shut my mouth, and asked the bosses instead, and they didn't mind telling me anything I wanted to know, for they were charmed with the speed with which I rattled off their letters and specifications. In fact, I soon earned another nickname from them, and was known throughout the building as 'The Flying Scots-woman'.

Oh but I longed to be assured, sophisticated like my typing companions. I had thought my accent was pretty acceptable until I went into this office and listened to the voices of girls who had been educated at the best schools, and for whom the expressions of workaday Glasgow were a source of rippling amusement. They would send each other into shouts of laughter by parodying their 'dailies', and saying, 'I was *that* annoyed', or 'Oh she was *that* nice'. How could I laugh when I lived among people who spoke like that every day of their lives, and when I wasn't above saying such things myself? Feeling I was speaking a foreign language, I began forcing myself to say, even at home, 'Oh it was *so* nice, Mother,' and to my surprise the heavens didn't fall, and nobody seemed to notice. I had been afraid people at home would think I was stressing inadequacies in their own speech but my altered vocabulary went right over their heads. I was so glad. I'd have hated to have hurt them, but I did want to fit into my new smart office background. Other expressions culled from those oft-quoted 'dailies' were 'I'm a done day this wumman', and if they were in a rush in the afternoons they'd exclaim, to peals of laughter, 'Two o'clock and no' a peenie on the wean', or 'Two o'clock and no' a wean washed'. I hadn't realized such expressions were comical; to me they were quite normal, for I'd heard the women in the back courts use them all my life. I was base enough to curry favour by adding one of my own, which I'd heard from my brother, and which even struck us as being funny, although we knew perfectly well what was meant. Our typists had to have it translated. Describing a bus conductor who'd infuriated him, one of my brother's mates had said, 'He wis wan o' thae fullas wi' eyes a' sewn wi' rid worset.' When I translated this as 'One of those fellows whose eyes were all sewn with red wool', a perfect description of red-rimmed eyes, the typists fell about holding their sides, and making such a noise with their gasping laughter that the boss on the other side of the glass rapped it to make them be quiet. But on that warm gale of laughter I was admitted to their friendship. I was accepted as one of them. I knew I wasn't, and I hoped they would never think of coming to Springburn, where nobody knew what a 'daily' was, and where they said without a blush, 'Oh I'm *that* hoat', or 'I'm fair sweatin'.'

There were some in that fine office, though, who knew coarse Springburn words. I was walking along the corridor with an old commissionaire one day, to recover something from postal department, and he said, observing a plump young girl walking ahead of us, 'My the young lassies nooaday have awfu' big bums!' I jumped in fright. I was absolutely scandalized. Fancy hearing such a word in the office. I pretended I hadn't heard him. But my heart sank. I betted to myself he would never have used such a coarse word in front of any of the other typists in my room. He obviously knew I was from the tenements, like himself, and that he needn't choose his words, as he'd have to have done if I had been a lady. Just wait till I had my elocution lessons, though, he'd soon change his tune.

From *Best Foor Forward* by Molly Weir

For my Grandmother Knitting

There is no need they say
but the needles still move
their rhythms in the working of your hands
as easily
as if your hands
were once again those sure and skilful hands
of the fisher-girl.

You are old now
and your grasp of things is not so good
but master of your moments then
deft and swift
you slit the still-ticking quick silver fish.
Hard work it was too
of necessity.

But now they say there is no need
as the needles move
in the working of your hands
once the hands of the bride
with the hand-span waist
once the hands of the miner's wife
who scrubbed his back
in a tin bath by the coal fire
once the hands of the mother
of six who made do and mended
scraped and slaved slapped sometimes
when necessary.

But now they say there is no need
the kids they say grandma
have too much already
more than they can wear
too many scarves and cardigans—
gran you do too much
there's no necessity.

At your window you wave
them goodbye Sunday.
With your painful hands
big on shrunken wrists.
Swollen-jointed. Red. Arthritic. Old.
But the needles still move
their rhythms in the working of your hands
easily
as if your hands remembered
of their own accord the pattern
as if your hands had forgotten
how to stop.

Liz Lochhead

NOTES

There is a wide range of available material on this theme. Of recent novels
from the area William McIlvanney's *Docherty* (mining) (Allen & Unwin),
Gordon Williams' *From Scenes Like These* (farm-work) (Secker) and Archie
Hind's *The Dear Green Place* (slaughter-house work) (Hutchinson) might be
mentioned. Among earlier novelists Edward Gaitens and George Blake are
outstanding. Both deal with Glasgow industrial workers, especially ship-
builders.

The vicissitudes of the working life are a major element in the short stories
of the young Glasgow writer, James Kelman. 'The Cards' and 'This
Morning', from his collection *An Old Pub Near the Angel* (Puckerbrush Press,
Maine) are recommended. A new collection, significantly called *Short Tales
from the Night-Shift* (Print Studios, Glasgow), has just appeared. Bill
Naughton's *Late Night on Watling Street* (Longman Imprint) could be usefully
compared with Kelman's work.

'First Day at Work': Roddy McMillan's *The Bevellers* (Southside) is a realistic
treatment of a boy's first day at work.

A good companion piece is Edward Gaitens' short story 'Growing Up'
which was reprinted in the Glasgow University magazine *Oasis* (Vol 2 no 5).
Unfortunately the work of Edward Gaitens (a novel *The Dance of the Apprentices*
and a short story collection *Growing Up*) is long out of print and difficult to
find. *Growing Up* is about a boy getting his first job.

'For my Grandmother Knitting': it is interesting to note that when this
splendid poem first appeared (in *Glasgow University Magazine*) it contained a
full range of punctuation, instead of just full stops, and was accompanied by
the writer's own line-drawing of her grandmother.

The anthology *And So to Work* (edited by Parker and Teskey, Blackie)
contains a selection of poems about a variety of jobs.

Scottish Literature in the Secondary School (HMSO) contains some useful
references to Scottish material on this theme.

I I

LANGUAGE

If Folk Spoke One Way

'Aye, right, Craig', he said. That was the proper way to address the farmer, although it sounded strange to call the old man by his surname. Willie had explained to him that his father was entitled to be called Craig—he was *the* Craig. Only men who didn't own land needed to be called Mister. Even Willie called his own father Craig.

'Hrrmmph.' The old man cleared his throat and spat a lump of catarrh the size of a penny. Then he squinted through his eyebrows. 'Is this suiting you better than being a scholar, Logan?'

'Oh aye,' he said, grinning. Craig must like him. He walked back to the two carts. It was very strange how the old man changed accents. Sometimes he spoke to you in broad Scots, sometimes in what the schoolteachers called proper English. They were very hot on proper English at the school. Once he'd got a right showing up in the class for accidentally pronouncing butter 'bu'er'. Miss Fitzgerald had gone on (him having to stand in front of the class) about the glottal stop being dead common and very low-class, something that would damn you if you wanted a decent job. A decent job—like a bank! His mother spoke proper English, but then she was hellish keen on proving they were respectable. His father spoke common Kilcaddie, which he knew his mother didn't like. When the Craigs spoke broad it wasn't quite the same as common Kilcaddie—some of their expressions sounded as though they came straight out of Rabbie Burns! Telfer had a Kilcaddie accent, but he pronounced all his words properly, no doubt from seeing too many pictures. McCann spoke very coarse and broad, but there was something false about him, as though he put it on deliberately.

He still spoke the school's idea of proper English, he knew that all right because every time he opened his mouth he could hear himself sounding like a real wee pan-loaf toff. (Maybe that was what annoyed McCann?) Why did Auld Craig and Willie change about? Did it depend on what they thought of you? He remembered Nicol the English teacher saying that broad Scots was pronounced very much like Anglo-Saxon or middle English or some such expression. If that was so why did they try and belt you into speaking like some English nancy boy on the wireless? He'd asked Nicol that and Nicol said right or wrong didn't come into it, proper English was what the school had to teach you if you weren't going to be a guttersnipe all your life. Was it being a guttersnipe to talk your own country's language? It would be a lot healthier if folk spoke one way. Sometimes you hear them say 'eight' and sometimes 'eicht', sometimes 'farm' and sometimes 'ferm'. Sometimes 'ye' and sometimes 'youse' and sometimes 'yese' and sometimes 'you'. Sometimes 'half' and sometimes 'hauf'. Was it your faither or your father? Your mither or your mother? He felt he was speaking to his audience again. You see, if school was any use it would teach you things like that, not just jump on you for not talking like a Kelvinside nancy boy. Why teach kids that Burns was the great national poet and then tell you his old Scots words were dead common? What sounds better—'gie your face a dicht wi a clootie' or 'give your face a wipe with a cloth'? One was Scottish and natural and the other was a lot of toffee-nosed English shite.

'See me, I'm Peter Cavanagh, the man with a million voices,' he said to Big Dick as they walked along the track road to the pits. 'Gi'es a len' o' yur pen, hen? What was that my good man? Sorry, lady, give us a wee loan of your fountain pen, madam. Otherwise Ah'll melt ye. And here is that ancient man of the moment, that crazy comic from Kilcaddie, Sir Crawly Craig, what song are you giving us the night, Sir Crawly—what's that "gin lowsing ye'll ging for a wee donner doon the heather"? Very nice, I hope it isn't dirty.'

From *From Scenes Like These* by Gordon Williams

Unrelated Incident (*1*)

its thi lang-
wij a thi
guhtr thaht hi
said its thi
langwij a
thi guhtr

awright fur
funny stuff
ur
Stanley Bax-
ter ur but
luv n science
n thaht naw

thi langwij
a thi
intillect hi
said thi lang-
wij a thi intill-
ects Inglish

then whin thi
doors slid
oapn hi raised
his hat geen
mi a fare-
well nod flung
oot his right

fit boldly n
fell eight
storeys
doon thi
empty
lift-shaft

Tom Leonard

Ah Fell an' Bumped ma Heid in the Sheuch

'Docherty!' Less a voice than an effulgence of sound falling across
their suddenly stricken silence. Outwith its paralysing glare, others

160

freeze. Conn stands up slowly, carefully doesn't look at anybody else, as if a glance might prove infectious. They all wait. 'Simpson! Would you two creatures come out here.'

They are allowed to stand on the floor for a moment, to become the relief of the others, a moral.

'You'll excuse us, Miss Carmichael. I wouldn't want to get blood on your floor.'

Some titters are gratefully offered, withdrawn. Silence is safest.

'Certainly, Mr Pirrie.'

They pass into the next room. Their small procession isn't a unique sight but they gain a brief attention here too. Beyond this room, a small cloakroom area, where they stop.

Conn almost swoons with the staleness of the place. It is a small passageway, foetid with forgotten children, a knackery for futures. He sees the drifting motes as clear as constellations. Two coats hang damp. Their quality of sadness haunts his inarticulacy. Mr Pirrie inflates, enormous in the silence, hovers like a Zeppelin.

'Well, well, well. Who started it?'

On one of the floorboards an accentuation in the grain makes a road. It runs winding, vanishes under Mr Pirrie's boot.

'It doesn't matter. You'll both be getting the same. What's wrong with your face, Docherty?'

'Skint ma nose, sur.'

'How?'

'Ah fell an' bumped ma heid in the sheuch, sur.'

'I beg your pardon?'

'Ah fell an' bumped ma heid in the sheuch, sur.'

'I beg your pardon?'

In the pause Conn understands the nature of the choice, tremblingly, compulsively, makes it.

'Ah fell an' bumped ma heid in the sheuch, sur.'

The blow is instant. His ear seems to enlarge, is muffled in numbness. But it's only the dread of tears that hurts. Mr Pirrie distends on a lozenge of light which mustn't be allowed to break. It doesn't. Conn hasn't cried.

'That, Docherty, is impertinence. You will translate, please, into the mother-tongue.'

The blow is a mistake, Conn knows. If he tells his father, he will come up to the school. 'Ye'll take whit ye get wi' the strap an' like it. But if onybody takes their hauns tae ye, ye'll let me ken.' He thinks about it. But the problem is his own. It frightens him more to imagine his father coming up.

'I'm waiting, Docherty. What happened?'

'I bumped my head, sir.'

'Where? Where did you bump it, Docherty?'

'In the gutter, sir.'

'Not an inappropriate setting for you, if I may say so.'

The words mean nothing. Only what happens counts.

'I'm disappointed in you, Docherty. You'll soon be coming up to the big school. And I'll be ready for you. I used to hear nice things about you. But not any more. You might've had the chance to go to the Academy. You still could. Do you know what that means? But what's the point? I wouldn't waste the time of highly qualified men. But while you're here you'll behave like civilised people. Brawling in the playground!'

His voice shudders the wood around them. The words have worked, mystically invoke his anger. It possesses him. The veins in his nose suffuse. The strap snakes out from its nest under the shoulder of his jacket.

'Simpson first!' It is a ritual. He holds the strap in his right hand, drops it over his shoulder, reaches back with his left hand, flexes the leather, begins. 'I will *not*. Have. Violence. In my school.'

Four. Conn can prepare.

'Docherty!' One. Conn recites to himself: *Ah bumped ma heid in the sheuch.* Two. *Sheuch.* 'You're getting as bad as your brother was.' Three. *Fat man.* 'I was glad to get rid of him.' Four. Conn's hands drop, stiff as plaster-casts. 'Up, Docherty, up! Two more for insolence.' Five. *Bastard.* He is watching for signs of tears. Six. *Big, fat bastard.*

He has become his hands. His will huddles round them, containing the radiations of their pain, refusing them the salve of tears. The two of them are led back to the room.

Mr Pirrie says, 'I've just been tickling these two's hands. As a little warning. The next boys I catch behaving like savages won't be able to use their hands for a week.'

The room is dislocated by his departure, becomes for a moment no more than his absence. Patiently, Miss Carmichael shepherds their attention. Her talk moves delicately across the film of her own thoughts, a fly walking water. Her sympathy, limed by circumstances, flutters half-heartedly and subsides. No doubt Mr Pirrie knows best. He comes from a working-class home himself, he says. He isn't afraid to admit what his father was—a pig walking upright. Troughing it at the table. Swearing. They're all the same. Afraid to better themselves. They need the comfort of the herd. They have the place they want. They have to be taught to keep it. He blesses his mother, who married beneath herself and found that you couldn't convert them. No wonder Livingstone left Blantyre. Africa was an easier proposition. But she at least managed to save her son. He will be forever grateful for what she has helped him to become.

A dull sense of irony exists in Miss Carmichael's mind without the hardness of conviction to sharpen it against. Her thoughts shift to High Street. There is a family there that she visits. From them she has heard about Conn's father. Once he was pointed out to her in the street. The stories about him have fused in her head with the white gash of a face, the hard-heeled walk. The image has occasionally troubled the demureness of her thoughts, like an uncouth and uninvited guest at a tea-party, and has become the extension of a vague unease in her own life. A brief confrontation of pictures occurs in her mind. Mr Pirrie seated in his own house, a book in his hand, people listening, his words incontrovertible in the atmosphere of the room, the whole scene held in a self-generated luminosity, bright and delicate as a soap-bubble. Tam Docherty walking down a street. The bubble bursts.

Briefly there comes to Miss Carmichael a swamping and frightening sense of chaos, thousands of uncontradictable and contradictory opinions, unimaginable ideas, invisible angers, millions of directions, pains, all hopelessly entangled. What is there that can possibly be done? She teaches spelling.

In the room there is a snuffling sound, contained, private. Alan Simpson is crying. Conn, on the brink of tears himself, is sorry but grateful. Poor Alan. He lost the fight too. Conn knows now that he won't be crying. Alan Simpson is doing it for him.

It was an unimportant incident and yet significant beyond itself, the hundredth sparrow alighting that snaps the twig. Within minutes, Conn was taking an almost aesthetic interest in the look of his wrists, pebbled lightly with blisters. Inside the puffiness of their pain his fingers hardened again. He flexed them. The rawness of the experience had already refined itself into separate constituents, not without their uses. The blisters weren't unimpressive. There would be the admiration of the boys, the sympathy of the girls. He would have to enlist his mother's help, though, in making sure that his father didn't take it any further.

Conn's conscious adjustment to what had happened didn't go much deeper than that. But more important, registering beyond the reach of his awareness, the small incident in the cloakroom was like a crucial digit affecting an immensely complicated calculation. Relating to it, realignments were already taking place in him. He was coming to understand through his own experience the attitudes Mick and Angus had expressed towards school. More and more he was beginning to envy Angus his escape and involvement in what was to Conn the real life of his family, work and the bringing in of a wage. He knew his father's contempt for the way they had to live and his reverence for education. But against that went Conn's sense of the irrelevance of school, its denial of the worth of his father and his family, the falsity of its judgements, the rarefied atmosphere of its terminology. It was quite a wordless feeling, but all the stronger for that, establishing itself in him with the force of an allergy.

While Miss Carmichael gave him sympathetic exemption from her questions, he took a stub of pencil in his fingers. Slowly across a scuffed piece of paper a word moved clumsily. Opposite it another word was manoeuvred and settled, the way he had seen in a dictionary Miss Carmichael showed him. His hand shook as he did it. It was a painful and tremulous matter, like an ant trying to manipulate stones. He sat buried inside himself while the words spread themselves across the paper. Minutes later, he was stunned into stillness, looking at the big awkward shapes they made before him.

sheuch	*—gutter*
speugh	*—sparrow*
lum	*—chimny*
brace	*—mantalpiece*
bine	*—tub*
coom	*—soot*
coomie	*—foolish man (Mr Pirrie)*
gomeril	*—another foolish man*
spicket	*—tap*
glaur	*—muck what is in a puddle after the puddle goes away*
wabbit	*—tired*
whaup	*—curloo*
tumshie	*—turnip*
breeks	*—troosers*
chanty	*—po*
preuch	*—anything you can get*
I was taigled longer nor I ettled	*—I was kept back for a more longer time than I desired*

One side of the paper was filled. He didn't start on the other side because he now wanted to write things that he couldn't find any English for. When something sad had happened and his mother was meaning that there wasn't anything you could do about it, she would say 'ye maun dree yer weird'. When she was busy, she had said she was 'saund-papered tae a whuppet'. 'Pit a raker oan the fire.' 'Hand-cuffed to Mackindoe's ghost.' 'A face tae follow a flitting.' If his father had to give him a row but wasn't really angry, he said 'Ah'll skelp yer bum wi' a tealeaf tae yer nose bluids'.

Conn despaired of English. Suddenly, with the desperation of a man trying to amputate his own infected arm, he savagely scored out all the English equivalents.

On his way out of school, he folded his grubby piece of paper very carefully and put it in his pocket. It was religiously preserved for weeks. By the time he lost it, he didn't need it.

From *Docherty* by William McIlvanney

Unrelated Incident (3)

this is thi
six a clock
news thi
man said n
thi reason
a talk wia
BBC accent
iz coz yi
widny wahnt
mi ti talk
aboot thi
trooth wia
voice lik
wanna yoo
scruff. if
a toktaboot
thi trooth
lik wanna yoo
scruff yi
widny thingk
it wuz troo.
jist wanna yoo
scruff tokn.
thirza right
way ti spell
ana right way
ti tok it. this
is me tokn yir
right way a
spellin. this
is ma trooth.
yooz doant no
thi trooth
yirsellz cawz
yi canny talk
right. this is
the six a clock
nyooz. belt up.

Tom Leonard

NOTES

A. J. Aitken's essay, 'The Scots Language and the Teacher of English in Scotland', is an excellent introduction to this theme. It appears in *Scottish Literature in the Secondary School* (HMSO, 1976).

'If Folk Spoke One Way': Dunky Logan's reflections constitute an amazingly comprehensive and penetrating summary of the language situation in the west of Scotland. The bromide, that social class does not matter in Scotland, is most cruelly untrue where language, especially urban working-class usage, is concerned. See also the Molly Weir passage, 'The New Office', elsewhere in this anthology.

'Unrelated Incident (1)': Tom Leonard succeeds in expressing complex philosophical concepts in 'thi langwij a thi guhtr' in his remarkable series 'Unrelated Incidents' (*Three Glasgow Writers*, Molendinar Press).

The reference to Stanley Baxter's *Parliamo Glasgow* is significant and suggests a possibly fruitful consideration of the language used by another Glasgow entertainer, Billy Connolly.

'Ah Fell an' Bumped ma Heid in the Sheuch': no better example of the fact, that language is an integral part of the individual's notion of self, could be found.

This extract could also be usefully compared with the George Friel passage 'Corporal Punishment', which is included in 'A Violent World'.

12

A VIOLENT WORLD

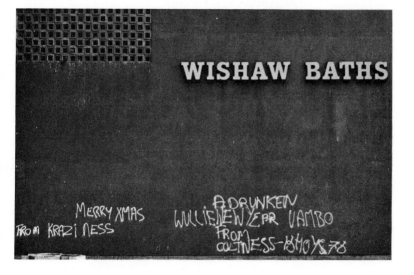

Whit Kinna Fight is This?

Well, it's all very well talking about fights, but it's a different thing fighting them except when you know you'll win and you won't get hurt. I never liked getting hurt. There was one afternoon I deliberately picked a fight with a boy in the class who wore an expensive blazer and had curly hair and a transparent complexion and talked like a jessie, and maybe he was a jessie, but his arms were about two feet longer than mine, and every time I made a run at him I ran my face straight into one of his fists, and when I started running back from him his arm could still stretch faster than my feet could move and all I wanted to do was be somebody else, in another country for preference. It wasn't the humiliation that worried me so much as the discomfort of being punched on the face, and once he had discovered the thing could be done, he was all for doing it all night. But I knew later how he felt because I had it the other way round and this time I didn't want the fight in the first place.

To be frank, I had given up the fight game for life. But there was a crowd of older boys with a pack-sheet tent pitched on the coup one evening, and they sponsored the match after this other boy of my own height and weight had landed an unprovoked stone on the back of my head. They wanted sport, and I felt that I was armed with justice, so we squared up. I'm not even sure of the other boy's name, but I think it was Hannah.

We sparred for a few minutes, and the big boys got impatient and shouted for action, and at last I forced myself to aim straight at his face, and hit him hard in one eye. I was ashamed at once and sorry for him because I knew what it was like to be punched. But although he was half-hearted about it and didn't fly into a killing rage, he went on fighting, and I hit him in the face again. The big boys cheered me and patted me on the shoulder, and I felt flushed with victory, but I hated them too and they disgusted me, for they were risking nothing themselves and nobody was punching their faces, and I hated myself a bit for playing up to them. I was hoping Hannah would run away, and I wouldn't chase him very fast, but he suddenly kicked me.

Dirty foul! One of the spectators was so hot on fair play that he was making to kick Hannah from behind to prove it, but missed him, and I was smarting slightly from the kick on the shin and justifying myself while I hit him again. And then it got hellish. He was either blinded or posing as blind, and it doesn't matter which, because he just stood with his hands in front of his face and I punched through his hands and hit him again and again until a man working in a garden across the street came over and stopped the fight and gave the big boys a telling off and said I was a bully.

'He hut me furst!' I said.

'Get away home out of here,' the man said, and I went.

It was always bad to see older boys urging young boys on to a fight, because they were always liable to throw in a clout or two themselves, if they didn't like one of the fighters, and they were just as liable to turn nasty with their favourite if he didn't produce enough action. Even among ourselves I didn't often see a fight that was deliberately sought and willingly fought. There was a standard practice at this time for satisfying honour. Fights usually started in the playground, and the contestants couldn't fight there. They would promise or threaten to meet up the Muck at four o'clock, and by four o'clock the thing would be forgotten.

The Muck is a piece of made ground with a cinder track on it used for training by Shettleston Harriers. It may have another name, but nobody knows it.

In the playground one afternoon I was tripped on my face by Willie Cairns. He was one of a big family of Cairnses who lived in a little low old row of cottages in Shettleston Road, since demolished and gone, and the Cairnses, about five of them all at school, were known for two things. They were all sneaky wee pukes and their mother was a terror.

After I was tripped, Willie was laughing in his Cairns way. I said:
'Ah'll get you.'

'Ah'll ge-e-et ye!' he mimicked. It was a catchphrase. 'An' if ah don't get ye, the coos'll get ye!'

The bell rang. 'You wait,' I warned him. 'I'll see you up the Muck at four.'

'Gi'e him a towsin', Willie,' one of his supporters said. 'Don't worry,' Willie said. We glared at each other as the lines went in and made a threatening gesture with our right fists. For this gesture, the left shoulder is pushed up and forward and the right forearm is tucked well into the body pointing towards the chin, and the fist is clenched, but with the thumb poked through between the first and second fingers. We regarded this form of fist as correct for a killer punch. In practice, if you landed a punch with the thumb like this, a stab of pain shot up your arm to the shoulder and paralysed the thumb.

I knew my Willie. There would be no fight up the Muck at four. In the crowd leaving school at four o'clock, it was easy to get quietly lost before anybody could find you. But I had friends, and Willie had friends, and friends love somebody else's fight. Willie would have got clean away at four o'clock, and good luck to him, but for his friends who wanted his honour defended, and my friends had me trapped before I was out of the classroom. We took our positions before an audience of fifty or sixty, or rather, inside an audience of fifty or sixty, for everybody wanted to crowd round for a ringside view.

I had no fear of Willie. On the other hand, even a Cairns fist can be sore against the nose and was undesirable. We set to in the first position, arms tucked into the body and right shoulders forward, and then we did the usual thing. I said:

'Well?'

And Willie Cairns said:

'Aye—well!'

'Well, whit'll ye dae?'

'You'll see!'

'Well, whit?'

'Ah'll dae a loat.'

Somebody in the crowd shouted:

'Aye—in yer troosers!' Shouts from every direction. 'Hit 'im wan!' 'Gi'e it tae 'im!' 'Whit kinna fight is this?' 'Baste 'im!' 'Gi'e 'im the auld wan-two!' Some of the spectators would demonstrate the kind of uppercut they fancied, and accidentally nudge another watcher, and arguments spurted up here and there. Willie Cairns and I were breathing heavily at each other, then I made the first attack, by leaning forward and bumping him on the shoulder with my shoulder and upper arm. He missed balance and staggered back a step, then stepped up and gave me a dunt with his shoulder.

'Well?' I said. 'You want a fight—let us see ye fight.'

169

'Ah never wanted a fight—you asked for it!'

'Ah don't want a fight.' These were the only honest remarks made all day.

'Well, yur gonny get wan!' a spectator shouted. Everybody was blood-mad to fight; except me and Willie Cairns. Somebody shoved Willie from behind to get him started, but he kept his balance and swung round angrily to curse the shover. It was a diversion that might end the main fight, but the crowd stayed in a solid ring and he finally had to give up arguing and turn back to face me. It never occurred to me to punch him while he was off guard. I don't say I was too honourable. He might have punched me back.

Somebody shoved me, and I was off balance. I cannoned into Willie and he fell back shocked. 'Hit 'im!' 'Uppercut!' 'Solar plexus!' I didn't know where the solar plexus was. Willie straightened up and aimed a swinging punch at a point two feet in front of my chin. 'Get in therr!' I aimed an uppercut about eighteen inches from Willie.

As I swung it, somebody shoved him again from behind, and his face crashed on to my fist. 'Uppercut!' the crowd shouted. 'Oh boy, did ye see that?' Spectators demonstrated the uppercut that I had landed. I danced about now, red and heavy breathing and looking as if I meant business. I had put an uppercut right on the button. I was a real fighter. Willie swung like a woodsman again, but this time he was peevish and didn't care even if he hit me. He hit my shoulder and I lashed out, terrified of myself, at his face, and struck bone. I never liked Willie, but I was grateful to him then. He didn't get angry, he surrendered the fight. He put his hands to his face as if he expected the jaw to be smashed, and reeled about drunkenly and decided not, after all, to fall down. It was a poor fight, as usual up the Muck. But my friends loyally made the best of it, and there were even some sycophants from Willie's camp who wanted to shake my hand and pat me on the shoulder. Soon I let them persuade me that I was a real killer. I lapped it up. I went home with fans on both sides of me and behind me shouting:

'You basted 'im! It was a massacree! Wan, two, bang!'

They stopped shouting. One or two of them left the procession and hurried ahead, or turned aside. We had reached Shettleston Road, and a big red woman was ten yards away facing us. She had Willie Cairns by the hand, and he was weeping floods and moaning. His eyes, which I had never laid a finger on, were raw red where he had rubbed them himself, and he had apparently sprained a knee and broken both arms on his way home, from the way he was walking. The big woman was Mrs Cairns.

'Aye, it's me! You come 'ere tae ah get ye, yah wee devil! Proud ae yersel', eh? Ah'll soart ye!'

'He started it!' I retorted. I was just as angry as she was, and I wasn't afraid either.

'Aye, an' ah'll feenish it!'

I ran like hell. She shouted after me:

'Ah know where ye live, ya bullyin' wee nyaff! Ah'll get ye!'

That was something I could worry about later, as long as I got out of reach of Mrs Cairns in the meantime. She wasn't like Willie. Mrs Cairns *could* fight.

From *Dancing in the Streets* by Clifford Hanley

Trouble on the Buses

'Oh,' the small man next to him said. 'Was that your foot Ah stepped on?'

Jim looked at him incredulously.

'Not at all,' he said. 'It's really ma brother's. Ah'm just wearin' it in for him.'

'Ye don't need tae get narky,' the small man said, bridling slightly.

'Ah'm no' narkin', Mac,' Jim said. 'Ah enjoyed it. Anyway, Ah've got another one in the hoose. Ah just use this one for walkin' wi'.'

'A funny man, eh?'

'They have been known to die laughing, friend.'

'Look. It wis an accident.'

'An accident? More of an atrocity, Ah wid say maself.'

'Anybody could step on your foot.'

'It just wouldny be the same, some way. You've got that professional touch. What are ye to trade? A foot-powderer?'

'Now, listen, you,' the small man said, anxious to get back to first principles. 'Ah just asked ye a civil question. If it was your foot Ah stepped on. All right?'

'Whose bloody foot is it likely to bloody be on the end of my bloody leg?'

'Ah've just about had a bellyful of you.'

'An' Ah've had a footful of you, friend.'

The small man was beginning to dance slightly, like a ferret on fire. He was thrusting his face as near to Jim's as he could get it. Jim put his hand flat on the small man's chest.

'Keep back,' he said. 'Ye're standin' so close Ah can see the reds of yer eyes. Get away from me. Before Ah do yer dentist out of a job!'

Their argument had begun to assert itself on the other people in the bus and an insidious silence came just as Jim spoke, so that the volume turned up even further on his remark. The little man looked as if Jim had been trying to crucify him.

'D'ye hear that?' he said to a jury of strap-hangers.

Their eyes put Jim in the dock.

'Did you hear him threatenin' me?' The little man appointed someone with a paper as foreman. 'Did ye?'

The other man almost ate his paper with embarrassment. But someone further along the bus took up the cry, smelling blood.

'Ah heard him all right, Sam,' he said loudly. 'It's the polis ye want for that kind.'

There was a round of ominous murmurs on Jim.

'Ah'll go quietly!' Jim said dramatically.

His jest was not appreciated. Mutters of 'Enough o' that!' and 'Who does he think he is?' 'No' safe in yer ain house any mair!' were spat at him like poisoned arrows.

'Ya buncha mugs!' Jim stood nobly defiant, Rome surrounded by Huns. 'Morons. All you can count up to is "Bingo"! Dae ye want me to stand here an' let this wee runt do a tango on ma taes?'

'Right, Jim. Here's our stop,' Andy said hurriedly.

They were a stop too early. But Andy decided a diplomatic withdrawal was called for. They managed to get Jim hustled off before he realized it. A woman sitting on one of the side seats by the door snarled at him like a maenad. Sneers and angry voices pursued them.

Outside, Jim ran to the front of the bus. He stood to attention at the kerb as the bus pulled away and gave all the inmates the fingers with both hands, bowing when they mouthed out at him.

'Come on, ya half-wit,' Andy said. 'You're definitely buckin' for a pair o' handcuffs the night.'

'Not at all,' Jim said. 'An' what did ye get off there for anyway? That's no' our stop. Ah was enjoyin' it fine.'

'Aye, that's right,' Andy said, catching up with Charlie. 'Ah heard ye laughin'. Ah just didny fancy goin' up to yer father the night an' handin' in a paira shoes an' a coupla fingernails. "Hello, Mr Ellis. Here's Jim. Divide him out among the weans." You want to watch yer mouth, man.'

'Me? Me? Ah want to watch? What would ye make o' that, Charlie?'

Charlie said nothing.

'Me?' As they cut through the side streets, Jim expostulated with the world. 'It's no' me. It's all a bloody plot. Ah'm tellin' ye. Ah mean, don't think this is anything new. Ah'm hardened to it. If Ah go into the pictures just, they're waitin' for me. Somebody there is goin' to pick me out. Specially. Some sixteen-stoner is goin' to decide to use ma head for a footstool. Or else the smoke from ma fag is definitely goin' to go into someone's eyes.'

The door of 'The Hub' came like a hyphen in Jim's diatribe, introducing a smoky parenthesis of brightness and noise.

'Look at them,' Jim continued, crossing to the bar. 'They've got the word already. He's here. Have your insults ready. Will you have first nark, Cedric? Or shall I? Have a little mercy, friends. Ah, lead me to the malmsey-butt. Ah'm goin' to do ma Clarence. Drown ma persecution complex in its depths.'

'Three pints, please,' Andy said. 'Heavy.'

'Very heavy,' Jim added.

From *Remedy is None* by William McIlvanney

The Coming of the Wee Malkies

Whit'll ye dae when the wee Malkies come,
if they dreep doon affy the wash-hoose dyke,
and pit the hems oan the sterrheid light,
an play wee heidies oan the clean close-wa',
an blooter yir windae in wi the baw,
missis, whit'll ye dae?

Whit'll ye dae when the wee Malkies come,
if they chap yir door, an choke yir drains,
an caw the feet far yir sapsy weans,
an tummle thur wulkies through yir sheets,
an tim thur ashes oot in the street,
missis, whit'll ye dae?

Whit'll ye dae when the wee Malkies come,
if they chuck thur screwtaps doon the pan,
an stick the heid oan the sanit'ry man;
when ye hear thum shauchlin doon yir loaby,
chantin, 'Wee Malkies! The gemme's a bogey!'
—Haw, missis, whit'll ye dae?

Stephen Mulrine

The Tiny Rastus

Fifty yards past the Palace, Scow comes to a sudden halt: sounds of shouting and the scud of feet drift faintly from behind the houses. Apprehensive, instinct tells him that the noise has something to do with Murray's disappearance and, enticed, he skulks up the nearest close into the back yard. Patched with light from the rear windows, wash-houses wall off the lane. Scow can hear yapping and yelling quite audibly now, though the direction of the sound is still mysterious. He has the urge to turn tail and gallop for the safety of the Gower, but curiosity prods him on. Using the bin lids as ladders, he clambers over the edge of the midden, finds a foothold on the window-ledge, a hand-hold on the decayed stump of a boiler stack, hauls himself on to the wash-house roof and goes up the steep short slope on all fours like a cat. Oblivious to the effect of the chipped slate and rusty girders on the knees and elbows of his best suit, he claws for the ridge. Over it he hopes to find answers to the questions which taunt him. Fingers fastened to the crest he lowers himself to his belly and, by bending his elbows, draws his head up over the edge. Below him the narrow lane is laid off by rain into an archipelago of sunken cobbles, surrounded by puddles of standing water. A rone, torn from a wash-house gutter, splatters its load constantly to the ground. Black and silver twists of water, sculptured by the pipe-mouth, shred in the gust wind which moans up the lane like a sad demon beset by spiked railings, telephone poles and broken masonry. At first Scow sees nothing, but the noises are louder than ever. He scans the vacant ground over the opposite wall but the only movement there is the tattered dance of some bit of rubbish, and in the far corner the whipping of an elm tree's naked branches. The sounds burst behind him with the suddenness of mortar bombs. He jerks his head round so fast he almost dislodges himself from his perch.

They spill out of the black close of the adjacent yard and head straight for the gate in the lane wall. Willie leads only by the length of a billiard cue, but gains a few additional feet by slamming the plank gate on his pursuers and cutting sharply into the lane. Arms akimbo, hands flared for balance, he dances from cobble to cobble as if bullets are spitting off the stones at his heels or the ground itself is riddled with quake-like fissures which, on peril of his life, he must avoid. Dismayed but clinical, Scow thinks how well Willie runs: for all his hopping and slithering he is very fast indeed. The jacket tail sticks out stiff in his slipstream like the painted tarpaulin hood of an old motorcar. Willie glances back, splashes through a deep puddle, leaps again to the cobbled track and plunges directly for the lane's end. Behind him the yard door crashes open and hordes of Rastus Tinys pour out in pursuit.

Scow ducks, pressing his nose and mouth against the slates, only his eyes, agog with horror, periscope above the roof. A better man might crib a leaf from comicbook fiction, leap like a giant avenger to straddle the ridge and deftly slice off a score of heads with a barrage of skimming slates, but there are no ridiculous stirrings of heroism in Scow. He cannot find it in himself to draw the mob's fire and allow Willie to escape. Cowering, he prays they won't notice him. Only by recognising the Couper brothers is he able to identify the Rastus Tinys: dim light and feverish motion blur the others' features. He knows they must all be Rastus, but is at a loss to understand what has aroused them to such a passion of hatred. Until now the Tiny Rastus have been only names on hoardings and walls, seemingly as remote as a tribe of Congo pygmies. The dozen in the lane below however are anything but remote and are fully accoutred with an armoury of crude weapons—wooden clubs, lengths of metal, cheap knives. A snaking black-knobbed object whirls above one head like a bolas. Frightening connotations rear into Scow's brain. He hugs the ridge tightly and gapes down at the army of raging children.

Unbroken voices shrill out. 'There he goes. After'm. Nail the bastard. Plant'm one.' Then, in a gutteral chant, *'Ras-tus: Ras-tus: Ras-tus.'*

The Coupers and a boy in orange boots lead the vanguard, the rest string out behind like athletes in a Marathon. Sweeping up the rear come two small boys, hand in hand, each crying in pitiful treble, 'Wait for *me*: wait for *me*,' as if the mountain was about to close on them.

In vain Scow searches for Bison, Veitch, Rikki, Karloff, or any of the leaders of the gang, hoping that in their directions he might unearth a clue to the motivating force of the attack. Scow's fear bears no resemblance to the prickling excitement, unlocked bladder and damp armpits, which precede a street fight. Murray is a stranger to them all and this total absence of motive is the most dreadful aspect of the Tinys' night-run, suggesting forms of unimaginable madness. Scow does not connect this chase with Friday's party; he knows the Toner kids too well to take chivalry into account. Boys this young will not rush to defend maidenly virtue, or assert their manly pride in bloody revenge. What Willie Murray must be suffering, Scow can't conceive; Willie, compelled to find his own escape route through a maze of lanes and alleyways, streets and waste lots, with a pack of alien children howling on his tail. Dumbly Scow watches as a fresh squadron of Tinys debouches from a blind alley at the lane's end. Bawling in triumph, they spread out to trap the victim. Their silhouettes are squat and dwarf-like and, in the murky glow of High Street's distant lamps, the shapes of their clubs swell into gargantuan shadows. Showing quicker wits and reflexes than Scow can credit, Murray instantly veers right and hurls himself at the iron fence which, at this point, unites the rear walls of disused garages. Willie wriggles his fingers through the *fleur-de-lys* spike-heads, tucks up his legs and, using hip and knee for purchase, struggles to surmount the spears without impaling himself. For a moment he balances on the rail-top like a mammoth frog, but before he can leap to safety his jacket snags on the tips, and a dozen eager hands snatch and grapple at his thighs. Still clinging to the railing, Willie sways, then, with the dead weight of a dozen boys tearing at him, yields to exhaustion, and sags backward into the bunch. The pack close around the struggling figure and blot him out. Scow stifles a whimper, and slides into hiding behind the roof lest they should spot him and pick him as their next victim.

Tenement windows open, faces peer out, but no stupid householder runs from the close to interfere in the strife. Muttered excuses pass between husband and wife, son and mother; the local code of ethics apportions blame equally to hunter and victim, white-washing caution and cowardice with apologetic cliches. The fight in the lane has nothing to do with them; it is nobody's business. Gangs are not accidents of nature. To pit oneself alone against such a cancer is to ask for infection. Fire, flood and violent storm all bring forth their heroes of the hour, but some quality other than courage is needed to tempt a man to tamper with a human situation—a touch of a similar caffard, or senseless hatred. Apparently nobody of that stamp lives in the High Street tenements; Scow's prayer for help goes unanswered. The Tiny Rastus, however, the first flush of temper spent, realise that noise could mean their downfall. They sink into a muttering silence which is more awful than the shouting; silence which implies coldness and makes their handling of Murray seem even more cruel. With his head swaddled in his jacket and the rest of his body as naked as scraped bone, Willie is hoisted high on the boys' shoulders. Even the smallest seems anxious to run under the spreadeagled body, as if it was a Roman shield. They lug him, hissing, back up the lane to some unthinkable destination.

From *The Saturday Epic* by Hugh C. Rae

Glasgow 5 March 1971

With a ragged diamond
of shattered plate-glass
a young man and his girl
are falling backwards into a shop-window.
The young man's face
is bristling with fragments of glass
and the girl's leg has caught
on the broken window
and spurts arterial blood
over her wet-look white coat.
Their arms are starfished out
braced for impact,
their faces show surprise, shock,
and the beginning of pain.

The two youths who have pushed them
are about to complete the operation
reaching into the window
to loot what they can smartly.
Their faces show no expression.
It is a sharp clear night
in Sauchiehall Street.
In the background two drivers
keep their eyes on the road.

Edwin Morgan

Death of a Cafe

Three lanky hairy youths in donkey-jackets and tight trousers came in hipswaying as if Enrico's cafe was a saloon in a Western and they were tough hombres on the trail who had just hitched their horses to the rail outside.

'Lucky strike,' said the first.

His mates loitered behind Granny Lyons.

'Excusa-me,' said Enrico to Granny Lyons.

He attended to his strange customers. Eyebrows raised, eyes questioning.

'Lucky strike,' repeated the gunless cowboy.

Enrico's eyebrows came down to a puzzled frown. The cowboy tried again.

'Day ye sell Lucky Strike?'

'Ah!' said Enrico. 'American cigarettes. Some I have.'

He turned to the shelves.

'But not Lucky Strike. Chesterfield, Stuyvesant. And I have—'

Even as he began naming the brands he had in stock he had a dim feeling he was being silly. But he was that bit slow. One of the cowboys behind Granny Lyons charged at her like a football-player giving away a penalty. She tottered and teetered, lost her balance and fell. Her handbag remained on the counter. The other cowboy snatched it. The one that had asked for Lucky Strike knocked over a jar of hardboiled sweets and threw a tray of Wrigley's PK at Enrico's face. In a split second the three bandits ran out together.

Granny Lyons clawed at the counter and got back on her feet. Enrico raced out of his shop like a whippet. Granny Lyons wept and trembled.

'Oh, not again,' she whimpered. 'Not again.'

Enrico came back, a lot slower than he had gone out.

'Hopeless,' he lamented, pulling his hair. 'They dive in a close round the corner. I see them. By the time I get there, gone. Up the stairs, across the back-court, through another close? Who knows?'

'Oh well, it might have been worse,' said Granny Lyons.

Her hands quivered as she tidied her grey hairs and smoothed her coat and skirt. She felt handless without her handbag. The loss diminished her.

Enrico saw how she felt. He wept in vexation.

'It's as well I was here,' she comforted him. 'Or it might have been the till they tried. And God knows what they might have done to you if you'd been alone. Lucky it was only me. They didn't get much. My God, let them ask for it if they're that hard-up and I'll give them it.'

'I give in,' said Enrico.

He wiped his brimming brown eyes with the cuff of his white jacket.

It may have been the saying of it made him think of surrender, or he may only have been saying what he wouldn't admit before. But from that day he lost heart. He was ashamed of his shop. He hadn't the spirit to fight its invaders any longer. He was sick of non-paying customers, bullies and rioters. The booths where he had hoped to encourage a cafe-society of young people discussing politics and literature and foreign affairs were an offence to the eye. The wood-work was hacked and scratched, the walls were defaced with the sprawling initials of his patrons, the floor was fouled with discarded wads of chewing-gum. The local lads and lasses had annexed his shop as a colony for revelry and disorder. They quarrelled at the drop of a joke and fights over nothing happened every night in the week. Enrico was always expecting to see blood shed but it never quite came to that.

In an attempt to get some peace and quiet he put the juke-box out of commission. Too often it caused a fight between rival fans of different singers. But without it the boys and girls made their own noise, and that was worse.

He made a last effort to get control. One wild night some laughing youths tested the solidity of the table in the back booth by kicking it from underneath and then jumping on it from the bench. They threw crisps across the cafe and poured coke into the coffees of the mixed company in the next booth. There was a lot of recrimination, and a threat and a challenge were heard. The uproar led to some punching and wrestling and somebody got up from the floor with a knife in his hand and a nasty look in his eyes. The girls screamed, some in terror, some in delight. Enrico phoned for the police.

By the time two policemen arrived the cafe was empty except for Gerald Provan sitting in the middle booth with Poggy, having a quiet conversation with Wilma and Jennifer. Gerald wasn't intimidated by a phone-call. He knew Enrico knew what would happen if he named anybody.

Enrico told the policemen about the disturbance. He said the culprits had run away as soon as they heard him phone from the back-shop. He didn't know any of them. The boy who had drawn a knife? He had never seen him before. They were all strangers. Gerald sat back listening, his face solemn and sympathetic.

'It's a shame, Mr Ianello, so it is,' he said.

The two policemen gave Gerald and his company a hard look but said nothing. They went away. Enrico felt very foolish. After midnight his windows were smashed. For a week after that he had nuisance-calls, sometimes at one and two in the morning. The various speakers threatened him and his wife and family. One call particularly alarmed him.

'Do that again,' said the voice in the earpiece, 'and I'll cut your throat from ear to ear.'

And then the speaker laughed at him.

He was going over some bills and his bank statement one night after the shop was closed. His flat above the cafe was quiet, his wife and two children were asleep. Into the hush there moved a vague scuffling and a susurrus of hostile voices. He looked up from his counting and listened. He was always frightened until he located and interpreted what he was hearing. It was youths quarrelling in the street. He waited for them to pass. They didn't. Then his shop-door was battered and young voices were raised, calling him. He could have thought his house was on fire, the way they were carrying on. He tiptoed downstairs and stood behind the door to the street. It was double-leaved, made of stout wood, double-locked and double-bolted. He felt safe enough. They would need an axe to break in. He heard his name called again.

'En-RI-co I-a-NEL-lo!'

'Who are you?' he asked, close to the wood.

There was no answer.

Upstairs, his wife and family wakened and listened, puzzled.

'What do you want?' Enrico shouted through the wood.

He tried to sound tough and abrupt, a dangerous man to annoy.

'You,' said a bass voice, no less terrifying because it was disguised.

The appalling monosyllable was followed by a crescendo of insane screeching and hysterical laughter, male and female. Enrico trembled in the dark. The assault on the door was renewed. He half expected it to come in, so fierce was the hammering and kicking. It didn't. But while he waited for signs of it cracking and shouted to his wife to phone the police, one of his windows had a brick through it. He pulled his hair and cursed when he heard the glass shatter. His wife screamed on her way to the phone. Then there was silence.

That was when he gave in. He made his surrender public and got his name in the papers. He had a nephew Gino who was a football-reporter on the local evening paper, and Gino put a colleague in the news-department on to it. Enrico's rambling account of his grievances was printed in an edited version.

'I cannot continue to live in this city. I must think of the safety of my wife and children. This has been building up. These people have made my life a misery with threats of violence over the phone. They have made my shop a shambles. I tried to give them service. They do not seem to want it. I am not saying where I will go. They said they will follow me if they find out.'

He went away, and nobody ever knew where, except Granny Lyons. She missed him, but she told him to go. He tried to sell his shop with the flat above it but nobody wanted that kind of shop and house in that kind of district. The abandoned cafe became a derelict site where children played, and all the metal fittings and lead guttering were stripped by nocturnal raiders.

From *Mr Alfred MA* by George Friel

Keystone Cop

I knew a policeman once
Though out of uniform and
Out of role he was still
My polisman my fuzzy wuzzy
My piglet my bobby my
Own fair cop.
That's how it was therefore
I'm prejudiced anti-establishment
(The many) and
Pro polis
(The one).

It was the fuzz after all who
Placated the fisherman
In the Chinese Restaurant
Shouting it was shrimp
Not prawn curry;
He should know he said
As he spat out mouthfuls of
Chewed pink proof.

It was the fuzz who
Waltzed around a lamp-post
In the street late for loneliness
Pretending it was Raquel Welsh;
Who whistled at girls from his box
And pretended he didn't;
Who tripped over a drunk in the dark
And pretended he hadn't.

It was the fuzz who
Collected a lost dog and
Took it home, who
Propped up the old unsteady man
And held him with kind hands
As his tears fell down
Plop onto the pavement,
Who came after the Sudden Death
To take away Jessie's Charlie
(He was sick all weekend and the
Doctor came just too late)
To a stone-cold mortuary.

That's how it was
So none of your proletariat games
Don't try to kick his teeth in
Don't call him nasty names;
My fuzzy wuzzy my polisman
My law and order custodian
My piglet my bobby my bluebottle
My own fair cop.

Catherine Lucy Czerkawska

Corporal Punishment

The teachers in Collinsburn used corporal punishment. Every time somebody wrote to the papers about the wrongness of it they laughed in the staffroom and agreed about the rightness of it. An English immigrant's letter complaining about the place of the tawse in Scottish education set them off again.

'The way these folk talk,' said Mr Brown, Deputy Head and Principal Teacher of English, 'you'd think we spent our whole day belting defenceless weans.'

'You give some pest one of the strap to keep him in line,' said Mr Campbell, Principal Teacher of Mathematics, 'and they call it corporal punishment.'

'Then in the next sentence it becomes flogging,' said the Principal Teacher of Modern Languages, Mr Kerr.

He read aloud from the offensive letter.

'Hyperbole,' said Mr Brown.

'They think we're a shower of bloody sadists,' said Mr Dale, the youngest member of staff. 'They've no idea.'

'The strap is only a convention here,' said Mr Campbell. 'Up to second year anyway. You don't need it much after that. But if you abolished it altogether you'd raise more problems than you solved.'

'It's like the language of a country,' said Mr Alfred from his lonely corner. 'You've got to speak it to be understood.'

His colleagues hushed and looked at him. He seldom opened his mouth during their discussions. He seemed to think himself above them. They were surprised to hear his voice.

Mr Alfred acknowledged their attention by taking his cigarette out of his mouth. He went on chattily as if he was giving a reminiscent talk on the Light Programme.

'I remember one school I worked in. There was a young Latin teacher next door to me. Very young he was. He wouldn't use the strap he told me. He thought the language of the strap was a barbaric language. He would speak to the natives in his own civilised tongue. He would be all sweetness and light like Matthew Arnold.'

'Hear, hear!' cried Mr Dale.

'Bloody fool,' muttered Mr Brown.

Mr Alfred smiled agreeably to them both and continued his talk.

'But when the natives found he refused to speak their language their pride was hurt. They felt he was insulting their tribal customs. They regarded him as a mad foreigner. They sniped at him till they saw it was safe to make an open attack. Within a week they were making his life hell on earth.'

'Boys can be cruel to a weak teacher,' said Mr Campbell.

'He was baited and barbed,' said Mr Alfred.

'By defenceless children,' said Mr Brown.

'Until he broke under the torture,' said Mr Alfred.

'Once they think you're soft they've no mercy,' said Mr Kerr.

'He went berserk one day,' said Mr Alfred. 'He thrashed a boy across the legs and buttocks and shoulders with the very strap he had wanted to put into a museum.'

'Probably the least troublesome boy,' said Mr Campbell.

'It usually is,' said Mr Kerr.

'It was,' said Mr Alfred. 'I heard the row. I heard the boy run screaming from the room as if the devil were after him. I nipped out in time to catch him in the corridor and managed to pacify him. I took him to the toilets and had him wash his face and calm down. I like to think I stopped what could have been a serious complaint from the parent.'

'It would never have happened if he had used the strap just once the day he arrived,' said Mr Campbell.

'Precisely my point,' said Mr Alfred.

'I always let a new class see I've got a strap and let them know I'll use it,' said Mr Dale. 'After that I've no bother. If you show the flag you don't need to fire the guns.'

'And you know,' said Mr Alfred, 'the tawse of the Scotch dominie is never wielded like the Jesuit's pandybat that distressed the young

Stephen Dedalus. Not that the pandybat did Joyce any harm. It gave him material. It showed him what life is like. These letterwriters would have us deceive the boys by pretending they'll never be punished later on in life when they do something wrong. And even if a boy is strapped unjustly it isn't fatal. Life is full of minor injustices. A boy should learn as much while he's still at school, and learn to take it without whining. I admire the heroes of history who fought against social injustice, but one of the strap given in error or loss of patience is hardly a wrong on that scale.'

He put his cigarette back in his mouth and withdrew from the discussion. He thought he had said all that needed saying about corporal punishment.

'The way I see it,' said Mr Campbell, 'the strap is our symbol of authority within a recognised code. The boys know what to expect and we can get on with the job.'

'You must have something to maintain discipline,' said Mr Kerr. 'Some quick sanction. Even if you never use it.'

'No discipline, no learning,' said Mr Brown.

'But tell me this,' said Mr Dale. 'What do you do if a boy refuses to take the strap?'

'Only a stupid teacher would create a situation where that would happen,' said Mr Campbell.

'But supposing,' said Mr Dale.

'It's a case for the headmaster then,' said Mr Brown.

'I've never met many cases of a boy refusing the strap,' said Mr Campbell. 'And those I have, they all came to nothing. The boy had to submit in the end and apologise. Then of course once he gets a public apology the teacher acts the big man. He won't condescend to strap the boy. The rebel ends up looking a bit of an ass.'

'Well, I'm deputy-boss here,' said Mr Brown, 'and I've never had any boy refuse the strap. We don't seem to get that kind of stupid defiance.'

From *Mr Alfred MA* by George Friel

Attending a Football Match

It sneaked past watchful attendants,
warned to be on the look-out for It
among the male together-noise.
White faces on dark clothes
cohered, shading the terracing
to the anonymous crouch of a crowd.

The ninepin players trotted in.
Kinetic muscles moved in play,
and Matt, John, Jock and Wullie
bounced on their excitement's cheers.

But as the ball began to score
goals spent in a stretched net,
It wedged Itself between the roars
of the single-backed, two-minded thing,
for *game*, insinuated *name*,
a syllableless, faceless feeling
of nothing words identified.

Then suddenly It broke loose—
bottles hit fists and screams.
Police tore the crown apart
to get It. It eluded them.

From spectators crushed by shock,
a swearing vanful of louts,
the cut-up quiet in hospitals,
no real evidence could be taken.
Charges were, of course preferred—
disorderly conduct, obstructing the police—
but no one found out what It came from
or whose It is, or where It was.

Maurice Lindsay

NOTES

'Whit Kinna Fight is This?': Alex Hamilton's short story, 'Gallus, did you say?' (*Three Glasgow Writers*, Molendinar Press), which is written in Glasgow dialect, describes how a bully is beaten by an underdog, while Chapter 9 of George Friel's *The Boy who Wanted Peace* (Calder) describes the opposite situation.

The well-known fight sequence in Keith Waterhouse's novel, *There is a Happy Land* (Penguin), has some features in common with 'Whit Kinna Fight is This?'

'The Coming of the Wee Malkies': possible companion pieces are Maurice Lindsay's 'Glasgow Nocturne' (*This Business of Living*, Akros) and Duncan Glen's 'Glasgow Problems' *(Follow! Follow!*, Akros).

Thom Gunn's poems 'On the Move' and 'Black Jackets' (both in *Poetry 1900 to 1965*, edited by MacBeth, Longman) convey the restless search for excitement and identity often characteristic of teenage gang members.

'The Tiny Rastus': Hugh C. Rae's *The Saturday Epic* (Blond) is a frank treatment of Glasgow teenage gang warfare. The same writer's *Night Pillow* (Blond) also deals with violence in a Glasgow setting. A relevant short story is Alan Spence's 'Brilliant' *(Its Colours they are Fine*, Collins).

James Patrick's *A Glasgow Gang Observed* (Eyre Methuen), a study of the pathology of teenage gang life in Glasgow, is an exceptionally vivid work of sociology, which is recommended. The author 'joined' a Glasgow gang for several months as a 'participant observer' and so his book is unusually detailed and authentic. An interesting discussion of possible solutions to the problem of violent teenage gangs is included.

'Glasgow 5 March 1971': this is one of Edwin Morgan's instamatic poems. These are usually derived from press reports and aim to record events in an almost 'photographic' manner. A collection of *Instamatic Poems* appeared in 1972 (Ian McKelvie, London). Recommended instamatic poems are 'Glasgow November 1971' and 'Fallin Stirlingshire October 1970'. Those set in Glasgow usually depict moments of violence.

It should be remarked that the selection of Edwin Morgan's poetry in this anthology does not do justice to his wide range of themes and techniques. Quite apart from his 'conventional' and 'Glasgow' poems, Morgan is a leading concrete poet and a masterly translator.

'Death of a Cafe': George Friel's masterpiece, *Mr Alfred MA* (Calder & Boyars), is a searching examination of the violence and anarchy underlying modern urban life. The hero, a middle-aged schoolteacher, moves through a terrifying world of graffiti, vandalism, defiance of authority and gang-warfare, culminating in the nightmarish vision of 'The Writing on the Wall' (Chapters 29 and 30), which was Friel's original title for the novel.

13

THE ORANGE AND THE GREEN

Colours

I spent that Christmas in hospital. I remember lying there in the dim ward, paper decorations on the ceiling, and an older boy calling out to me from the next bed. He asked if I was a Protestant or a Catholic. I didn't know. I had never heard the words before. He laughed at that, thought I was stupid. Then he asked if I supported Rangers or Celtic. 'Rangers,' I said, thinking of the little castle on the roof of Ibrox stadium. 'Well then,' he said. 'Ye must be a Protestant. That's OK.'

When I got home I asked my parents about Protestants and Catholics, but they weren't able to explain, in any way I could understand, just what the words meant, or what the difference was between them.

*　　*　　*

The earliest holiday I remember was for the Coronation. Every child received a tin of sweets with the Queen's portrait on the lid. I went with my mother to visit my aunt, one of the first people in the area, perhaps in the whole of Glasgow, to have a television set. The set was tiny, with a nine-inch screen, and the house was full of neighbours, crowding round to watch. Afterwards, in the back court, somebody gave a party for all the local children, with crisps and ice-lollies and paper hats, party-games and songs and jokes. It was a great, great day. God save the Queen.

The Queen was a Protestant. My uncle had told me that. My uncle was in the Orange Lodge, and had undertaken my education in such matters. He and my father had already taken me to see Rangers play at Ibrox. I had felt the elation at their victory, the depression at their defeat; I had been initiated. Emotionally now I could feel the connections; the Queen and the Union Jack, being a Protestant and following Rangers; it was all noble and good, all part of some glorious heritage that was mine. And the opposite of all this was Catholic, was darkness, was bad and in some way a threat.

I remember one day my uncle teaching me about colours. I was wearing a blue jersey and he said it was good, was a fine colour.

How about orange, I asked, was that a good colour? The best, he said.

Purple? That was good too.

Red was fine.

Black and white were OK, not good, not bad.

But green was bad. The worst.

I thought of the green park where we went on those summer evenings, and how beautiful it was. But no. It was the colour of Celtic, of the Catholics. They had made it their own, had made it bad.

I was eating further of the tree of knowledge.

My uncle said I was growing into a good Protestant. He said when I was a little older he would get me into the Juvenile Orange Lodge. The thought excited me.

I could march in a parade, perhaps even learn to play flute or drum in a band. But my mother said no. They were all mad she said, just making people hate each other all the more, and for nothing.

Reality was growing more complex and confusing. Nothing, it seemed, was clear cut.

From *Boom Baby* by Alan Spence

A Billy or a Dan

The Glasgow gangs never made any money for anybody. They existed for fun. Gangs' bosses never graduated to Cadillacs or even Austin Sevens, far less villas on the coast and political pull. They just wanted a fight. They started poor and they finished poor and they stayed poor in between.

One of their best excuses for fighting was religion. The Billy Boys took their name from the remote Protestant gentleman King William of Orange and the Sally Boys took theirs from Salamanca Street, where the founders lived. But I never yet saw a Billy Boy or a Sally Boy to identify, though my father once had to nip up a close smartly to escape being mixed up in a brawl and maybe arrested since he was small-built and not likely to give the police trouble.

It's odd that not only Glasgow's Catholics but Glasgow's militant Protestants take their aggressive inspiration from Ireland, for Ulster is the home of the Orangemen and a place given to good rousing religious bigotry just as Eire is the fount of the Fenians. Not that I would deprive Glasgow of any of the credit for Billy and Sally. Long afterwards, when I had read Sean O'Casey and heard about the 1916 Rising and once even met face to face the late Jim Larkin, senior—the titanic Irish patriot who came to Liverpool and told the authorities candidly that the purpose of his visit was to overthrow the British Government—these years later, I acquired a kind of astonished liking for the Fenians, astonished because such a thing denied the very principles of my childhood. And even before that I had taken a kind of scunner at the Orangemen, and not on religious grounds at all. It was the music of an Orangemen's band that drove me away.

It must have been the day of an Orange Walk—'The Twelfth of July, the Papes'll die'—the formidable anniversary rally of the Orangemen when they gather from all airts to spend a day dedicating themselves to the downfall of Rome and the restocking of their fervour. It's a poor Lodge that doesn't have a band.

This one marched up Cubie Street on the way to some railway station to join the rally, and I caught the words 'Orange Walk' from passers-by with a strain of apprehension in them that infected me too. If they were Orangemen, then naturally I was on their side, but the way people said it suggested that they might decide to hit somebody, and how would they know I wasn't a Catholic? But they didn't hit anybody. They just marched up Cubie Street, wearing fancy blue sashes over their good suits and playing the strangest things—flutes. Now there's nothing wrong with a good flute, but a chorus of flutes and nothing but flutes has a surprising quality, like a first acquaintance with those twenty-four-note Oriental scales, and the oddity of it combined with the tangible unease in the people listening, put me off;

and to tell the truth, I thought that in spite of the blue embroidered sashes they looked a bit scruffy, and pretty silly too.

The reason for the flutes, I imagine, is only partly historical and partly because a flute is cheaper than a trumpet, and Glaswegians of any denomination were not too rich. But who would ever expect a thing like a flute to be a recognised religious symbol? One of the oldest Glasgow jokes is about a new Irish immigrant who went looking for work to a Glasgow Corporation building foreman, who he had been warned was Irish.

'Hallo,' he said, making the sign of the cross, 'have ye ony jobs, I don't suppose?'

'Aye,' said the foreman, imitating a flute player, 'start on Monday, I don't think.'

So on the twelfth of July, although at any other time we played with the Catholics of the neighbourhood and never noticed it, we would be exclusively Protestant, and always ready for the challenge from any other wandering gang—

'A Billy or a Dan or an auld tin can?' The wrong answer might mean a stand-up fight and personally, I always said an auld tin can because there was no known procedure for that. I suppose it meant a religious nothing, so it was prophetic. Still today, the day of the Orange Walk produces its little spots of trouble in Glasgow, for there's nothing like religious zeal to put a man in the mood for a fight, and, not to shilly-shally about it, after the Walk some of the boys are not above taking a dram.

And then there are the songs to go with that flute music. Because people in Glasgow are always singing or dancing or both, as you can find in any side street in the slums any dry day of the year. Whether I was an auld tin can or not I could sing the fighting Orange songs with the best.

From *Dancing in the Streets* by Clifford Hanley

The Good Thief

heh jimmy
yawright ih
stull wayiz urryi
ih

heh jimmy
ma right insane yirra pape
ma right insane yirwanny uz jimmy
see it nyir eyes
wanny uz

heh

heh jimmy
lookslik wirgonny miss thi gemm
gonny miss thi GEMM jimmy
nearly three a cloke thinoo

dork init
good jobe theyve gote thi lights

Tom Leonard

King Billy

Grey over Riddrie the clouds piled up,
dragged their rain through the cemetery trees.
The gates shone cold. Wind rose
flaring the hissing leaves, the branches
swung, heavy, across the lamps.
Gravestones huddled in drizzling shadow,
flickering streetlight scanned the requiescats,
a name and an urn, a date, a dove
picked out, lost, half regained.
What is this dripping wreath, blown from its grave
red, white, blue, and gold
'To Our Leader of Thirty Years Ago'?

Bareheaded, in dark suits, with flutes
and drums, they brought him here, in procession
seriously, King Billy of Bridgeton, dead,
from Bridgeton Cross: a memory of violence,
brooding days of empty bellies,
billiard smoke and a sour pint,
boots or fists, famous sherrickings,
the word, the scuffle, the flash, the shout,
bloody crumpling in the close,
bricks for papish windows, get
the Conks next time, the Conks ambush
the Billy Boys, the Billy Boys the Conks till
Sillitoe scuffs the razors down the stank—
No, but it isn't the violence they remember
but the legend of a violent man
born poor, gang-leader in the bad times
of idleness and boredom, lost in better days,
a bouncer in a betting club,
a quiet man at last, dying
alone in Bridgeton in a box bed.

So a thousand people stopped the traffic
for the hearse of a folk hero and the flutes
threw 'Onward Christian Soldiers' to the winds
from unironic lips, the mourners kept
in step, and there were some who wept.

Go from the grave. The shrill flutes
are silent, the march dispersed.
Deplore what is to be deplored,
and then find out the rest.

Edwin Morgan

A People Once United

In this extract from 'The Sash' by Hector MacMillan, a modern play set in Glasgow, Una, a young Catholic woman from Northern Ireland, talks about the troubles there with Cameron, a young Glasgow Protestant. Una and her sister have been victims of a bombing incident.

CAMERON: ...Was it true what she said, then?

UNA: Who?

CAMERON: Your...Aunty Bridget. Aboot your sister.

UNA (*looks away into the past*): She lost an eye too...and a big bit of her face. (*Cameron is troubled*)...But they say her hearin'll be restored.

CAMERON (*incredulous*): And you were there?

UNA (*apparently unemotional, though the fingers continually make small nervous movements*): We were in this shop. I went outside again, t'take another look at a pram in the winda. She was buyin it for me...I was stannin there, tryin t'make up me mind about the colour, when this car beside me went off... (*Turns to him*) Explosions are funny things. Did you know that? (*He can only shake his head*) It's not always them that's nearest gets the worst...M'sister was inside, and a big bit a the winda near cut'r in half. (*Cuts across the top of her thighs. It seems oddly hard, callous*) B'here...I had nuthin wrong but shock... (*remembers*) Oh an for a time my hearin was away too.

CAMERON: Was this recent?

UNA: Five weeks, come Thursda...They said only I was an awful strong girl, I woulda lost the baby all together.

CAMERON: ...Funny how things work oot.

UNA: Ay. Funny.

CAMERON: You an me, sittin here noo.

UNA: Scotch Prodisants in Ulster. Ulster Catholics in Scotland.

CAMERON: Yeah. (*Sardonically*) Right bloody mix-up.

UNA (*nods*): Right bloody.

She looks away out into the past again. Silent so long that Cameron begins to wonder why she has broken off the conversation. Then she begins to sing, and all nervousness slips away.

(*Quietly, slowly, freely*)

> Last night in dreams I met the men
> Known only by the date,
> The men who stood United,
> The Men of Ninety-eight
> And through the sleep I thought I heard
> A soft and bitter cry,
> 'Twas not for you we lived and fought,
> Nor yet for you did die,
> For you are Orangemen—or Green;
> You are Orangemen—or Green.
> A People once United
> Are Orange, now—or Green.'

CAMERON (*puzzled by Una, and the song*): You're no a real Catholic. Staunch.... Are you?

UNA (*wry*): Your father would say yes,... and me Aunt would disagree!

CAMERON: But Ah mean d'you believe in Heaven, Purgatory, an aw that?

UNA (*bitterly*): I know where there's a Hell...

He understands that.

(*Shakes her head*) The writins a James Connolly have always been more the family bible. An the priests were never too fond a that.

CAMERON (*it seems to ring a faint bell*): *James* Connolly?

UNA: Commandit the forces a rebellion at the Easter Risin.

CAMERON (*remembers*): Oh ay... (*Flat*) Dublin.

UNA: The General Post Office.

CAMERON: Were they no aw kill't?

UNA (*nods, a hard bitterness showing*): An afterwards, they sat Connolly, woundit, in a chair. They strapped him into it, upright, so that your British soldiers could have a decent-size target!

CAMERON (*mixed feelings about that*): ... Well,... t'them, Ah suppose he wis a traitor.

UNA (*realising it for the first time*): ... I suppose, technically, he *wasn't* Irish.

CAMERON: Wasnae?

UNA: ... (*looks over at him*) He was... Scotch.

CAMERON (*sharp*): You're at the kiddin!

UNA: Born, bred, an educatit in Edinburgh.

CAMERON: Well even so!

UNA: Worked for the Corporation there.

CAMERON: That doesnae make'm Sco'ish! Look at the Pakistanis in Glesca! (*She has heard it all before*) Listen, wi a name like Connolly, ... he'd be a Catholic. Right?

UNA: He was a socialist. An for that, he was continually persecutit (*quietly bitter*) b'the Holy Roman Church!

CAMERON (*insistent*): He still went t'Dublin!

UNA (*slightly weary now*): He went t'many places.

CAMERON: Including Dublin?

UNA: He helped t'organise the workers in America.

CAMERON: But finished up in Dublin!

UNA (*nods, quite weary*): Foundit the Irish Citizen Army there, t'protect the dockers.

CAMERON (*almost relieved*): Ay. That's it. (*Rises*) That's whit it aye boils doon tae. (*Going to King Billy's portrait*)

UNA: What?

CAMERON: Whit you're born. (*Bitterly*) A Billy, ... or a Dan!

UNA: ... Not always ...

Takes up the song again—not to tell Cameron anything—for herself.

> (*Softly*) Twas Henry Joy McCracken
> The Ulstermen brought forth,
> And a Croppy priest led Wexford out
> To join the gallant North.
> Ay North and South, United were
> The year of Ninety-eight,
> With liberty their only bond,
> Twas brotherhood,—not hate,
> But now we're Orangemen—or Green,
> We are Orangemen, or Green,
> What were United Irishmen
> Are Orange now, ... or Green

(*Very softly, poetically, looking back into the past to see—and know—the people involved*) ... The Unitit Irishmen, and the Unitit Scotsmen, they worked together at that time; ... for a free Ireland; a free Scotland; and even for an England (*softer still*) free from that drive for domination that has always diminished her.

CAMERON (*had never thought about it before*): ... Ah suppose we are quite close.

UNA (*immediately back to the present; matter-of-fact*): Fourteen mile.

CAMERON: Naw, Ah wasnae meanin the dista- ... fourteen mile? (*She nods*) Between Sco'lan and Irelan?

UNA: At the nearest.

CAMERON: Christ it's three times that f' Glasgow t'Edinburgh!

UNA: We were all the one Gaelic-speakin people annyway ... A thousan years, an more, of comin-an-goin, (*shrugs*) mixin together.

193

CAMERON (*swithers about offering whisky*): D'you use this stuff?

UNA (*nods, half-smile*): But not at the moment.

CAMERON: Make it an addict?

UNA (*mainly to herself*): We're bound t'make it an addict t'somethin. Maybe whisky would be less damagin than prejudice.

He studies the bottle a moment.

CAMERON: Your health.

There might have been the suggestion of bitter amusement from Una as he drinks.

It is funny how things work oot.

UNA: Ay... You an me. Your father. Bridget.

CAMERON: Whit aboot your faither?

UNA: ...(*looks away*) He's in the place they used t'call,... Long Kesh.

CAMERON (*sharp*): A Terrorist?

UNA: T'some.

CAMERON: Aw you cannae go along wi that noo! No eftir whit's happened t'you an your sister!

UNA (*flaring*): Second-class citizens, with first-class entitlement?

CAMERON: Even so!

UNA (*rises abruptly*): Dominatit b'foreign troops?

CAMERON (*rises from settee, away from her*): S'nae excuse for the things that've been done!

UNA: Denied the human rights that youse have here?

CAMERON: There's other ways t'change things!

UNA (*loud, hard, and elemental*): O christ, an this world'll always see you get justice! (*Before he can interrupt*) Just so long as you first catch its attention with a big-enough bloody bang!

From *The Sash* by Hector MacMillan

NOTES

Antagonism between Catholic and Protestant in the west of Scotland is not the explicit theme of any recent major novel, but it is a significant element in almost all autobiographies by writers from the area.

The Greenock television dramatist, Peter McDougall, has written several plays on the theme, notably *Just Another Saturday* about an adolescent's participation in a Glasgow 'Orange Walk'.

'Colours' delineates the cultivation of prejudice in the young in a simple devastating way.

The title story of Alan Spence's short story collection, *Its Colour they are Fine* (Collins), is an acute analysis of the insecurity which underlies prejudice.

'The Good Thief': this remarkable little poem manages to synthesize a cluster of key elements in the west of Scotland male experience: religion, football, drink, the search for identity and (lurking in the background) incipient violence.

In his *Poems* (O'Brien, Dublin) Tom Leonard included the following transcription into Standard English and note:

THE GOOD THIEF: Hey Jimmy! Are you allright, eh? Still with us, are you? Eh? Hey Jimmy! Am I right in saying you're a Pape? Am I right in saying you're one of us, Jimmy? (One can) see it in your eyes—one of us. Hey! Hey Jimmy! (It) looks like we're going to miss the game. Going to miss the GAME Jimmy! (It's) nearly three o'clock the now (just now). Dark, isn't it? Good job they've got the lights (i.e. floodlights).

N.B. The author was brought up to believe that Christ died on the cross promptly at 3 p.m. on Good Friday. 3 p.m. is also usually the time at which football matches start. In Glasgow, Catholics generally support Glasgow Celtic, while Protestants usually support Glasgow Rangers. The Good Thief is therefore assumed to be a Celtic supporter, who addresses Christ shortly before 3 o'clock, as darkness descends on the earth. The reason for assuming that the Good Thief was a Celtic supporter is because Christ said to him, 'This night thou shalt be with me in Paradise'—and 'Paradise' is the nickname for Celtic's football ground.

Billy Connolly's famous monologue 'The Crucifixion' (from *Solo Concert*, Transatlantic Records) has some associations with 'The Good Thief' in method and tone.

'King Billy' succeeds in being both sociological and compassionate.

'A People Once United': Hector MacMillan's play, *The Sash* (Molendinar Press), from which this extract is taken, had a popular, but, it must be remarked, ambivalent success in Glasgow, because the charisma of Andrew Keir in the leading part of a Protestant bigot, rather worked against the ultimate intention of the text, which was to expose the futility of prejudice.

14

ROMANCE

Genuine Ghastly First Love

Mixed schools are a mixed blessing. In an ideal situation they ought to mean that boys and girls grow up in a simple comradely atmosphere and pay more attention to their work than they otherwise might. But we were only human and the teenage years were fraught with far more distractions than one could possibly experience at single-sex schools. Sex, after all, is a pretty distracting thing normally, and even more so in an academic desert. (I suppose that's why it's such a popular university pastime.) We were not immune. One needs some relief from 'O' Levels. Also we, the girls, felt separate, forced into extremes of femininity by the very presence of boys, and not perhaps as free in our academic choices as we might have been. I expect that the same applied to the boys. In some subjects, e.g. Domestic Science or Woodwork, the school inhibited us. But then most of us had never dreamed that girls could do such patently masculine work. Neither we nor our parents queried the status quo and often we simply inhibited ourselves. Equality was only a vague idea filtering through. I suspect that even now it has little support in most Scottish secondary schools. I remember the son of a friend being laughed to scorn for his desire to learn cookery instead of technical drawing. In many ways I was lucky. As an only child I had fulfilled the functions of both a son and a daughter and consequently I was ready to tackle most things. As it turned out my natural favourites were the 'feminine' Arts subjects but I certainly passed my pre-adolescent years as a tomboy who swarmed up walls and took to the woods occasionally wearing a Davy Crockett hat and carrying a rifle.

In our early teenage it was not our classmates who appealed to us: not the 'clever' boys who seemed to be so emotionally and physically immature. But the C classes with their cave-man appeal attracted us enormously. Many of them were big tough boys, raring to get away from school and into a job. They scorned uniform and slouched around in jeans. Their hands were horny from frequent strappings and they were afraid of nobody. Often their home backgrounds were unhappy; most of them had been deprived of books, if nothing else.

In my fourth year I was a prefect. Leon was a big, blue-eyed, black-haired Irish-Scots ruffian, who led a gang of boys on forays every lunchtime. It was a primitive and enchanting game. They pestered us, using all possible strategies to get into the school building. We—the girls—threw them out with maddening insistence. But they were bigger and stronger than us. The encounters frequently erupted into delicious physical contact with just the right threat of violence. Leon never let things get out of hand. Nobody got hurt. Like so many of those boys he was a clever troublemaker who infuriated his male teachers and left them frustrated and angry. But there was no real malice in him and memories of him live on to substantiate the female fantasy of the rough diamond. Or perhaps it's just that no judgement of anyone can ever be final; no one can ever see the whole picture.

Later, we became more sophisticated in our tastes, or so we thought: went to parties where we drank cheap wine and played Postman's Knock, fixing the numbers, giving and receiving chaste, wet passionless kisses outside the door, or danced smoochily to Jim Reeves and the Beatles. The Beatles pursued us through our teens. John Lennon was my great idol. I sat through *A Hard Day's Night* and *Help* repeatedly; changed my allegiance from John to Ringo and knew all the words of all the songs, a fact which now severely dates both myself and my friends.

The parties were a disappointment. The gap between fantasy and reality was too wide for me really to enjoy myself and like the Postman's Knock kisses, there was always that inexplicable feeling of let-down afterwards. Sex was all-pervasive at that time, although we did not admit it blatantly. We felt a certain amount of guilt. We were at the awkward age; certainly not honest enough to say, as one friend later so ruefully remarked, 'You know, almost all my thoughts are dirty.'

I had a crush on a tall blond boy who wore a long fringe, cuban-heeled boots and black-rimmed spectacles, following the fashion of the time. He was clever and popular and he never gave me a second glance. But then I hardly expected it. I fell in love—genuine, ghastly, first love—a little later with the boy who was to marry one of my best friends. It was my one and only experience of love at first sight and it was utterly shattering. The crisis came several months later, at the big event of the year—the senior dance.

We talked about those dances for weeks beforehand, planning dresses and make-up; speculating as to who liked whom. One month before, the P.T. fiends donned their dancing shoes, herded us into the gym, forced the reluctant boys to take random partners, more often than not much taller than themselves, and tried to teach us civilised dances, like foxtrots and waltzes and the Gay Gordons. Eightsome Reels were the worst and always ended in utter chaos with boys setting gingerly to other boys and Mr Blank in his tracksuit bellowing directions and manipulating Jimmy Shand on the rickety gramophone.

At that particular dance all those first and worst agonies of unrequited love seemed to be focused on me. I felt like the only soul left on earth with everyone else in paradise. In the grubby, slogan-scrawled station waiting-room on the way home, the blackness in my head alarmed me. 'Do you know,' said one of the boys, looking at the back-to-front reflections on the window of the train, 'that Troon is Noort, backwards.' I wondered how I could even hear anyone talking through all the misery.

Later, we went to other, less innocent dances at the crumbling Pavilion, down by the seashore and I was consoled by a gentle brush salesman with a wolfish face—another ruffian—who kissed me tenderly in the rain. Nothing had ever felt so good. He wanted to take me home in his big green van but I wouldn't let him. I was sixteen and scared as much of myself as of him. It was all touch and then go as far as most of us were concerned.

From *A Sheltered Wilderness* by Catherine Lucy Czerkawska

Lady of Shalott

Fifteen or younger
she moons in the mirror.
Penny for your thoughts,
Lady of Shalott.
In her bedroom tower
with mother and father

watching T.V. downstairs,
she moons in the mirror
and swears she will never
lead a bloody boring life like theirs.

Maybe you'll find True Romance
at the youth club dance,
Lady of Shalott.

She paints her nails scarlet,
she moons in the mirror.
Ingenue or harlot?
The mirror is misted,
every mirror image twisted.
Like Real Life—but larger.
That kid-glove
dream love
a Knight on a Charger.
Sure
you can lure
him, keep him enslaved.
Buy him Christmas aftershave.

She moons in the mirror
asks it to tell her
she's every bit as pretty as the other
gadfly girls.
Yes, you'll tangle him in your curls
my Lady of Shalott.

Maybe tonight's the night for
True Romance.
You'll find him at the youth club dance,
Lady of Shalott.

But alas
no handsome prince to dare
ask Rapunzel to let down her hair.
Her confidence cracked from side to side,
by twelve o'clock her tattered pride
is all Cinders stands in.
You're the wallflower the fellows all forgot,
Lady of Shalott.
Oh, how she wishes she could pass
like Alice through the looking glass.
You're waiting to be wanted,
my fairy-tale haunted
Lady of Shalott.

Silver dance shoes in her pocket,
no one's photo in her locket,
home alone through the night,
on either side suburban gardens lie,
bungalows and
bedded boxed-in couples high and dry.
But you're
lovely in the lamplight,
my Lady of Shalott.

Liz Lochhead

Dunky at the Dance

Dunky stood on his own at the men's side of the hall, watching for
Alec and his woman in the eerie light thrown on to the dancers by the
revolving globe in the middle of the canteen, reds and greens and
purples and blues, the kind of light they had in a lot of dance-halls,
moving rays of light flickering across the walls and the people. It was
supposed to make the joint glamorous. Diseased, more like it. He had
to keep thinking of his date with Elsa Noble to stop himself becoming
depressed. Dances were all the same, no matter how much you looked
forward to them thinking *this* time it would be different. You shaved
and your collar burned against your raw neck. You wiped Brylcreem
and water into your hair and combed it and combed again in the
lavatory mirror. You tried not to let your hands get dirty or sweaty in
your trouser pockets. Your shoes were shining and your best trousers
creased.

You didn't come too early, when there were only a few guys there
and the lights were still up and everybody could see you. But you
came before the pubs closed and the boozers had fights with the men
at the door. About half-past eight was a good time. You paid your six
shillings (at private dances there was a ticket, stiff cardboard with
curly edging and a pink border) to the two men sitting at the trestle
table in the entrance and then you went to the lavatory and had a
run-off and a last comb at your hair.

Then you went inside, trying to look as casual as possible, hands in
your trouser pockets. Private dances were better because there weren't
so many hard men as there were at the Town Hall jigging and also
because there were a lot of olde-tyme dances. Pride of Erin, St
Bernard's Waltz, Gay Gordons, Military Two Step—they were easy
to do, easier than quicksteps. The band always looked the same, three
or four men in red jackets and evening-dress trousers and bow-ties, a

pianist, a drummer, an accordion player and a saxophone player. They always sounded the same, not like a real band on the wireless, thinner and more harsh, loud and a bit squeaky.

You stood with all the other blokes at one side of the hall, looking across the empty floor at the dames. You looked for girls you knew, because you weren't so embarrassed at the start if you got a dance with a girl you knew from school or from some other dance. You discussed the talent with your mate, trying to make it sound as though you were a couple of bigtime guys who'd been to bigtime places and thought this was smalltime jigging for kids. You felt you'd never have the nerve to walk across the floor, all the way across, and ask a girl to dance with you.

There was always an M.C.—'Ladies and gentlemen, take your partners for a slow tango?'—and you decided you'd wait this one out, saying to your mate that you wanted to eye up the talent a bit more. Maybe a guy you knew from school or the football would come up and have a chat with you. You'd tell him about your game that afternoon, he'd interrupt you to tell you about his game. He'd say he was winching steady, a smashing piece who'd had to stay at home that night with her sick mother. You'd say you'd been winching steady but you'd chucked her in, going steady was a mug's game. You knew you were lying so you took it for granted he was lying.

The first dance was the worst. As soon as the M.C. said what it was all the blokes started across the slippy floor, walking fast in case some other guy got in first, not so fast so that you actually broke into a run. She always looked away when the rush started, pretending not to notice, chatting desperately casual to her pal. You touched her elbow and said 'May I have the next dance, please?' or just 'May I?' If you knew the girl or if you were a hard case, you might say something else, a joke, like 'Lend us your body for the next struggle' or maybe just nod your head towards the floor.

If the girl you headed for was grabbed by some other guy you kept on walking hoping to see something good-looking. You might be unlucky and be left with only the horrors, the wallflowers, and then you had to turn away and move round the hall, back to the men's side. She might even say 'No thank you' and everybody would see you getting the brush-off, that was the worst thing of all.

You felt tense, most of the time, except when your mate and you were standing together between dances. Twice or three times at every dance the M.C. would announce a ladies' preference. That could be worse than ever. You'd no idea what girls thought of you but this was when you found out. You might not be asked at all—quite a lot of girls didn't get up for ladies' preference. Or you might find your elbow being touched by a tremendous horror. You couldn't refuse, that would be too difficult. You had to go round and round the floor with her, all the other guys knowing she was the best you could manage.

You could take the easy way out at a ladies' preference and nip out to the lavvy—but you could get tired of going to the lavatory.

Older guys had it easy, they knew what to say to dames and some really bigtime guys would actually stand *at the ladies' side*, chatting up the dames they were going to dance with.

Once you'd danced a few times you had to start thinking about getting a lumber, the only reason you went to a dance, a girl who'd let you take her home. By about ten o'clock you had to have some idea, maybe danced with her twice. You asked her where she lived. Sometimes it might be the first thing you actually said to her.

From *From Scenes Like These* by Gordon Williams

The Miracle of the Burd and the Fishes

ach sun
jiss keepyir chin up
dizny day gonabootlika hawf shut knife
inaw jiss cozzy a burd

luvur day yi
ach well
gee it a wee while sun
thirz a loat merr fish in thi sea

Tom Leonard

First Date

Jean was standing at the corner and smiling as he arrived.

'It's *terrible*,' he said. 'Twenty minutes late. How dare you?'

'You just don't have any respect for me,' Jean said, and took his hand. 'What do you want to do?'

Peter affected to think deeply, feeling awkward and gloomy. He had been counting on Christine's arriving home before he left because, although he still owed her five shillings, he needed another loan to see him through the evening, and he knew she would have plenty. He had no objection to Jean's paying him into the pictures, but he found himself unable to break this news with the devil-may-care casualness that he wanted. He cursed Christine.

'I thought that maybe...' Jean said. '...Maybe you wouldn't want to, though. If we got out early would you like to come home for a cup of tea? But the pictures get out late, we'd miss the big picture.'

Peter was suddenly confused and apprehensive and excited.

'Are you sure it's all right?'

'Yes, of course.'

'All right, if it's all right. We could just go for a walk, then.'

'All right,' Jean said doubtfully.

'I wish it was dark.' Peter felt unsure of himself. 'It's dark across the waste ground. I bet you would hate that.'

She took his arm and laughed into his eyes.

'It must be frightening.' They walked along the path across the waste ground, out of the light from the street lamps.

'Mm. This is the only dark place for *miles*.'

'We're practically at the other side, that's the snag. What do we do then? It's all a conspiracy to get us into the light again.'

'We could walk back again,' said Jean.

'Just think of the amount of energy we could save if we just stopped in the middle.' Peter's heart was hammering in his chest and sounding in his ears.

'All right, if you like.' Jean stopped, uncertainly.

'I couldn't even see your face if I wanted to kiss you good night,' Peter said. His voice came out cracked, and before he could turn to face her he heard footsteps ringing on the tar macadam. 'Oh, great,' he said. 'There's a whole army using the path for maze-marching.'

'Come on.' Jean took his hand and started running away from the path. Peter plunged after her, breathless across the uneven grass.

'I think you're a disgrace to your sex,' he whispered. 'Dragging innocent schoolboys into bits of waste ground in the dark.' He stood uneasily beside her. 'We could sit down, but the grass must be soaking.'

'I've got a plastic mac.'

He could hear the plastic rustling.

'Will it not tear?'

'Shut up and sit down.' Her voice came from low down and he strained his eyes to see her. 'Down here,' she said. 'You can see better if you shut your eyes.'

'That sounds logical.' He sat beside her and clasped his hands round his knees. 'I've never kissed you at all, except twice at your gate and twice in the pictures.'

'Eleven times in the pictures.'

'It only counts as twice. I must have supernatural powers of self-control.'

'Yes.'

Without moving his hands, he turned his body uncomfortably and twisted towards her till their lips touched momentarily.

203

'That's the first time I've ever kissed you alone, in the dark.'

'Yes.' Jean sighed happily and sat waiting, without impatience. Peter lay back until he felt his head touching the grass. The waste ground was hardly much more than an acre of grass that had been left uneven and scarred from the places where brick air-raid shelters had been built on it during the war.

'This should be in the sunlight,' he said. 'On a cliff somewhere. You can hear the sea bashing on the shore. I've got an open-necked shirt on and I'm chewing a long bit of grass and looking at wee white clouds scudding across the sky. There's always a lot of wee white clouds scudding across the sky at the time.'

'I like it just as nice in the dark.' She giggled. 'With the lamp-posts scudding across the street.'

'Mm. No, it's always sunlight in these pictures. It's so nice that I can look up and see you turning round and smiling down at me. The girl always does that as well.'

'Well, can't you see me?'

'I can see the light reflecting on a wee shiny bit in the corner of your left eye. And one of your teeth.'

'And then the girl bends down.' She bent and kissed him, and relaxed against him as he put his arms around her. They held each other closely until Jean rolled off and lay on her back. Peter raised himself on one elbow and looked down at her face, faintly visible in the darkness, and kissed her gently again and again.

'I'm supposed to feel passionate and fierce,' he said.

'Are you?'

'I don't think so. I just feel... pleased with myself.' He felt her cheek lightly with his fingers, then laid his hand gently on her cheek so that his fingertips were tickling her ear. 'I don't really know *anything* about sex,' he admitted ruefully.

'Tickle my ear again.'

'I must be immature.'

'No, you're not. You're far brainier than me.'

'That's got nothing to do with it,' he corrected her plaintively. 'I just know a lot facts. A child can do that.'

'I don't know *anything*. I'm the most ignorant person you ever met.'

'Oh, Jean, you're so beautiful and wonderful. It doesn't seem possible that this is happening to me.'

'It is, honest.' She took his hand and began to kiss the fingertips gently, one after the other. Peter lifted the hand away and kissed her in long-drawn warmth. 'Not true, not true,' he muttered.

'True, true.' She strained up to kiss him again. 'See?'

'It's funny that I don't feel fierce. People are supposed to.'

'Maybe it's too cold.'

'I think you're a very wicked girl.'

'Am I? Why?'

'Don't listen to me. I can't see the two wee lines between your eyebrows. Did I tell you I thought they were marvellous?'

'They're just lines. Bad temper, probably. Peter?'

'Um.'

'Will you tell me all about sex? Maybe not now, if you like. Some time. Honestly, you would never believe how ignorant I am.'

'That's silly. You must know the basic facts.'

'Oh, I know. But I don't *know* if I know. People never talk about it sensibly. I've always wanted to get a book about it, but I would be afraid to get one. Anyway, my mother would throw a pink fit if she found it.'

'Parents are incomprehensible. You would think it was the nineteenth century. A hundred years ago they used to put frilly covers on piano legs because they thought legs were rude.'

'They didn't!'

'Oh, laugh again!'

'I *can't* laugh. Only by accident.'

'Of course you can. Laugh, instantly! See, you're laughing.'

'Oh, I love the way you can make me laugh.'

'I love the way you can make me make you laugh. Would you kiss my nose?'

'Yes.'

'I bet you wouldn't bite my ear.'

'It would hurt!'

'You don't need to bite right through it. It's just an experiment. I keep reading about people biting each other. Frankly, I don't get it.'

'All right, but tell me if it hurts.'

'No, it doesn't hurt. It's quite nice.'

'Very nice?'

'No, just quite nice. Is it nice when I bite yours?'

'It's all *right*.'

'Maybe it's an acquired taste. Would you not feel embarrassed if I started to tell you about sex?'

'No, not if it was you. I know you wouldn't be laughing at me.'

Peter was filled with quiet, calm pride, at the discovery that he could contemplate talking about sex to Jean without inhibition and without any urge to exploit it.

'Well,' he said. 'No, just a minute. I'll lean on my elbows. I don't want to touch you while I'm talking.'

'All right.'

'Would you rather I talked or kissed you?'

'It doesn't matter. I mean, I like it whatever you do. I never get tired of listening to you.'

'You're mad, girl, mad. Still, all right. Well, men and women are a different shape. Right?'

'Yes.'

'No, don't touch me. Try to curb your insensate lust, woman, you'll have your opportunity after the lecture.'

'All right, I didn't mean any harm.'

'Right. Blast, we'd better start at the beginning.'

'The birds. And the bees.'

'No, no, just the perpetuation of the species. It all begins with the reproductive process and the perpetuation of the species, which is a damn dull idea when you think of it.'

'Ye-es.'

'Well, it's all worked by evolving a human race divided into two types. Each type is highly specialized for different jobs, and they have a different shape so that they're built for their job.'

'Yes. Funny, it sounds so natural, that way. What's all the fuss about, that puzzles me. I mean, I know what it's about, but why?'

'Well...' Peter cupped his hands under his chin and stared across the waste ground; and talked and talked. Jean lay on her back and nodded her head in the darkness, warmed and flattered by the feeling that she, too, was candid and reasonable and un-silly about what were—after all what were they? Simply scientific facts. It was infuriating to think of how childish people could be about them.

'There, you know everything in the world,' Peter said. 'Hee hee.'

'What's funny?'

'I was wondering if that's what happens in these pictures—you know, on the top of the cliff, when it slowly fades out. Does the girl look down at the man and say "Tell me all about sex", and the man says "Well, we'll start with the perpetuation of the species"?'

'No, no. The girl kisses him, like this. And then she says, "What are you thinking?"'

'What a question.'

'It's a perfectly sensible question.'

'And does he say, "I'm thinking about the perpetuation of the species"?'

'Don't be silly.' She took his hair in both her hands and shook his head, and then kissed him. 'What are you thinking, anyway?'

'It's impossible! I'm thinking about three thousand four-hundred and eighty-two things at once.'

'I'm not.'

'Yes, you are. I'm thinking that the street lamps are shining over there, and what's the time? And this plastic mac feels shiny, and the colour of your hair, and the first time I took you home, and how nice it is to be here with you, and the rough nail on my pinkie, and the soft bit on your cheek, and I can't see any stars, and the dark colour of your eyebrows—how do eyebrows get that shape? It's sensational. I'm even thinking about other things I don't even understand. Things keep reminding me of some feeling. Maybe it was a feeling I had in a dream and I've forgotten it, but I can feel it away at the back of my mind.'

206

'Is it a nice feeling?'

'I don't know, there are a lot of them. Do you know what it's like? You know when you watch a play on television, and somebody comes into the house halfway through it and asks what it's about? It takes twenty minutes or half an hour to explain what happened before they came in, and yet you know it all *in an instant*. It's all in your head . . . you know . . . the whole story, even if it took an hour to watch, you know it all, phfft.'

'Yes! That's funny.'

'Well, if you ask me what I'm thinking, it's like that. By the time I explained a quarter of the things I'm thinking, it would be twenty minutes later and I would have thought of a million other things.'

'Oh, it's horrible! You could never catch up!'

'There, there. You don't need to ask me. We can just do this. Then you get it all through my lips by electricity.'

'I haven't quite got it.'

'All right, we'll try again.'

'Maybe the electricity takes a long time to get through.'

'Oh, Jean, don't let me talk ever again. Just let me kiss you.'

'Mm.'

Jean wore a wrist-watch, but neither of them carried matches, and they had to get up and walk towards the lamplight to find the time. It was just after nine o'clock. Jean started to pull a comb through her hair in quick, decisive strokes.

'There isn't any grass at the back, is there?' she giggled.

'No. Do you just have to do that—comb it like that?'

'Yes.'

'You don't go to bed with curlers in it, do you?'

'No!'

'If you had, I would have emigrated, honestly.'

'Well, I don't, so you'd better stay here.'

'What is this all about? Is the family going to inspect me under a wee microscope?'

'Don't be foolish, I would take any of my friends home.'

The statement gave a small jolt to Peter's euphoria, and the name of Archie Horne, which had lain forgotten under his consciousness all evening, shot into his mind and hovered on his tongue, but he left it unuttered.

From *The Taste of Too Much* by Clifford Hanley

Saturday Night

The pattern of so many such Saturdays came back to mind, a pattern that must have been obeyed by so many young men besides himself, automatically, unquestioningly, as if it had been coded through their blood, the orders of the day to which they responded en masse. Early in the evening, the compulsion came on you, like a distant bugle. You washed and shaved with special care and felt good with a fresh clean shirt against your skin.

When you got to the dance-hall, you checked in your coat and went to the toilets to comb your hair. There would be a group of young men there, talking gallous, already drunk on one part whisky and nine parts determination, exorcising the timidity of John and Joe and instilling themselves with the fearless spirit of Johnnie Walker. When you came out the band would be at the stage of quiet perspiration and the drummer would be hunched in that professional attitude of ecstatic boredom that must be stipulated by the Drummers' Union. From then on you divided your time between the stag line and dancing. You learned to categorize your partners roughly. About the worst thing that could happen was that she might be a singer. 'I was waltzing one night in Kentucky... ta-ra-ra-ra... too sune... and the bee-eutiful Kentucky mune.' Running this a close second in the Boredom Stakes, was a congenital hummer so that, dancing, you felt as if you had a hive on for a hat. You established contact in various places and tried to consolidate and assess during the evening, by the scouting pressure of a hand or the suave brush of lips on the forehead at the dance's end. And between sorties you returned to the peacock patter of the knots of apprentice men, talk puffed up with hyperbole and gaudy with swearwords.

'Hell! Talk about walk. She lives at the North Pole. Igloo-Strasse. Knock three times and ask for Chinook. An' fur whit? Ye winch her fur a year, and then maybe ye get tae put yer haun' on her left lug. A write-off, definitely.'

'Jist at that meenit her auld man comes out, ken? Doing his Willie Winkie, ken? Wearin' his stupit pyjamas. See aboot every two meenits efter that? He shoves his neb oot like a cuckoo-clock tae tell us the time. Ah politely puked an' left. Ah felt like askin' him whit he wanted tae be when he grew up, or givin' him a bob to lose himself.'

'Look. You're wrong! Ah know fur facts ye're wrong. Dempsey never seen Walker, never mind fighting him. Dempsey took the title off Lewis Firpo, an' he was a heavyweight. Mickey Walker was a bloody middle-weight. Ten stone seven. An' Ah've got the books in the hoose tae prove it.'

'Ye shoulda been with us last night, boy. Fantabulous. One of the most best nights known to man. Ah don't remember a thing.'

So the night would pass, a hothouse of pleasant sensations, small seeds of fact blooming from inspired mouths into exotic fictions, mascara'd eyes ogling over shoulders, cigarette smoke veining dark corners, neat bottoms bobbing into sight, only to submerge again in a sea of bodies, artesian laughter suddenly unstopped, until you began to notice fewer people in the toilets and more room on the floor. And reading the signs of the night working to a close, with the body of dancers now in slower revolution like a wheel running down, and many stilled altogether, holding each other, swaying slightly like plants in a gently breathing wind, and girls with their heads drooped bouffant on their partners' shoulders like dying flowers, and the faint musk of perfumed sweat, and the drift beginning towards the door, couples leaving with collars up, the boys lean waiting, weaving minute silvered webs of cigarette smoke till their girls come clicking to them, swathed in raincoats and fresh powder, magnetizing the swivelling attention of the lobby-loungers with a whiff of perfumed promise that says 'Don't you wish it was you?' and then mounting the stairs hand-in-hand until the big door is unbarred and swung open and with the sputter of a cigarette-stub in a puddle and a clack of eager heels they are gone.

You would walk with her, enjoying the tingle of strangeness, the first fumbling verbal contacts, making conversation out of a puddle you had to skirt or a drunk man coming towards you, steering her subtly towards one of the familiar parts of the geography of your relationships with girls, where you felt more confident—the archway leading to disused stables where when it rained you stood in a dry arch of darkness with a beaded curtain of rain on each side of you, or the Burns Monument in the park, a building deft at darknesses, giving sudden black shadows, shallow but deep, which shut behind you like a door, so that someone standing a yard away couldn't tell you from the brick, a building sworn into the freemasonry of courters, that mush-roomed lovers in its shadows after dark, under stairways, in clefts and corners, while above them the Bard stood in stone, conniving with the moon, his hand raised in apparent benediction of their efforts, smiling, and, when the sun rose, revealing nothing to the respectful visitors who came to do obeisance to a dozen dusty, illegible books and a score of faded prints.

Once there, you might talk a while. Sometimes talk wasn't very necessary. But sometimes it was and wouldn't come, and the situation would freeze on you. At other times sudden intimacies sprang up in the crevices of darkness like tropical flowers, the sweeter for their transience, the richer because you felt you wouldn't always be capable of such sudden depth of contact with a girl. You could talk about pictures, people, places, anything, and what you said seemed to matter entirely. Nothing was trivial. Things you had done or known were rediscovered in her reaction to them, and you were surprised to find how interesting they were.

You would talk and kiss and go off into a twin trance, lost in each other, grown together like statues shaped from a single piece of clay, until the chaperoning owl hooted the night and the trees back into your awareness and the poplared avenue beneath you laid with moonlight, down which you would be able to see the lake ringed with lamps whose lights were elongated, wavering in the water like tapers of cold fire, and you would embrace and kiss and become industriously involved in each other again, happy in the collisions of your flesh and the feel of wall on hand and the smell of hair and the taste of mouths, and would break off from time to time to talk or smoke or just stand happy, and would start again and stop, continuing and leaving off casually and deliciously, with conversation growing in the interstices of your activity.

You continued, wrestling pleasantly, resting between rounds, and the decision would vary from girl to girl. You would walk her home, usually in the region of midnight, and wait at her door until an irate mother or father, depending on whether the household was matriarchal or patriarchal, called or appeared. Then you came up home alone with most of the town asleep and a pleasant taste of morning in your mouth.

From *Remedy is None* by William McIlvanney

NOTES

'Genuine Ghastly First Love': two short stories which could be compared with this extract are Fred Urquhart's 'The Bike' (*Ten Modern Scottish Stories*, edited by Millar and Low, Heinemann Educational) and Alan Sillitoe's 'A Trip to Southwell' (*Down to the Bone*, Wheaton 'Literature For Life' Series).

'Lady of Shalott': the same writer's 'Cloakroom' (*Memo for Spring*, Reprographia) is a similar treatment of romance and disillusion.
    Antonia Fraser's *Scottish Love Poems* (Penguin) is a useful anthology.

'First Date': George Friel's *The Boy who Wanted Peace* (Calder) has (in Chapter 10) a tragi-comic description of the hero's first date with a girl.

'The Miracle of the Burd and the Fishes': the author included the following transcription into Standard English in the 1973 edition of his *Poems* (O'Brien):—

Ach, son. Just keep your chin up. (It) doesn't do going about like a half-shut knife. And all just because of a bird! Love her, do you? Ach well. Give it a wee while, son. There's a lot more fish in the sea.

THE WRITERS

Stewart Conn, born in Glasgow in 1936, is a poet and playwright. He works in Edinburgh with BBC Scotland as a radio drama producer. His main poetry collections are *Stoats in the Sunlight* (1968), *An Ear to the Ground* (1972) and *Under the Ice*, all published by Hutchinson. Among his published plays are *The King* (in *New English Dramatists 14*, Penguin 1970), a historical drama *The Burning* (Calder and Boyars 1973) and *The Aquarium and Other Plays* (Calder and Boyars 1976). The latter includes his well-known Glasgow play *I Didn't Always Live Here*.

Billy Connolly was born in Glasgow in 1942. He was originally a folk-singer but has attained great popular success as a comedian. Much of his stage material is derived from his Glasgow childhood experience. He is also a playwright.

Catherine Lucy Czerkawska was born in Leeds in 1950 and brought up in Ayrshire. Her poetry has appeared in *White Boats* (Garret Arts 1973) and *A Book of Men: Poems* (Akros 1976). A historical monograph, *Fisherfolk of Carrick*, was published by the Molendinar Press in 1975.

Jane Duncan, who was born at Renton, Dunbartonshire in 1910 and died in 1976, is mainly known for her 'My Friends' series of novels, beginning with *My Friends the Miss Boyds* (Macmillan 1959), but (under the pseudonym Janet Sandison) she has also published the Jean Robertson quartet which began with *Jean in the Morning* (Macmillan 1969).

Douglas Dunn was born at Inchinnan, Renfrewshire, in 1942. He is a poet and free-lance writer. His first collection, *Terry Street* (Faber 1969), was followed by *The Happier Life* (1972), *Love or Nothing* (1974) and *Barbarians* (1979). He has written for BBC radio and television.

Ian Hamilton Finlay was born in 1925. He is well-known as a concrete poet who uses a variety of materials as well as the written word. His poetry includes *The Dancers Inherit the Party* (Migrant Press 1960) and the famous short sequence *Glasgow Beasts an a Burd*. A collection of short stories, *The Sea-bed and Other Stories*, was published in 1958.

George Friel, who was born in 1910 and died in 1976, was a Glasgow schoolteacher. His novels, all with Glasgow settings, include the well-known *The Boy who Wanted Peace* (Calder 1964) which was televised, *Grace and Miss Partridge* (Calder and Boyars 1969) and *Mr Alfred MA* (Calder and Boyars 1972).

W. S. Graham was born in Greenock in 1918. He now lives in Cornwall. His volumes of poetry include *The Nightfishing* (Faber 1955) and *Malcolm Mooney's Land* (Faber 1970).

Clifford Hanley was born in Glasgow in 1922. A journalist for 20 years, he is now a free-lance writer and broadcaster. His most notable publications to date are his autobiography *Dancing in the Streets* (Hutchinson 1958) and the novels *The Taste of Too Much* (Hutchinson 1959) and *The Hot Month*

(Hutchinson 1967). He has also written plays for stage, radio and television and a series of thrillers under the pseudonym Henry Calvin.

Archie Hind was born in Glasgow in 1928. He has been Writer in Residence to the community in Aberdeen. His novel *The Dear Green Place* (Hutchinson 1966) has a Glasgow background.

James Kelman, who is a short story writer, was born in Glasgow in 1946. A collection of his stories *An Old Pub Near the Angel* was published by Puckerbrush Press, Maine, in 1973. His work also appears in *Three Glasgow Writers* (Molendinar Press 1976).

Tom Leonard was born in Glasgow in 1944. His poetry is notable for the phonetic transcription of Glasgow dialect. His publications include *Poems* (E. & T. O'Brien 1973) and *Bunnit Husslin* (Third Eye, Glasgow 1975). *Three Glasgow Writers* (Molendinar Press 1976) includes a selection of his work.

Maurice Lindsay was born in Glasgow in 1918. As journalist, critic, broadcaster, television executive and director of the Scottish Civic Trust, he has been an influential figure in Scottish cultural life. He has published books on a variety of Scottish subjects, including an assessment of Burns, *Robert Burns: the Man, his Work, the Legend* (McGibbon & Kee 1968) and a *History of Scottish Literature* (Hale 1977). Of his many anthologies, *Modern Scottish Poetry: an Anthology of the Scottish Renaissance* (Carcanet 1976) is the most significant. His *Collected Poems* was published by Hale in 1979.

Liz Lochhead was born in Motherwell in 1947. She is a teacher of art in Glasgow. A selection of her poetry appeared in *Made in Scotland* (Carcanet 1974). *Memo for Spring*, her first collection of poetry, was published by Reprographia in 1972.

George MacBeth was born in Lanarkshire in 1932. He works with the BBC in London. His *Collected Poems* (Macmillan) appeared in 1971. Other publications include an autobiographical collage *My Scotland* (Macmillan 1973) and, more recently, several novels.

Carl MacDougall was born in Glasgow in 1941. He is known mainly as a folk-song and short story writer. He has published two volumes of short stories based on Scottish folk tales, *A Cuckoo's Nest* (1974) and *A Scent of Water* (1975), both published by the Molendinar Press.

William McIlvanney was born in 1936 in Kilmarnock, where he still lives. Formerly a schoolteacher, he is now a full-time writer. His novels are *Remedy is None* (Eyre and Spottiswoode 1967), *A Gift from Nessus* (Eyre and Spottiswoode 1968) and *Docherty* (Allen & Unwin 1975). He has also published a volume of poetry *The Longships in Harbour* (Eyre Methuen 1970) and a thriller *Laidlaw*.

Hector MacMillan was born and brought up in Glasgow's East End. Among his plays are *The Rising* and *The Sash*, the latter published by the Molendinar Press in 1974.

Roddy McMillan was born and raised in the Finnieston district of Glasgow. He is a well-known actor on the stage, and in television and films. His play *The Bevellers* was published by the Southside Press in 1974. He died in 1979.

Edwin Morgan was born in 1920 in Glasgow where he is titular Professor of English at Glasgow University. A distinguished scholar, critic and translator, his original poetry is extremely varied, both in theme and technique. Three major collections of his poetry have appeared, *The Second Life* (Edinburgh University Press 1968), *From Glasgow to Saturn* (Carcanet 1973) and *The New Divan* (Carcanet 1977).

Stephen Mulrine was born in 1937 in Glasgow where he is a lecturer at the School of Art. He has written several radio plays, scripted a television series on modern Scottish writing and published *Poems* (Akros 1971).

Ian Niall is best known for his naturalist non-fiction such as *The Poacher's Handbook* (Heinemann 1946), but he has written a series of novels set in rural Galloway, including *The Galloway Shepherd* (Heinemann 1970) and *The Village Policeman* (Heinemann 1971).

Patrick O'Connor was born and raised in Ardrossan, Ayrshire. A former merchant seaman, he has published two novels largely based on his childhood experience, *Down the Bath Rocks* (Gill and Macmillan 1971) and *In a Marmalade Saloon* (Hutchinson 1974).

Hugh C. Rae was born in Glasgow in 1935 where for some years he worked in a bookshop. Since 1964 he has been a full-time writer. Among his novels are *Skinner* (Blond 1964), *Night Pillow* (Blond 1967), *The Saturday Epic* (Blond 1970), *The Rookery* (Constable 1975) and *Harkfast* (Constable 1976).

Alan Spence was born in Glasgow in 1947. His collection of short stories, *Its Colours they are Fine*, was published by Collins in 1977.

Sydney Tremayne was born in Ayr in 1912. His working life was spent as a journalist in Fleet Street. Among his collections of poetry are *The Rock and the Bird* (Allen and Unwin 1955), *The Swans of Berwick* (Chatto and Windus 1962) and *The Turning Sky* (Hart-Davis 1969). *Selected and New Poems* was published by Chatto and Windus in 1973.

Molly Weir was born in Glasgow. Well-known as a stage, television, radio and film actress, she has also written several volumes of autobiography, including *Shoes were for Sunday* (Hutchinson 1970), *Best Foot Forward* (Hutchinson 1972) and *A Toe on the Ladder* (Hutchinson 1973).

Gordon Williams was born in Paisley in 1934. He is now a full-time writer in London. Among his novels are *The Camp* (1967) and *From Scenes Like These* (Secker & Warburg 1968). He has also created and written the television series *Hazell*.

SELECT BIBLIOGRAPHY

N.B. Significant books, which are noted in the section, 'The Writers', are not listed again below.

FICTION

Chaim I. Bermant	*Jericho Sleep Alone*	(Chapman & Hall 1964)
Evelyn Cowan	*Portrait of Alice*	(Canongate 1976)
Margaret Thomson Davis	*The Breadmakers*	(Allison & Busby 1972)
George Friel	*The Bank of Time*	(Hutchinson 1959)
George Friel	*An Empty House*	(Calder & Boyars 1974)
Clifford Hanley	*The Red-haired Bitch*	(Hutchinson 1969)
Alexander Highlands	*The Dark Horizon*	(Jarrold 1971)
Robin Jenkins	*The Changeling*	(Macdonald 1958)
Robin Jenkins	*A Very Scotch Affair*	(Gollancz 1968)
James Kennaway	*The Cost of Living Like This*	(Longmans 1969)
Alastair Mair	*The Ripening Time*	(Heinemann 1970)
Hugh Munro	*The Clydesiders*	(Macdonald 1961)
Robert Nicolson	*Mrs Ross*	(Constable 1961)
Robert Nicolson	*A Flight of Steps*	(Constable 1966)
John Quigley	*The Golden Stream*	(Collins 1970)
Alan Sharp	*A Green Tree in Gedde*	(Michael Joseph 1965)
Alexander Trocchi	*Cain's Book*	(Calder 1963)

DRAMA

Bill Bryden	*Willie Rough*	(Southside 1972)
Bill Bryden	*Benny Lynch*	(Southside 1972)
John McGrath	*The Game's a Bogey*	(EUSPB 1975)
Robert McLellan	*The Hypocrite*	(Calder & Boyars 1970)
Cecil Taylor	*Bread and Butter*	(*'New English Dramatists to'*, Penguin 1967)

POETRY

Tom Buchan	*Dolphins at Cochin*	(Barrie & Jenkins 1969)
James Copeland	*Some Work*	(Bramma 1972)
Duncan Glen	*Clydesdale*	(Akros 1971)
Duncan Glen	*Follow! Follow!*	(Akros 1976)
Maurice Lindsay	*This Business of Living*	(Akros 1971)
Edwin Morgan	*Wi the Haill Voice*	(Carcanet 1972)
Walter Perrie	*Poem on a Winter Night*	(Macdonald 1976)
John Purser	*The Counting Stick*	(Aquila 1976)
Tom Scott	*The Ship and Ither Poems*	(Oxford 1963)

AUTOBIOGRAPHY

Janetta Bowie	*Penny Buff*	(Constable 1975)
Janetta Bowie	*Penny Boss*	(Constable 1976)
Jimmy Boyle	*A Sense of Freedom*	(Canongate-Pan 1977)
Evelyn Cowan	*Spring Remembered*	(Canongate 1974)
Jack House	*Pavement in the Sun*	(Hutchinson 1967)
Ian Niall	*A Galloway Childhood*	(Heinemann 1967)

GLOSSARY

a' by: all over
ahint: behind
ain: own
back-het: re-heated (of chips)
bampot: an idiot
beardie: a loach
bine: a washing-tub
blether: to speak nonsense (also a noun)
blooter: to smash
burd: a young woman
burroo: Social Security office
causey: a pebble
caw: to knock over
chap: to rap
Chapel: a Catholic Church
chib: a knife
chiel: a man
chuck: to stop, abandon
chuck: to throw
claes: clothes
cloot: a cloth
close: entry from street
coo: a cow
coup: midden, dung-heap
craythur: a creature
dead: very
dicht: to wipe
donner: to stroll
dreep: to drop down carefully
duke (jouk): to dodge
feartie: a coward
fly: cunning
forbye: also
gallus: bold, brave, flashy
gaun (gawn): going
gemme's a bogey: there's nothing to be done
gie: to give
gonny: going to (often interrogative)
guid: good
hale (haill): whole
haud: to hold
hen: a young woman
het: term in children's games

hoachin: full of
howk: to dig
hudgies: children's game of stealing lifts on backs of lorries
hurl: a ride (on vehicle)
jigging: dancing
jink: to dodge
keepie-up: a ball game
ken fine: to know well
knock: to steal
land: a landing (of a stair)
leerie: a lamplighter
leeved: lived
lowsing: the end of work
lug: ear
lumber: a girl escorted home from a dance
manky: very dirty
meenie: a minnow
mell: a mallet, hammer
melt: to hit hard
mogre: a bad situation or mess
narky: irritable
neb: nose
never-never: hire-purchase
noo: now
nyaff: an annoying person (usually of small stature)
owerbye: quite near
oxter: arm-pit
pair: poor
pan-loaf: snobbish
pawn: a pawnshop
peenie: a pinafore dress
peever: hopscotch
pit the hems oan: to put out of action, stop
plunk: a beginner
sair: sore
sannies: sandshoes
shauchlin: shambling
skelp: to smack
skint: penniless
sojer: a soldier
steamie: a communal washhouse

steer: to stir
stumor: an idiot
sugerally water: mixture of water and liquorice
tatties: potatoes
that: so
themorra: tomorrow
towsing: a rough time
trauchle: troublesome situation or hard toil

tummle thur wulkies: to roll head over heels
wan: one
wapenshaw: an expanse of water
wean: a young child
wheesht: command to be quiet
winching: courting
yase: to use
yin: one
yirra: you are

SUGGESTIONS

1 TO BE A CHILD

1 'That is what it was like to be a child. The place, the people.' Write down your earliest memories.

2 Ask your parents to tell you about when you were very young. They will have some funny and perhaps strange things to tell you. Use the material to write an essay called 'My Amazing Early Life'.

3 Imagine you are a five-year-old on his or her first day at school. What are your thoughts?

4 Write about your memories of primary school.

5 Describe a primary teacher whom you remember.

6 After some class discussion, compile a sheet of useful advice for new first year pupils in your secondary school.

7 Liz Lochhead and Douglas Dunn describe unpleasant incidents which they still remember clearly. Is there an unpleasant childhood experience which still disturbs you? Would you be prepared to write about it? Discuss this with your friends in the class.

8 We are often confused about things when we are very young, just like Jean in 'Jesus Loves Me' and Aleck in 'Sheaves'. Try to remember some of the things which confused you.

2 FAMILY MATTERS

1 The whole family tends to be involved when there is a baby in the house. Explain how to do *one* of the following: change a nappy, feed a baby, talk to a baby, get a baby to sleep. To make it more interesting, include stories from your own experience.

2 Organize a 'baby-show' consisting of photographs from everyone's childhood. How many members of the class are still recognisable? Write a humorous paragraph contrasting your class friend as a baby with him or her today.

3 After some discussion compose a set of instructions for inexperienced baby-sitters.

4 Improvise the dialogue for some common family situations. Possibilities are 'Getting Me Out of Bed', 'I've Lost My ——', 'Can I Have Money For ——?', 'Can I Go Out, Mum?', 'Just Wait Till Your Father Comes Home!'.

5 Big brothers or sisters can be nasty. Younger brothers or sisters can be pests. Write about one of your brothers or sisters.

6 Talk about family jokes or special family sayings.

7 'They were all conscious of having made something among them. A night had been baptised. That was The Night That Uncle Hughie Fought The Egg.' Describe a funny and memorable incident that took place in your family.

8 Describe your favourite aunt or uncle.

9 Write an affectionate tribute to one of your grandparents.

10 Script a dialogue between parent and child in which an important subject such as jobs is discussed.

11 Write about a family outing or holiday which you will never forget.

3 STREET GAMES

1 Make a class collection of the street songs and rhymes you can remember. Into what sections or subjects does your collection divide? You might like to record the collection for playing to younger classes.

2 Molly Weir remarks that 'these songs were surely handed down from generation to generation and we acted and changed them, following a ritual which came from we didn't know where'. Identify any lines, words or names in your collection which show that the rhymes are quite old. Is there anything you can't explain? You could send a group to the school library to do some research.

3 'We were merciless on those who couldn't or wouldn't learn the movements fast enough, and who spoilt the rhythm.' Explain a well-known street game as clearly as you can. Include a labelled diagram if you think it necessary.

4 Some boy's games are described by Billy Connolly as 'initiation rites' which involve courage. The poem 'Children Playing' suggests reasons for this. Do you agree with these reasons?

   Spin some stories of your own young days when you did daft, dangerous things.

5 'Geordie' shows that dangerous games can have unhappy endings. Write about the worst accident that ever happened to you.

4 MAN AND BEAST

1 Think of stories, films and cartoons in which animals are treated as if they were human. Which is your favourite and why?

2 Script a conversation between a Glasgow alsatian and a very different dog, such as a royal corgi.

3 Discuss the hunting of animals. You could hold a class debate on the subject, with two speakers in favour of blood-sports and two against.

4 Describe your experience of keeping pets. If you have a family pet, write an affectionate description of it.

5 How should people treat animals?

6 People often fear or dislike certain creatures such as snakes, spiders, mice or dogs. Express your fear or dislike of some creature as vividly as you can.

5 HAPPY DAYS

1 Describe a family celebration that you remember very well: perhaps the first wedding you attended; the return of a relative from the army or from abroad; a birthday or engagement party; a particular Christmas.

2 Write a poem or story about a time of the year when people celebrate. It might be about guising, or a Hallowe'en witch tale, or a Christmas ghost story.

3 Cities, towns or districts often have their own special days. There might be an annual fair, gala, sports-day or festival in which nearly everyone takes some part. Describe a special occasion of this kind which you know about or took part in.

4 Does your town or district have any special customs connected with a particular day or time of year? It might be interesting to find out.

6 THE PITY OF IT

1 Although Maurice Lindsay's poem is called 'Accident Report' identify the ways in which it is not really a 'report' in the usual sense of the word.

2 Edwin Morgan sees in the blind man the

> 'persisting patience of the undefeated
> which is the nature of man when all is said.'

Carl MacDougall's narrator remarks that 'everywhere life is full of heroism'.
   Discuss examples from your own experience of the heroism of apparently ordinary people who are less fortunate than most of us—for instance the old or the sick. You might prefer to write your tribute to such a person.

3 'Accident Report' and 'The Blind Reading' both involve policemen. Discuss how your ideas about policemen might be changed by reading these.

4 The blind man in Edwin Morgan's poem 'depends on many who would evade him'. Discuss how far we should be prepared to go to help other people. Where do *you* draw the line? At family, friends, neighbours, the amount of trouble involved for you?

7 A SENSE OF PLACE

1 Americans call the city of New York 'the big apple', a huge tough place with many problems, but still the dominating city, the influence of which stretches across America. Glasgow is the west of Scotland's 'big apple', fascinating and slightly frightening. Even if you don't stay in Glasgow you have probably been there quite a few times for shopping, football, exhibitions etc.

Write down your ideas about Glasgow and its people. If your school is outside Glasgow it would be interesting to exchange your class essays for those of a class in a Glasgow school and to discuss the differences.

2 Defend Glasgow from her critics.

3 Clifford Hanley has some criticisms to make of Glasgow's housing schemes. Discuss these and decide how far they are justified.

4 If you live in a housing scheme, compose a letter to your local councillor in which you point out the ways in which your area needs improvement.

5 'I don't know what such guide-books as there may be of the town and district would say, but I'm fairly sure they wouldn't mention very many of the places that have mattered to me.'—William McIlvanney.

Write about the places of your childhood that meant a lot to you, but would not find a place in any guide-book: the back-courts, hide-outs, patches of wasteground, trails, woods, burns, farms etc.

6 W. S. Graham and William McIlvanney both 'pour out' their memories of their childhood towns. Try the same thing for your town or district, using some of their methods if you can.

7 In 'Landscape and History' Catherine Lucy Czerkawska tells how she was fascinated with the literature and history of the Ayrshire landscape. See what you can discover about your own area. You could start from local place-names, the registry office, old buildings and the files of local newspapers.

Here are a few specific things to investigate:
(a) Is there a local historian (there usually is) who can come into school and talk about the history of the district?
(b) Has your district produced any writers, such as Robert Tannahill, the weaver poet of Paisley?
(c) Is there, or was there at one time, a prominent family in the district who owned an estate or 'big house'?
(d) Was a particular industry or craft once associated with your district?
(e) Did any well-known historical events take place in the neigh-bourhood?
(f) Are there any very ancient or even pre-historic remains?
(g) Were there any trials for witch-craft in the district?
(h) Were there any connections with the covenanters?
If you collect enough material you could produce an interesting magazine.

8 Even if you live in the middle of Glasgow, if you travel ten miles in any direction you will be in the wilderness or out at sea! The west of Scotland is like that, town and remote country are unbelievably close. Try the 'ten-mile test' with the aid of a map and see what it reveals.

Describe some of the 'remote' places in your area which you have visited. Find out about those you haven't.

8 DAY-DREAMS

1 Collect the words of the current 'Top Twenty' songs and discuss them in terms of *dreams* and *reality*. What are your conclusions?

2 Discuss the advantages and disadvantages of day-dreaming.

3 Both Alan Spence's short story and Ian Hamilton Finlay's play show how we blend dream and reality in our daily lives. Try to trace this blend in your own life. You could think of love, jobs, money, your future, your appearance and so on. The result might be a short story, sad or funny.

9 GROWTH PAINS

1 Discuss why teenagers often find it more difficult to get on with their parents than younger children do.

2 Compile a list of reasons for rows between teenagers and their parents. In groups, script the dialogue for some typical rows.

3 How much control do you think parents should have over their teenage children?

4 When does a boy or a girl become an adult? Is there a clear answer to this question? A group could be formed to discover the ages at which teenagers can legally do various things.

5 Write about the things which annoy you, as a teenager, about older people.

6 Try to trace your own development over the past few years. Think of your changing taste in records, books, television and so on; of attitudes to your family, school and the opposite sex. From your notes, write an essay about your development.

7 Do you want to be the same as other people?

10 WORK

1 G ting the job you want when you leave school is obviously the most important thing in your immediate future. You should be thinking of how you will go about it. Perhaps you have worked out the whole thing. On the other hand, you may not have thought very much about the subject.

'The First Trip is the Hardest' contains some good tips about getting a job. Read it again and make a list of the useful pointers which you notice.

2 Take a class census to discover how many of you have done part-time jobs. It might be useful to make up a questionnaire for each of you to fill in. The questions could be about hours, pay, type of job, advantages, disadvantages, problems etc. You could form groups to examine particular parts of the questionnaire and report the results back to the class for discussion.

3 Write an account of your experience of a part-time job.

4 Is there a gap between your *ideal* job and the job you are likely to get? Try to make an honest list of your qualifications and abilities and compare them with those required for your ideal job.

5 Obviously, a good way of finding out about the world of work is to ask people who are working about *their* jobs. You could interview your own class teacher first. Members of your family and friends might also answer questions about their jobs.

6 Discuss with your teacher how to write a letter of application for a job. Look at the vacancies in a local newspaper and write a letter of application for a job that interests you.

7 Form groups to discuss some of the jobs applied for in 6. Imagine you are the interviewing-board and script the questions you would ask the applicant. 'Interview' some of the applicants. Discuss the results, especially the question of what makes a good interview. A sheet entitled 'How to Have a Good Interview' could be produced for future use by members of the class.

11 LANGUAGE

1 Perhaps you find the subject of language just as confusing and annoying as does the fifteen-year-old boy in Gordon Williams' novel. Why do folk not speak one way? Is one way of speaking better than another? Is there a 'proper English'? Is there a 'langwij a thi guhtr'? Do you have to speak a certain way to get a good job? Should you just speak naturally?

You will have to answer these questions for yourselves, but you should consider these facts:

(a)   Language is a means of communication. What you are saying must be understood to be effective.

(b)   All of us in the west of Scotland speak English in a particular way, in the accent of our region, just as someone from Liverpool or Yorkshire or Cornwall speaks in his regional accent. This is not wrong—it is natural!

(c)   Most regions of Britain have their own particular forms of English. These regional forms are called dialects. Dialects contain words and expressions which will *not* be understood outside the region. Some of the writing in *this* book is in Glasgow or west of Scotland dialect. Perhaps *you* did not understand some of it!

(d)   Nobody speaks *only* in regional dialect. We can all understand *and* speak the English of radio, television and newspapers, which is called Standard English.

(e)   Nobody, in fact, speaks 'one way'. We all change our language to suit the person we are speaking to and the situation.

12 A VIOLENT WORLD

1 Talk about playground fights that you remember well. What are your honest feelings about fighting?

2 Script the dialogue for an incident between two pupils which ends in a challenge to fight. It could start from a collision in the corridor, an insulting remark or a misunderstanding.

3 Try to write a story in which a bully is unexpectedly beaten by one of his victims.

4 What does the word 'gang' mean to you? Each member of the class could write down ten words they associate with the word 'gang'. Compare the various results.

Through class discussion build up your picture of a typical teenage gang. Does your picture differ from the one usually presented in newspapers and on television?

5 Why do young people join gangs?

6 Do you think that, if you have gangs, you will also have fighting and vandalism?

7 Discuss the causes of vandalism. What would you do to prevent vandalism in your area?

8 What do you think of the police?

A policeman is talking to a group of teenagers and moving them on. Improvise the dialogue.

9 Discuss the use of the belt in schools. Were you ever belted 'for nothing'?

You could have a debate on the motion that 'the belt should be abolished immediately in schools', with two speakers for and two speakers against.

10 Is the world more violent today than in the past? A group could do some research in the school library to help you decide.

13 THE ORANGE AND THE GREEN

1 The aim of this theme is to enable you to discuss *prejudice*, particularly the religious prejudice which often exists in the west of Scotland. Two things are worth stressing:

(a)   the right of each individual to live by and defend his or her sincerely-held religious beliefs.

(b)   the equally important need to tolerate the different beliefs of others and to defend their rights to those beliefs.

2 Discuss whether you thought the extracts were 'fair' or not.

3 Discuss the word 'prejudice' and try to work out its meaning as fully as you can. It might help you if you can think of particular examples.

4 Do you dislike groups of people who are different from you and your friends? Discuss why this should be so. What are the differences and are they really important?

5 Have you ever had the experience of being 'picked on' because you were different in some way? Describe the experience and your feelings as honestly as you can.

14 ROMANCE

1 Improvise the dialogue for these situations;
   (a)   a boy and a girl on their first date
   (b)   two girls discussing a boy at a dance
   (c)   a boy chatting up a girl at a dance
   (d)   a first meeting between a boy and his girlfriend's parents
   (e)   a girl's parents waiting for her late return from a date
   (f)   an argument between a girl and her parents about her friendship with a boy whom they do not like.
You could divide into groups and assign each group a particular situation. Tape-record the best efforts from each group.

2 Can you remember how you felt at your first dance or on your first date? Try to describe the situation as honestly as you can.

3 What are the qualities you look for in the opposite sex?
Divide into groups of all boys and all girls and make up lists of these qualities. The whole class could discuss the results.

4 Use the material collected for 3 to make up descriptions of 'The Ideal Boyfriend' and 'The Ideal Girlfriend'.

5 Many pop songs have love as their theme. Make a collection of these songs and examine the words. How realistic are the ideas about love which are presented?
You could also make a collection of poems about love and compare these with the pop songs.

6 Collect some romantic magazines for discussion by the class.